More praise for
AWAKENING THROUGH LOVE

"You're in good hands with John; he has discovered how to love his way all the way to enlightenment."
—Lama Surya Das, author of
Awakening the Buddha Within

"Written from the heart, *Awakening Through Love* is bound to affect the hearts of all who read it…Practical, profound, and deeply moving."
—José Ignacio Cabezón, XIVth Dalai Lama Professor of Tibetan Buddhism, UC Santa Barbara

"*Awakening Through Love* presents a message of compassionate wisdom that is greatly needed in today's world. In this book Dr. John Makransky offers readers of all faiths and persuasions a profound guide to experience the deep and limitless love that has inspired and awakened Buddhist practitioners throughout the ages. Being both a learned scholar and an experienced practitioner, Dr. Makransky is well positioned to present the deep meaning of the Buddhist teaching to a contemporary audience. This book is an important contribution to the modern understanding of Buddhism that will serve as an inspiration and a friend for anyone who wishes to experience the great qualities of love, compassion, and wisdom that we all possess as our innermost being."
—Chökyi Nyima Rinpoche, co-author of
Medicine and Compassion

D0920644

AWAKENING
THROUGH
LOVE

Unveiling Your Deepest Goodness

John Makransky

Foreword by Lama Surya Das

Edited by Philip Osgood

WISDOM PUBLICATIONS • BOSTON

Wisdom Publications
199 Elm Street
Somerville MA 02144 USA
www.wisdompubs.org

Library of Congress Cataloging-in-Publication Data
Makransky, John J.
  Awakening through love : unveiling your deepest goodness / John Makransky ;
foreword by Lama Surya Das ; edited by Philip Osgood.
    p. cm.
  Includes bibliographical references and index.
  ISBN 0-86171-537-3 (pbk. : alk. paper)
  1. Spiritual life—Buddhism. 2. Love—Religious aspects—Buddhism. 3.
Compassion—Religious aspects—Buddhism. 4. Buddhism—Doctrines. I. Das,
Surya. II. Osgood, Philip. III. Title.
  BQ4302.M35 2007
  294.3'5677—dc22
                                              2007014697

16 15 14 13 12
5   4   3   2

Cover design by Emily Mahon. Interior design by Tony Lulek. Set in Bembo 11.5
pt/16 pt. Cover photograph by Michael Turek / Getty Images.

Wisdom Publications' books are printed on acid-free paper and meet the guidelines
for permanence and durability of the Production Guidelines for Book Longevity of
the Council on Library Resources.

Printed in the United States of America

This book was produced with environmental mindfulness. We have elected to
print this title on 30% PCW recycled paper. As a result, we have saved the following resources: 8 trees, 4 million BTUs of energy, 808 lbs. of greenhouse gases,
3,647 gallons of water, and 231 lbs. of solid waste. For more information, please visit
our website, www.wisdompubs.org. This paper is also FSC certified. For more information, please visit www.fscus.org.

Contents

Foreword

JOHN MAKRANSKY IS A MENSCH. You're in good hands with Lama John. And *I* should know that, having observed him closely over the last dozen years. He is my Dharma heir in the non-sectarian lineage of our Dzogchen master Nyoshul Khen Rinpoche. Every true teacher wishes to have students and protégés with the potential to surpass him or her. As my protégé, John is such a person, one who has discovered how to love his way all the way to enlightenment. Whether he achieved this more from the three decades he spent learning from Tibetan lamas in Nepal, India, and America, or from his long work as a professor and Buddhist scholar-practitioner, or from his life as a family man, it is hard to say. Undoubtedly his beautiful family—two sons and wife, Barbara—are implicated in making him the beloved teacher, esteemed colleague, and good spiritual friend he is on two continents, in both the East and West.

In 1978, shortly after finishing service in the Peace Corps, John met his first Tibetan Buddhist teachers, Gelug-lineage lamas closely affiliated with His Holiness the Dalai Lama. He spent fifteen years immersed in the study and practice of Tibetan Gelug teachings of love, compassion, and transcendent wisdom under their guidance. Then Nyoshul Khen Rinpoche, Khenpo Sonam Tobgyal, and I introduced him to the Dzogchen teachings of the Nyingma lineage, and Nyoshul Khen Rinpoche indicated to me that John would play a significant role in our teachings and transmission. After further years of spiritual practice, we all saw the practices of love and compassion really come alive in John through the Dzogchen view of innate wisdom—practices that take natural expression in the meditations transmitted here.

After Nyoshul Khen Rinpoche's demise in 1999, John and I traveled together on pilgrimage to Nepal and Bhutan. Upon meeting John at the Kagyu-Nyingma monastery near Kathmandu, its learned abbot, my old friend Chokyi Nyima Rinpoche, seemed immediately to recognize John's sterling qualities as a scholar-practitioner and asked him to teach annually at his monastery within Kathmandu University's new Center for Buddhist Studies. John is now senior faculty advisor to the Center and has been instrumental in it becoming partnered with Boston College, where John is a professor of Buddhism and comparative theology.

John has been teaching the love, compassion, and awareness practices in this book for years at our Dzogchen Center retreats. We are reminded through these practices and his example that love is not found outside of ourselves; love is found through loving. Drawing from his immersion in the mind-training teachings of compassion and the Dzogchen teachings of innate wisdom—using plain, practical instruction—he helps readers uncover the unity of love and wisdom in the very nature of their minds. Then he shows us how to actualize those qualities in each aspect of our lives—in family, community, work, service, and social action.

As John always emphasizes, the key to Buddhadharma is practice; this book is based upon his own life of practice, his very pragmatic path of awakening through love. Here he offers us the words of his own teachers and tells many stories past and present of those awakened through this path. He speaks about the power of unconditional love to transform ourselves and thus transform the world. As Buddha said of his own teachings: Don't take my word for it, find out for yourself, test it out. John has followed this wisdom.

Many readers who are not Buddhist will find these nonsectarian practices accessible and applicable to their fundamental beliefs and concerns. John urges all people of faith to explore how their own spiritual paths may be informed and empowered by the practices of love, compassion, and self-transcending wisdom transmitted here. As he teaches, and as the peace master Shantideva says in his classic *Way of the Bodhisattva:* selfishness is the real demon, egotism is the true enemy, and joy comes naturally from loving and caring for others. We need each other to become enlightened, as His Holiness the Dalai Lama often says, because we need to develop deep compassion in order to fulfill the journey of awakening. Here in these practical, useful teachings by a contemporary lama, we find the modern means to fulfill that promise.

Lama Surya Das
Dzogchen Center, Austin, Texas
October 2006

Acknowledgments

I AM GRATEFUL TO MY SPIRITUAL TEACHERS and mentors for their profound guidance and continual blessing: Nyoshul Khen Rinpoche, Lama Surya Das, Chokyi Nyima Rinpoche, H.H. Drukchen Rinpoche, H.H. the Dalai Lama, Khenpo Sonam Tobgyal Rinpoche, Tulku Thondup Rinpoche, Geshe Lhundub Sopa, Lama Thubten Yeshe, Lama Zopa Rinpoche, Geshe Ngawang Dhargyey, Geshe Thubten Tsering, Geshe Lobsang Namgyal, Charles Genoud, Lama Yeshe Gyamtso, Tsenzhab Serkong Rinpoche, Geshe Sonam Rinchen, Gyume Khensur Rinpoche, and Father Michael Himes of Boston College.

I thank my friend and editor, Philip Osgood, for helping me develop this manuscript from Dharma teachings I've presented at Dzogchen Center meditation retreats the past few years. It was because of Philip's deep knowledge of the creative writing process and tireless commitment to the spirit of enlightenment that the book could emerge in this form. To work with him was to receive a remarkable tutorial on good writing from a brilliant writing coach. Obviously, any infelicity of expression that remains is my own.

I thank my Dharma partner Julie Forsythe for her unfailing generosity and wisdom throughout this project, and my spiritual friends Brendan Kennedy, Lama Choying Palmo, Roger Walsh, and Jane Burdick for their insightful input in initial writing. Thank you Ana Hristic for your wise assistance in early drafts, and Bob Morrison, Leah Weiss, Jane Moss, Andria Whited, and Sheila Moir for your wonderful contributions. Thank you, Paul Crafts, for your selfless support. I am also grateful to my editor at Wisdom Publications, David Kittelstrom, for his perceptive input and assistance.

I dedicate this book to my wife, Barbara, and my children, Jonathan and David, and through them to all others.

Introduction:
Unleashing the Power of Love

EVERYTHING THAT IS MOST IMPORTANT to human beings is dependent upon love. Powerful and enduring love, grounded in wisdom, is the panacea to cure the ills of this world, starting with our own. We all have this curative power of goodness within us; all we need are the means to unveil it. This book provides those means.

Strong, impartial love is indispensable for everything that matters most to us. We seek safety and well-being for ourselves, our families, our communities. But what is it that makes us feel truly safe and well? What makes intimate relationships and family life into a nourishing, life-affirming enclave rather than a place of unfulfilled expectations and recriminations? What makes children sense they are growing up in a warm, welcoming home and community, rather than a callous place of indifference? What makes our world feel blessed; a place where we feel free to explore our lives together, creatively and joyfully? Enduring love is required to make all such things possible.

Every human act is an expression of a basic motivation—a force of intent and will. In any moment that our motivation is narrowed by brittle self-concern, we are incapable of being fully present or available for others. In contrast, in those moments when we are motivated by a genuine, impartial care for others—a strong love that actually wishes those around us to be well and happy—we are vividly present and attentive; we become a genuine help and port of safety. This may sound simple, but it is not simplistic. It is an inescapable human truth. Those who learn to embody this truth have a joyful and fulfilling life; those who do not find themselves caught in continual struggle.

This book is for those who want to realize their capacity of love to the fullest, to apply its vivifying and protective energy to every part of their lives and world. The meditations here can help you to unveil your deepest goodness—a capacity of enduring love and wisdom that you may not have realized you already own, a power to benefit others all around you. This capability is not given to just a few people at the whim of fate—a select few to be admired from afar. *Every one of us has this inner capacity*. Its power can be revealed through specific practices available to anyone with a strong interest; it is just a matter of taking them up with diligence. Thousands before us have entered into these practices and experienced their life-transforming results.

So what is love? And how can a greater force of love, grounded in wisdom, help us to achieve everything that we most care about? If we all have such a capacity of love and wisdom, how can we bring it out and make it real in our lives? In this introduction, we will begin to address these questions. The following chapters then provide specific means to awaken our potential of wise, enduring love for the sake of all.

Buddhist Methods to Unleash Love's Power

Many of the world's religious and cultural traditions affirm the central importance of love and compassion. Yet Buddhism seems distinctive in providing exceptionally clear and specific methods to bring out our human capacity for enduring love, compassion, and the self-transcending wisdom that informs them. The essentials of these methods can be learned by anyone, no matter their religious affiliation.

Unconditional love and compassion, supported by sympathetic joy and equanimity, are among the essential qualities that the Buddha taught his followers to cultivate. Buddhist texts refer to these four powerful states of mind as the *boundless attitudes*. *Love* here is the powerful and enduring wish for beings to be deeply well and happy and to possess the inmost causes of such happiness. *Compassion* is the enduring wish for beings to be free from suffering and its inmost causes. *Sympathetic joy* is joy in the happiness of beings and in the means to their happiness. *Equanimity* is the deep wisdom beyond self-centeredness through which the three prior attitudes become impartial, all-inclusive, and steadfast. Buddhist traditions teach specific ways for people to cultivate these potent attitudes and to apply their power for the benefit of many others.

In texts that focus on the teaching of *buddha nature,* the Buddha declared that all the qualities of his enlightenment—including the capacities for such enduring love, compassion, and wisdom—abide within the very essence of beings' minds. Our fundamental nature *is* that of the buddhas. But this innate goodness is thickly obscured by habits of thought that reduce others to mere objects of self-centered need. Buddhist traditions teach specific ways to cut through those obscuring patterns to unveil our natural goodness and to rediscover ourselves and all others as intrinsically holy.

In Tibetan Buddhism, one cultivates the four boundless attitudes to empower the emergence of what is called the *spirit of enlightenment,* or *bodhichitta* in Sanskrit—the resolve to completely realize one's hidden goodness in order to meet the deepest needs of beings. The spirit of enlightenment *is* the power of love, compassion, and impartial wisdom stirring within the individual, impelling her to the fullest realization of her best potential for the sake of all.

When this profound resolve takes hold of a person's heart and mind, it makes him or her into a *bodhisattva,* one whose life is directed to spiritual awakening on behalf of the world. For the bodhisattva, wise love and compassion become so enduring a motive power that her daily actions bring tremendous good into the lives of those around her. As the Dalai Lama frequently teaches, the challenge of our time is to learn how to take "universal responsibility." That is what the bodhisattva path of enlightenment actually means—taking the responsibility to rediscover your life as your link to all others, to awaken the tremendous goodness hidden within you, and to act from there.

Love Is the Motive Force for Genuine Help

Love is the power to commune with someone's fundamental goodness while wishing that person deep well-being and happiness. Any time we lack that genuine wish of love, we lack the motivation to be a significant help to others. Love *is* the motive power of help. We ache at the violence, pain, and hunger in our world, and inside us is a will to help. But "help" only helps if it is an active expression of love. Otherwise our attempts to help, limited by narrow self-concern, become rigid and too easily discouraged.

We may want to protect our dear ones, but who will protect them from us at those times when we worry just about ourselves and are not listening to them? The violence in the world that we hear about in the daily news and so decry—is it only caused by those "others"? Haven't we all contributed to the coarsening atmosphere of intolerance and distrust whenever we've lacked a loving response and indulged our most self-centered tendencies? How can we make the world safer if we ourselves are not a stable port of safety? Can we be honest about this?

Strong love that wills the well-being and happiness of persons is essential to accomplish everything we most value for ourselves and others. Yet this simple truth is hardly discussed in modern culture, virtually unmentioned in newspapers and magazines. This is because contemporary, secular societies have little knowledge of how to unleash an enduring power of love. Not knowing how to do it, modern societies assume it can't be done. So they look to experts for helping strategies while ignoring the role of motivation behind any attempt to help—as if only techniques mattered, not a *genuine will* to help.

Parents know it is love that nourishes their children. "Parenting strategies" are means to enact that love effectively. But the same principle applies everywhere else: helping strategies only help when they effectively carry out a genuine wish of care, of love—the wish for someone's well-being and happiness. Otherwise, so-called "helping strategies" don't help. Have you noticed?

After college, I entered the U.S. Peace Corps in the Philippines and worked in a tuberculosis program serving rural villages. Patients in this program needed to take their medicine each day for a year. If they stopped, their tuberculosis often returned in more virulent form. Unfortunately, monsoon rains deluged the region for several months each year, and the floods made it difficult for village patients to travel miles to the nearest clinic. Success required the health workers to carry the medicine to the villages during the rainy season, at great personal hardship.

Local government and international agencies invested many resources into the tuberculosis program, and many health workers were remarkably dedicated. But overall, the will to get the medicine to village patients during flood season was not strong enough to get the medicine out reliably. Lacking that, the human tendencies toward narrow self-concern, apathy, and prejudice against the rural poor rendered communities helpless to deal with the problem effectively. There just was not enough enduring love, care, and compassion to make the program work.

This experience partly motivated my exploration of Buddhist practice in Asia after my Peace Corps service. It appeared to me that real solutions to individual and communal suffering required more than material resources and techniques. Our methods for achieving social well-being may be sophisticated but in themselves are quite limited in effectiveness—wars, gross social inequities, and self-serving political battles continue to pervade our daily headlines. The problem is that the basic substance of social well-being isn't strategy or technology—it is love, the will in our hearts for others around us to have happiness and contentment. If that is absent, no policy, no political party, no army, and no technology will protect us. Without an enduring motivation of genuine care for persons, the common good simply will not hold together, no matter how clever the plan or how advanced the technology. When a strong motive force of genuine care is present, and when that motive force is enacted through wise plans and methods, great benefit does come. We see this in the effective work of exemplary providers of service and aid here and abroad.

Love Empowers Social Service and Overcomes Burnout

At meditation workshops, I meet many people involved in social service—teachers, therapists, social workers, doctors, nurses, and activists. Many say they have lost their energy for service and have become burnt out. They ask what can be done to help them go on. When any of us wants to help, we need to ask ourselves: What is the motive force, the will behind the helping? How powerful is that intention and how long lasting? Is it just the weak commitment of a frail ego? If our motivation for serving others is tied to a strong desire for specific outcomes or for praise, our potential is limited. Because we can never completely control the results of our efforts, we may become easily frustrated and disheartened.

On the other hand, in any moment that a person's motive is the simple, strong care for all involved, at least for that moment there is no burnout, no discouragement—love in action is sufficient. If one plan doesn't work, another can be sought; no narrow expectations limit the freedom of love to try anew. Such a way of being is its own reward, for it expresses our inmost nature of fundamental goodness. Have you known such a person in your life, someone who embodied in her service to others a genuine regard and affection for each one, inspiring them to realize their best potential, whatever the result of the moment? It is the clarity and power of genuine care, a strong, stable love wishing others well, that makes enduring service possible.

Indeed, those who learn to embody an indomitable love become virtually unstoppable in their activity for others, because the motive force of their action is unaffected by short-term outcomes—people such as Martin Luther King, the Dalai Lama, Aung San Suu Kyi of Burma, Thich Nhat Hanh, Nelson Mandela, Gandhi, and Mother Teresa. Some admire such figures from afar and think, "How special they are; I could never be like that." But according to the Buddha, the power of active love in such people is a natural capacity that we all share.

Without Enduring Love, Relationships Don't Work

The crucial importance of enduring love is obvious for family life. It brings a power of goodness and joy into our families, so children feel truly at home with us, fearless to explore who and what they are. It makes our relationships with spouse, partner, and friend profoundly safe, based upon deep mutual appreciation, reverence, and joy, instead of the brittle reactivity of mere self-protectiveness. It is the nurturing power of genuine love that protects and empowers all intimate relationships. But it is equally important for our lives at work. It is love, the operative wish for each person to have happiness, that makes our workplace into a zone of genuine care and protection for coworkers, clients, and customers, rather than an arena of unspoken jealousies and recriminations. Love protects us from our own worst tendencies to reduce others to mere objects of momentary need or want, triggering hostility and competition whenever our expectations are not met.

We can talk about "family values" as much as we wish, but the quality of our presence to partner, children, neighbors, colleagues, students, and clients depends *entirely* on the strength of our fundamental care for them. In simple terms: how strong is the quality of our love for those with whom we share our lives, how enduring our wish for their happiness? Whatever the strategies for a successful life promulgated in self-help books, and no matter how hard someone may thump a holy book to declare a particular belief as the answer to all life's problems, none of those approaches works if the basic motive of genuine love, of actual care for persons, is not present.

No Real Solution to Violence Without Impartial Love and Wisdom

Someone might object—isn't loving everyone unconditionally woefully unrealistic; being blind to how things work in the real world? According to the Buddhist teachings we will explore in this book, no such "real world" stands on its own, out there, apart from what we are all making of it. We make our world with each intention, each action, each thought we have of others, and each reaction to our own thought of them. Strong love and wisdom are what reveal the reality of self and others, so we *can* generate the kind of world that we really want.

In my own city of Boston there was a news story involving a jealous man who took revenge upon a former girlfriend by murdering her children. A friend of mine teaches in a school for youths from poor inner-city neighborhoods. Several of his students, deeply upset at the news, told him that they personally knew the murdered children. Then, one by one, these students recounted their own stories of friends and relatives who had been murdered, often by rival gangs who attacked others with little or no provocation. The students told him: "This *is* the world. This is how it is."

When individuals and groups do not experience being loved—when whole communities lose hope that anyone cares—fear and violence are often seized upon as seeming protectors in the form of gangs, mobs, and communal hostility. The only apparent protection is to be on the strongest, most violent side. Indeed, when violent tendencies become so omnipresent that they completely suppress love and compassion, their projections of fear and hatred appear simply to *be* the world—as these students declared.

The attitudes of prejudice, hatred, and violence are so radically cut off from the realities of persons—so lost in projections of fear and malice—that they present the appearance of *being* objectively what persons are, what the world is. Current perpetrators of violence here and abroad often perceive themselves as the historical victims who finally get "justice" through violence. Meanwhile their own victims fantasize someday becoming the perpetrators so as to inflict their revenge in the name of "justice." Hatred and prejudice drive a never-ending cycle of self-righteous revenge in the name of the good.

Fundamentally contrary to that dynamic are the all-inclusive attitudes of impartial love, compassion, and wisdom, which are attuned to the *actual* realities of persons beyond such projections. These attitudes sense and respond to persons accurately, as they really are, in the conditions shared by us all: layers of human suffering and fear that hide tremendous inner capacities for generosity and fundamental goodness. Unconditional love and wisdom embodied in a person's life are the most powerful forces for remaking the world we experience together and for holding open the door for others to learn similarly.[1]

The Aims and Audience of This Book

The purpose of this book is to provide fresh access to Buddhist practices of love, compassion, and wisdom for *anyone* who wishes to explore them. The freshness of this approach comes from the main tradition I speak from—the Dzogchen tradition of Tibetan Buddhism. *Dzogchen* is Tibetan for "natural great perfection," meaning that our fundamental being is already pure, perfect, and tranquil, primordially good, the very nature of the buddhas. Our intrinsic purity, however, is obscured by narrow self-clinging thought patterns that have become so habitual that we mistake these thoughts for our very being.

The path to embodying unconditional love and wisdom is not some overwhelmingly difficult struggle to make ourselves into something alien to our nature. Quite the opposite. Unconditional love and wisdom dawn as we come home to what we most deeply are. Our deepest wish is already impartial love; our deepest knowing already intuitive wisdom beyond self-clinging. We just need to learn to relax our grip on ourselves enough to allow those capacities to awaken within us and shine forth.

Efficient means of awakening have been passed down by great masters of Buddhist tradition, adapted to the hearts and minds of the people in diverse cultures throughout history. Such means are provided in the guided meditations of this book. My intention is to present them in a form that is readily accessible to our contemporary culture.

This book is aimed at two audiences: (1) people, no matter their religious affiliation, who seek fresh access to the heart of spirituality and clear, concrete ways to realize the power of love and compassion; (2) people long practiced in Buddhist traditions, who seek to reconnect with the simplicity of practice in a fresh way, to revitalize and deepen their continuing life in the Dharma.

While these techniques are transmitted from the Buddhist tradition, readers of other faiths are invited to take up the meditation practices and engage them through their own spiritual understandings. Feel free to explore how your faith may be informed and deepened by practices of love, compassion, and self-transcending wisdom transmitted here from Buddhism. For example, in the meditation of chapter 1 on receiving the wish of love, while I envision the Buddha at the center of a field of beings who radiate their wish of love, a Christian might envision Christ, a Hindu might envision Krishna, a Jew or Muslim simply the radiant power of God's love.

Replicating the Transformative Effect of an Ancient Tradition

The content of this book is not merely of my own making. It is thoroughly dependent upon my teachers who transmitted these practices and on those students who have come to me over the years to learn them.

Most of my teachers have been Tibetans, and the guided meditations in this book translate my experience of Tibetan Buddhist practices. But this translation does not seek just to reproduce the literal context of their ancient tradition. Rather, it seeks to replicate the effect of their words on me over several decades of practice. These practices have woven themselves into a heart and mind patterned by my life as an American, formed by the symbols, myths, and perspectives of my culture. These teachers instigated in me a learning process that revealed some of my distinctively Western channels of receptivity to Buddhist truths. And anything that my own students have found helpful in my teaching has further informed and sharpened this learning process.

For example, the traditional door of entry into the path of the buddhas is to take *refuge* in the liberating qualities and powers of enlightenment. This means to rely completely upon the powers of unconditional love, compassion, and wisdom that are fully realized in the buddhas, evoked by the practices they transmitted (Dharma), and embodied in mature spiritual community (sangha). In Tibetan practice, such refuge is further empowered through the profound practice of *union,* merging one's mind with the enlightened mind of one's spiritual teachers, beyond separation of self and other.

Tibetans engage such profound practices of union first by ritually receiving the blessings of the buddhas from stylized Indo-Tibetan arrays of holy beings. These "blessings" are actually the liberating powers of love, compassion, and wisdom—capacities anyone can learn to open to. But the symbolic depictions that Tibetans use for opening to such powers may not function to the same depth for Westerners, at least not initially. Over time, the practices taught by my Tibetan teachers helped me to recall and receive the love and compassion that I had sensed in caring people and mentors throughout my entire life as a Westerner. I began to realize that the "blessings" of enlightenment had pervaded my world all along, embodied in countless wise and loving gestures. This made such blessings real to me, strengthening my capacity to receive them deeply from my Buddhist lineage teachers as well, thus replicating a key effect achieved by Tibetans through their symbolic forms.

In the chapters that follow, we will explore how the practice of receiving the radiant wish of love from loving people and spiritual mentors, and merging into oneness with them in that radiance, provides a way for contemporary people of all backgrounds to access these powerful Tibetan practices of refuge and union. In this way, by using channels of receptivity natural to us, we learn to let our inmost goodness commune with the inmost goodness of all who have loved us. Then, through the power of such communion, we are brought to rest in the limitless, radiant ground of such goodness: the deep wisdom of pure awareness beyond self-grasping. Through such practice, we begin to sense each aspect of life and every being as holy.

In 1978, shortly after I had finished my service in the Peace Corps, I met my first Tibetan Buddhist teachers, Lama Thubten Yeshe and Lama Zopa Rinpoche, who connected me with other teachers close to His Holiness the Dalai Lama, including Geshe Ngawang Dhargyey and Geshe Lhundub Sopa. I spent fifteen years immersed in the study and practice of Tibetan teachings of love, compassion, and wisdom under their guidance, inspired especially by the ancient Kadam and Gelug masters of Tibet. Then I met Lama Surya Das, Nyoshul Khen Rinpoche, and Khenpo Sonam Tobgyal, who introduced me to the teachings of Dzogchen from their revered Nyingma lineage. After further years of practice under their guidance and inspiration, the teachings of love and compassion came newly alive for me in light of the Dzogchen view of innate wisdom, taking expression in the meditations transmitted in this book. In recent years, my understanding of the unity of compassion and primordial awareness has been further informed by the profound teaching and blessing of Chokyi Nyima Rinpoche and His Holiness Drukchen Rinpoche.

When Lama Surya Das asked me to help guide practices at meditation retreats, I found that, like him, the most effective way was not only to quote my teachers' words, which I cherish, but also to speak from the effect of their words on my practice and life—my own experience of their teachings, however limited. The same approach has shaped the content of this book. My hope is that this process of translation may assist you to tap into your own innate reserves of love and wisdom.

I. Receiving Love:
Key to Life, Key to the Spiritual Path

Love Pervades Our Existence

My root spiritual teacher, Nyoshul Khenpo, has said that a moment of enlightenment is a moment when we realize "the blessings that are always pouring forth." We are, by nature, endowed with qualities of absolute goodness—purest love, compassion, wisdom, and tranquillity. Those radiant qualities are intrinsic to our being. They are some of the "blessings" to which Khenpo refers.[2] A moment of enlightenment is the moment that we newly notice such "blessings" as having been all around us, and within us, from the beginning. Whenever we are ready to notice, we can sense their healing, liberating energy pouring forth right here, right now.

One such radiant quality is unconditional love; the kind of love that doesn't care what someone has thought or done but simply wishes him deep well-being and joy. It's like the unconditional and unreserved love that a wise, devoted parent has for her child. That capacity of love is within each of us and has been active all around us, pervading our world from the moment we were born.

The claim that love pervades this world may not sound real to you but not because it isn't true. Rather, many of us haven't learned to pay much attention to countless moments of love, kindness, and care that surround us each day: a child at the store reaching for her mother's hand, an elderly stranger at the park who smiles upon a young family, a grocery clerk or waitress who beams at you with kindness as she hands you the change.

The "blessings that are always pouring forth" include the pervasive power of love that has permeated our lives, peeking at us through the eyes of many persons all along. Think, for example, of someone whom you adored to be near when you were a child. A parent or grandparent, a special aunt or uncle, a family friend or teacher—someone it felt wonderful to be with. Why did you like so much to be near that person? Probably because they radiated a wish of love to you, the simple wish for your well-being and happiness, through the quality of their presence, their words, their play with you, or simply through their smiling eyes when you came near. Try to remember someone like that from your childhood right now. Hold that person in your mind for a moment. Recall how it felt to be near him or her. That's what it is like to receive the love that just wishes for your happiness. We like to be near people like that because we have a deep need to receive their unspoken love, their wish for our happiness, to drink up its life-giving goodness.

Rediscovering the Love in Your World

That radiant blessing of love has been coming to us from the start, not just from a few people close to us, but also from many not personally known to us or forgotten. So many have offered themselves to us quietly, unnoticed, and unremarked upon, such as those who served in our school parent-teacher groups, who coached sports for us as small children, who taught us music and clapped when we played, who watched over us with kindness and care wherever we ran and played. Countless such adults offered themselves each day from a simple, loving concern for the children of those towns, including you and me. Then there are all the adults who put loving care into their work for us, as our teachers, doctors, nurses, social workers, craftsmen, bakers, librarians, waitresses. Yet we may never have noticed the extent of such care and consideration. No one actually verbalizes: "Out of loving concern for all the children in this neighborhood, including you, I am helping to build this playground," or "I am now sending you the wish of love; that's why you like to be near me." And the child doesn't think, "I am now receiving the wish of love." We overlook it or just take it for granted. So we may never become conscious of how much loving care is in our world and how pervasive it has been all along.

Then as we grow older, we learn to pay attention to things that society considers more real and significant than the loving care of all those people. According to the social discourse around us, it seems much more important to identify those whom we should hate, fear, or compete with for affirmation, power, and wealth. Meanwhile, television news and magazines focus our communal attention each day on the horrible things that some people have done to others, as if that is all that happened throughout the entire world that day.

Much of our discourse is spent propping up this negative worldview: "Oh, yes, I know what you mean, my relatives are horrible too." "I can't stand that political leader either." "Can you believe how stupid those people are?" As adults our attention has become so focused on the unloving aspects of our life and world, we easily overlook the love embodied in countless small daily gestures of kindness. We've learned to ignore that and to shut it out.

We have become so smug in our cultural cynicisms that we don't notice how the fuller reality of everyone we talk about has routinely escaped our notice. Even the people we generally look down upon have had at least moments of integrity and kindness. Even in homes that we took to be unloving, there were some faltering gestures of kindness and support or social service workers and schoolteachers struggling to make the lives of children and families better.

The truth is that very few of us would have survived our childhood had it not been for countless, now mostly forgotten, acts of loving kindness extended to us.

In addition, there are people in the world and throughout history who have benefited many persons beyond their personal life, people whose way of being embodies such powerful concern for others and for the world that they epitomize our greatest human potential, such as Shakyamuni Buddha and Jesus, St. Francis, Martin Luther King, Gandhi, Mother Teresa, and the Dalai Lama. Such potent spiritual beings have radiated their love to all of us without discrimination. But within modern, secular worldviews, many of us have forgotten how to acknowledge and to receive the liberating power of such love. Instead, we've learned to ignore it.

Our society provides no curriculum or schooling on how to notice so much love or to recognize the many people who have transmitted its life-giving power. Most of us haven't been taught that to receive love deeply and transmit it wholeheartedly is a real human possibility, that it can be learned, and that to do so is the key to our deepest well-being, our spiritual life, and our capacity to bring more goodness into this world.

So, as adults, we need to become newly aware of the love that has infused our life all along, to turn our attention to it afresh with the eyes of a child. To do so is to become conscious of the tremendous capacity of love that even now permeates our being—to open to it, heal in its life-giving energy, and participate in its power to renew our world. We can awaken to the deepest goodness in ourselves and others. We can learn to recognize and commune with "the blessings that have always been pouring forth."

The first step is to learn to pay new attention to what has been ignored.

Reawaken to Love First by Noticing It

At the Corner Store

A poem by Alison Luterman

It was a new old man behind the counter,
skinny, brown and eager.
He greeted me like a long lost daughter,
as if we both came from the same world,
someplace warmer and more gracious than this cold city.

I was thirsty and alone. Sick at heart, grief-soiled
    and his face lit up as if I were his prodigal daughter

returning,
coming back to the freezer bins in front of the register
which were still and always filled
with the same old Cable Car ice-cream sandwiches and
    cheap frozen greens.
Back to the knobs of beef and packages of hotdogs,
these familiar shelves strung with potato chips and corn chips,
stacked-up beer boxes and immortal Jim Beam.

I lumbered to the case and bought my precious bottled water
and he returned my change, beaming
as if I were the bright new buds on the just-bursting-open
    cherry trees,
as if I were everything beautiful struggling to grow,
and he was blessing me as he handed me my dime

over the dirty counter and the plastic tub of red licorice
    whips.

This old man who didn't speak English
beamed out love to me in the iron week after my mother's
  death
so that when I emerged from his store

  my whole cockeyed life—
  what a beautiful failure!—
glowed gold like a sunset after rain.

  Frustrated city dogs were yelping in their yards,
  mad with passion behind their chain-linked fences,
  and in the driveway of a peeling-paint house
  a woman and a girl danced to contagious reggae.

Praise Allah! Jah! The Buddha! Kwan Yin,
Jesus, Mary and even jealous old Jehovah!

For eyes, hands
of the divine, everywhere.[3]

What is remarkable about this poem is not that the old man extended such love. Many people are extending such love, the simple wish for another's happiness—and have been since the day we were born. What is remarkable to me is that the poet, Alison Luterman, was willing to *notice* it. Even during the "iron week" after her mother's death, she noticed the love that a little stranger radiated to her from behind a store counter. It was natural to think of the clerk as a foreigner, someone who didn't even speak the same language. But moved by his simple love, which asked nothing in return, Alison found herself participating in a more subtle level of communication with him, a silent language of grace and blessing, "…as if we both came from...someplace warmer and more gracious than this cold city."

Even more remarkable than her willingness to notice such love was her willingness to *receive* it. The simple act of accepting this stranger's wish for her happiness empowered her to experience the world in a completely different way. To accept that wish of love evoked a natural awe toward her own "cock-eyed" life, which now "glowed gold like a sunset after rain." To accept that wish of love brought out her capacity to appreciate and revere all that was arrayed around her: the yelping dogs, the paint-peeling house, the mother and daughter dancing, and the reggae music.

To receive such a simple wish of love quietly opens our minds to an innate wisdom that recognizes the essential goodness of being, the intrinsic goodness of experience itself, the joy of being alive. It brings out the natural wisdom that was hidden in our minds—a purer vision that knows the beings and things all around us to be utterly holy, as if they were all messengers of the Buddha, of God. That is why Alison's poem ends with such appreciation, gratitude, and reverence for "eyes, hands of the divine, everywhere."

To receive love in this way is to become conscious of a fresh, holy world that was somehow obscured by our tired, socially constructed worlds of self-centered worry and cynicism. When someone awakens in a moment of receptivity, as Alison did, to the "blessings that are always pouring forth," the fresh, sacred world that was long ignored suddenly unveils itself. It is self-revealed as one's true home.

Discover the Benefactors in Your Life

We discover love's transformative and liberating power first by receiving love more fully, then by offering it more inclusively, and finally by becoming a reflex of it from the ground of our being. That is one way to describe the path to enlightenment. To enter into this process, we need to identify benefactors who have been emissaries of love in our lives. "Benefactor" here means someone who has sent us the wish of love, the simple wish for us to be well and happy, like the store clerk in the poem. Once we start to notice such beings, we find, actually, that there have been many that have radiated such love to us, but we had mostly overlooked or forgotten them.

A benefactor is someone you perceive as such in your own experience; not just someone you *assume* you should pick as benefactor. Your benefactors may be living or not. It makes no difference—the power of love transcends how we think of time.

Exercise: Learning to Recognize Benefactors

It's important to be mindful that benefactors need not be infallible or perfect people. Just allow yourself to become newly aware of moments when someone's unreserved love came to you— through a kind word, a gesture, a smile, or a comforting presence. It could be someone well known to you or a seeming stranger like the store clerk.

Try to recall someone like that from your childhood right now. Envision his or her smiling presence before you. Recall how good it felt to be near that person. That is what it is like to receive love. Hold that person in mind for a little while, communing with him or her in the simple goodness of their wish of love for you, their wish for your happiness and joy. Take a few minutes just to relax and receive that wish from him or her. Right now.

When you feel ready, try now to think of a few other persons you adored to be near as a child. An uncle or aunt, perhaps? A schoolteacher that you loved to be with? A friend of your parents whom you looked forward to seeing? When I began to do this exercise, my second grade teacher suddenly appeared in my mind's eye—Mrs. Kirchner, whom I liked so much that I accidentally called her "mom" at school. So that is why I liked to be near her, I realized. She wasn't just teaching; she was expressing her love for her students *through* her teaching. Another time, two close friends of my parents came suddenly to mind—Ted and Yvonne, with their smiling faces radiating kindness to me as a small child. Then there was my uncle Morton, who expressed his love with silly jokes and by snitching some of my french fries when I wasn't looking—while making sure I would catch him in the act.

When you have thought of a few such benefactors in your life, imagine them before you one by one or all together. Mentally hold the smiling faces of those benefactors before you; then relax and just accept the simple goodness of their wish for your well-being and happiness, their wish of love for you. Take time for this right now, accepting, receiving, and enjoying the power of their wish. There is nothing more important to do.

If you do this exercise repeatedly over time, you will progressively recognize more benefactors not only from your early life but from other periods as well, right up to the present. Even now there are persons you have probably overlooked who make a wish for your happiness, but you hadn't realized how important and life-giving it was to pay attention to them.

As practice progresses, you may find yourself widening your range of benefactors by spontaneously recalling instances when you were the recipient of unconditional love, even from people that you long characterized as unloving! One meditator, who had a particularly difficult relationship with his mother over the years, told me how he found himself recalling a scene from his early childhood during a meditation session on love. He had been in a fever, foggy with delirium, when his mother came to soothe him by placing her hand on his stomach—a gentle, healing touch. Even after all these years, the memory of that simple, loving gesture suddenly reawakened. Again, we are not looking for infallible persons; just moments when genuine, unreserved care came through.

Feel free to include your pet as a benefactor. Pets often take such joy in our happiness that it's natural to include them among our benefactors.

Importance of Spiritual Benefactors

Besides benefactors recalled from your personal life, it is important to learn to recognize a second kind of benefactor when it makes sense to you—deeply spiritual persons in your world, past or present, who function as spiritual benefactors for you. These are persons that you feel embody great goodness, a force of love and compassion that extends to all without partiality, including yourself. These may be people in your life whose fundamental goodness and way of being profoundly influenced you. If you have a mentor or teacher who inspires your spiritual practice, he or she would be included here. You could also include the teachers of your own spiritual teacher. Persons most profoundly holy to you, such as Shakyamuni Buddha or Jesus, would fall into this category. Try to identify ones *you* feel to be such sacred beings, true to your own maturing sense of that, without trying merely to conform to others' assumptions.

You probably have not had personal acquaintance with all your spiritual benefactors. Some may be people who inspire you from afar, whether still living or not—holy beings, prophets, and spiritual activists such as the Dalai Lama, Teresa of Avila, Martin Luther King, Mother Teresa, Martin Buber, Ramakrishna, St. Francis,

Rumi, Thich Nhat Hanh, Dorothy Day, Ramana Maharshi. Such beings may truly inspire or guide you as you read their writings, hear their stories, or gaze upon a picture of them and feel their goodness coming through. Indeed, you can keep a picture of such a person near you for that purpose. One meditator I know keeps a picture of Mr. Rogers, the fatherly television personality and minister who helped generations of American children feel at home in this world.

Because such spiritually weighty beings have communed so deeply with the very source of love and compassion, the very ground of goodness, we share in that ground when we open to their wish of love, their wish for the fullest well-being and happiness of ourselves and all others. It blesses our life. This is part of the reason that images of the Buddha, the Dalai Lama, and other revered spiritual teachers are so important to Tibetan Buddhists—such figures are sources of spiritual energy and inspiration for those who regularly commune with them in their love and compassion for all.

Try to bring to mind one or more spiritual benefactors now, whether personally known to you or admired from a distance, and imagine their smiling presence before you. Relax and gently open to receive their wish for your deep well-being and happiness, their wish of love that radiates to you and many others. Commune with them in that way for a little while, and enjoy.

Entering into the Practice of Love

Now you are ready for the meditation below. It can be done in daily practice for about twenty minutes per session. Pause after each demarcated subsection, to give yourself time to dwell on the instruction at hand. When first beginning, if you find it helpful, reread the instruction of one subsection a few times before meditating on it for a little while. Then move on to the next subsection and do similarly.

When you have repeated the meditation a number of times, you will need to look at the written instructions much less. If you would like an mp3 file for audio transmission of the meditations in this book, please consult the ordering information at the end of the book.

Meditation: Receiving the Healing, Transforming Power of Love

Part 1: Receiving Love

Sit in a relaxed way with back comfortably straight, on cushion or chair, eyes open, gazing slightly downward. Having identified both kinds of benefactors, ones from ordinary life and spiritual benefactors from near or far, bring one or more of each type to mind and imagine their smiling faces before you. Envision them sending you the wish of love, the wish for your deepest well-being, happiness, and joy.

Sensing these wonderful people before you, gently open to their wish of love. Imagine their wish as a gentle radiance, like a soft shower of healing rays. Bathe your whole body and mind in that tender radiance, all the way down to your toes and fingertips. Bask in the loving energy of that wish. Trust it. You don't have to trust every aspect of all benefactors, just the wish of love that they radiate, the simple wish for your well-being and happiness.

Receive the gentle, healing energy of that radiance. As other thoughts or feelings arise, let them be enveloped in this loving luminosity. No matter who you think you are, what you think you deserve, all such thoughts are irrelevant now—just accept the benefactors' wish of love for your deepest happiness. Trusting this wish more than any limiting thoughts of yourself, receive it into your whole being.

Let yourself rely upon this love, the goodness it comes from, and the goodness it meets in your heart. To rely upon this love more than on your own defensive reactions is to find profound refuge.

Be at ease, open, and accepting, like a puppy lying in the morning sun, passively soaking up its rays. Absorb the soft, healing energy of love into every cell of your body, every corner of your mind. Bathe in this, heal in this, rest in this.

After a little while, join your benefactors in their wish for you. While receiving the radiance of their love, mentally repeat the wish for yourself, using words like these: "May this one have deepest well-being, happiness, and joy." Affirm the words repeatedly in your mind. Try to mean them as you say them, just as your benefactors mean them for you. Like everyone else in this world, you most deeply need and deserve happiness and well-being. Repeat the wish for yourself while accepting your benefactors' love even more deeply into body and mind, communing with them through its radiance.

Part 2: Letting Go and Merging into Oneness with the Radiance

Finally, let go into utter oneness with the radiance, dropping the visualization of benefactors, and releasing any attempt to hold on to any frame of reference. Deeply let be into that gentle, luminous wholeness beyond separation of self and others. Enjoy just being thus for a little while, at ease, at rest, complete.

Good work! You have completed the meditation.

We Have to Receive Help if We Want to Offer Help

Why Pay So Much Attention to Myself?

Most participants I meet at retreats and workshops catch on quickly to the profundity of this practice of receiving unconditional love. There is much more to it than meets the eye! Indeed, it eases us experientially into what it means actually to enter the spiritual path. It does so by helping us to become newly conscious of our hidden capacities of unconditional love and wisdom (buddha nature), and to begin to rely on those capacities rather than on ego-centered habits of mind. That is the beginning of authentic refuge in the intrinsic goodness of being, which presages entry into the path of a bodhisattva, a holy one, the path to become a spiritual protector of this world.

Some people have a slightly defensive reaction when first introduced to conscious receiving of love: "I am not comfortable putting so much attention upon myself. I want to turn my attention to helping others, not to myself." Such a reaction is common here in the West, since many of us learned from childhood that to be a good person is to think first of others. Dharma teachings from Buddhism are also frequently misinterpreted to mean that the well-being of others is of a different order than the well-being of oneself. But that represents a failure to understand the deeper implications of concern for others.

If we want to be truly helpful to others, our help must express an authentic care that actually wishes others well. Otherwise, when the chips are down, our attempts at "helping" become brittle and self-serving. If we want really to help others, we need a strong, enduring attitude of loving care. But where does such an attitude come from? Does it happen simply by turning your attention away from yourself to others? Aren't others a lot like yourself in needing, wanting, and deserving such loving care? If you don't think you ought to receive such love, do you really think that others ought to receive it? After all, they're just like you.

In order to give loving care in a stable, enduring way, we have to be able to receive loving care in a stable, enduring way. Why? Because giving and receiving are of one piece, and because "self" and "other" are not so different from one another. There is a saying: "You can't give what you don't have." People who refuse to receive love find that they have little to give.

The Ability to Receive Love Becomes the Ability to Give Love

Indeed, one reason we have difficulty finding the enduring love we need to help others is that others often bother us. Many others just don't seem so good to us! On the streets, in the tussle of life, we are on our guard against strangers to a greater or lesser extent. But this is related to our brittle sense of self. What bothers us about others, what we dislike or fear in them, are aspects of ourselves that they mirror back at us, aspects we dislike seeing. Until we make deep peace with such aspects of ourselves, unwanted aspects we don't want to see, by learning to receive a love that touches in past them to the intrinsic goodness of our being, we can't open to the intrinsic goodness of others that also lies hidden from our view.

We need to receive love from those who have sent it to us just as we are, with all our flaws, in order to relax into the deeper goodness within us that always deserves such love and to heal there. Then we can offer a love in turn that embraces others with similar flaws, that touches in on their intrinsic worth, mirrors their goodness back at them, and doesn't give up on them no matter what. Perhaps you can recall someone who mirrored your own inner goodness back at you when you felt most low. Wasn't that a profound help? That is what we are learning to become—someone who has received love so fully that she can offer love to others unconditionally. Therefore, in the practices that follow, our ability to receive love will evoke an ability to give love more enduringly and inclusively than we may have thought possible.

Many people, over many centuries, have taken up a practice like this and have already included us in it—spiritual benefactors who first learned to receive the enduring wish of love from others before them and then radiated that wish to us all. Buddhas, bodhisattvas, holy beings, spiritual teachers—many have blessed us with that radiant wish even before we had heard of them. From them, we can learn to recognize this, acknowledge it, receive it, participate in it, and pass it on. Then our benefactors, by blessing us with their love and compassion, will continue to bless many others through us.

Establishing a Daily Practice

Try to do this practice of receiving and merging with the radiant wish of love each day for at least twenty minutes at a time. First thing in the morning is a fresh time for it. When first starting this practice, some people tell me they can't recall any benefactors. That's not uncommon, since we may never have been told to identify them. Remember, a benefactor is not an infallible person—just someone, at some time, who wished for you to be deeply happy, well, joyful. Many near or far have wished that, but we probably hadn't learned to notice. These days I pick many kind adults from my early childhood, several teachers and key mentors from school and summer camp, and many others throughout my life, but it required some excavating. In the beginning I didn't have these people in mind. I didn't even remember most of them. Over time the practice itself began to uncover many who had quietly held me in their wish of love. These are just examples; you will need to find the actual persons who embody that wish for you.

It is also important to make prominent within your array of benefactors the spiritual figures that most powerfully inspire you, such as the Buddha or a central spiritual being of your own tradition. Within the center of the field of benefactors, you would place that weighty spiritual figure, surrounded by your own spiritual mentors or teachers, around whom are all your other benefactors. In my own daily practice, the radiant figure of the Buddha is at the center, surrounded by my spiritual teachers and their lineages, around whom are the other benefactors I recall from this life. At the heart of each is the radiant image of the Buddha, which reminds me of the source of goodness in each of them that communes with my own. If you are a Christian, it would be natural to envision Christ at the center; if a Hindu, then Krishna, Shiva, or Mahadevi. If you are a Jew or a Muslim, you might simply consider God to be the source of your benefactors' radiant love and compassion.

Despite all that's been said, some people still find it difficult in the beginning to accept love for themselves just as they are. If that is true for you, you might try envisioning yourself as you were when you were a child and receive the radiant wish of love in that way. See if that helps you to get started in this profound practice.

I would recommend that you practice the meditation of this chapter daily for some weeks before focusing much on the meditations of the following chapters. The effect of such practice unfolds in its own time. It can't be hurried. I envisage a typical reader reading through this whole book for content but then rereading this chapter and doing a daily practice of its meditation for several weeks. Then you can reread the next chapter and do its meditation daily for several weeks or months, and so on. In this way, the practice can unfold in its own time, naturally and effectively. You can explore how it works best for you.

Familiarizing and Progressing

As you become familiar with the meditation of receiving love, several things unfold. First, more and more benefactors occur to you—so many people you had forgotten come crowding in upon you! Aunts, uncles, cousins, grade school teachers, a counselor at camp, a special coach, a smiling stranger who waved you ahead in line, persons who quietly mentored and influenced you in positive ways that you had never consciously acknowledged. Indeed, over time, this simple practice can reintroduce you to your whole life! Many people who were essential to your thriving, long lost to your conscious mind, are rediscovered through this practice. They become a potent influence in your life once again, as if you were joyfully reunited with a host of long-lost friends and mentors.

Through daily practice, the meditation of receiving love softens the hard edges of reactivity to self and other, the hard edges of our life. It helps us to acknowledge and rely upon the deep goodness within and beyond us—to take refuge in the power of genuine love and compassion, to sense it as a real and ever-present refuge whenever we recall it. By learning through this meditation how profoundly we can let be into the simple receiving of love, we also strengthen the skill of letting be into the natural ease of deep inner knowing and peace, the wisdom beyond self-grasping whose practice is introduced in the next chapter.

2. Letting Be:
Relaxing into Natural Wisdom

Reading Tips for This Chapter

This chapter introduces the perspective of the Dzogchen tradition of Tibet, drawing upon quotes from a few of its twentieth-century masters. Some readers will find this material tremendously fresh and beautiful. Others at first may find it daunting. The Dzogchen view is vast and all-encompassing. It is impossible to understand merely by thinking hard about it. Indeed, much of the language is intended to pull us beyond the narrow confines of our usual thinking process. Often the words have an aesthetic function akin to profound, evocative poetry that can transport us beyond our accustomed ways of seeing. Please read the chapter in that spirit, letting it engage not only your thinking mind but your aesthetic appreciation, intuition, and heart. As you first enter into the meditation below, don't worry if you've fully understood the material that precedes it. Rather, let the meditation instructions gently evoke your intuitive capacity to relax deeply and to enjoy the essential goodness of your being beyond self-clinging.

The Innate Pure Nature of Mind

The fundamental nature of mind is sheer lucidity, free and unfettered by concepts such as subject and object; a profound luminosity free from partiality and fixation, a free-flowing compassionate expression of indefinable, limitless emptiness, unobscured by thinking. Thought is bondage; the immeasurable openness of empty awareness is freedom. Compassion for those bound within their own illusory constructs, mind-forged manacles, and self-imposed limitations, spontaneously, unobstructedly, and inexhaustibly springs forth.

Nyoshul Khen Rinpoche[4]

What Nyoshul Khenpo calls "the fundamental nature of mind" is our fundamental, innate awareness. This pure awareness is the ground of all experience: all our thoughts, feelings, and perceptions. As such, it is naturally all-inclusive and wide open. Our dualistic thinking process tends to limit our attention to a very narrow sense of self (as "subject") that seems to stand completely apart from others (as "object"). Yet our fundamental, pure awareness, even as it gives rise to such dualistic thoughts, is a vast expanse of knowing that transcends all such limitations, "unfettered by concepts."

Nothing within our fundamental awareness is substantial or graspable in any way. Awareness per se has no color, no shape, no center or boundary, and nothing concrete to be found in it. Fundamental awareness is thus "a profound luminosity" that is not only cognizant but a "limitless emptiness," meaning that it is totally insubstantial and unobstructed by anything. For this reason, our basic awareness is also described as "primordially pure," for there has never been anything in it substantial enough to stain or obstruct it. Our awareness therefore has the potential to come to self-recognition as a vast expanse of infinite openness and cognizance, like a boundless sky pervaded by sunlight.

In sum, Dzogchen masters explain that our innate, basic awareness, which is also called *nature of mind,* has two essential aspects: (1) it is cognizant, knowing, aware, and (2) it is totally open, for it is empty of any substantial entity. The cognizance and openness are

infinite, undivided, and intrinsically free of any constriction or fixation on a "self" reacting against an "other."

Importantly, as Nyoshul Khenpo implies, the cognizant, knowing
aspect of our awareness possesses powerful energies. When our attention is limited to self-concerned thoughts and reactions, those energies take shape in deluded, self-centered emotions like fear,
possessiveness, and hatred, leading to harmful actions that throw us
repeatedly into suffering. Dzogchen practice cuts the root of such suffering, by letting our innate awareness come to vivid recognition of
its infinite, empty nature, which lacks any substantial self. Then all
aspects of experience are recognized as the expression of that same
pure awareness, like sunrays recognized by the sun as its own radiance.

Through that profound recognition, thoughts that had previously
formed into chains of self-centered thinking and emotion are spontaneously released within their own ground of empty knowingness,
like ocean waves self-releasing into their own watery bed. Then the
energies that had fueled deluded emotions are freed to manifest instead
as boundless energies of love, compassion, and liberating power,
directed to all beings who remain caught in ego-centered thought,
fear, and reaction. So Khenpo concludes: "Thought is bondage; the
immeasurable openness of empty awareness is freedom. Compassion
for those bound within their own illusory constructs...and self-
imposed limitations, spontaneously, unobstructedly, and inexhaustibly
springs forth."

Khenpo's tradition is called "Dzogchen," *natural great perfection,*
because when our innate, pure awareness comes to self-recognition,
all aspects of experience are simultaneously recognized as essentially
pure and perfect from the beginning. Through that recognition, the
innate capacities and energies of a buddha, previously hidden in our
minds, are freed to manifest spontaneously. Because such capacities
abide in the very nature of our minds, even now, they are said to
comprise our *buddha nature.*

To sum up, the practice of Dzogchen allows the fundamental nature of one's mind, the boundless expanse of pure awareness and openness, to attain stable self-recognition. That is enlightenment: the enduring recognition of all experience as the radiant expression of primordially pure awareness. This realization cuts through the self-imposed limitations of one's mind to unleash tremendous liberating powers of love, compassion, joy, and creativity from the ground of one's being, which can inspire and uplift many others. It is also the foundation of a wise equanimity that senses all others as essentially undivided from one's self, making one's love and compassion unconditional, all-inclusive, and inexhaustible.

> Inherent in this great emptiness—this openness and luminosity, the true nature of one's mind, the innate Great Perfection—are inconceivable qualities, all of the enlightened qualities of the Buddhas of all directions…. These transcendental qualities are inherently present…and accessible even today.
>
> Nyoshul Khen Rinpoche[5]

If such enlightened qualities are already given in the very nature of our being, why don't we notice them so much of the time? What hides our tremendous innate capacity of goodness even from ourselves?

Samsara: The Struggle of Self-Grasping

Ignorance Hides Our Innate Nature

Mistakenly perceiving the…innate wakefulness of primordial awareness for a fixed self or soul—our own egoic, individual existence—we enmesh and bind ourselves time after time, time without end. Ignorance is the sole cause of wandering in samsara. Buddhas know and understand what

ordinary sentient beings ignore, misunderstand and overlook: the true original nature of one and all. That is the sole
distinction between Buddhas and ordinary beings.

Nyoshul Khen Rinpoche[6]

As Nyoshul Khenpo declares, habits of thought work below the
surface of conscious awareness, hiding our innate nature from us.
Each moment there is a subconscious movement of anxiety within
our minds—a subtle grasping that seeks to fill the totally insubstantial and open nature of experience with a constricted, substantial,
and isolated sense of self. Moment by moment our thoughts close
off the natural all-inclusiveness of awareness to create and grasp on
to a narrow, concrete, and unchanging sense of self, seeking in that
way to feel safe and protected from the vast, intangible mystery of
experience as it really is. That patterning of thought is what Buddhist
masters call *ignorance,* because while trying to create a sense of safety,
it just constructs a deluded world of anxiety and suffering around
oneself—a world of fear and struggle, called *samsara.*

This Buddhist view of "the fall" from our pure, original nature
differs from the biblical view, for it is not perceived as having happened once and for all in some mythical beginning. Rather, this
"falling away" is constantly reoccurring here and now, as our subconscious fear of the openness of experience struggles each moment
to create and grasp on to the appearance of a narrow, unchanging
self—a self bound up within a small world of self-centered concern. Our ongoing stream of experience is patterned by momentary thoughts into an organized personality that can certainly be
referred to as "I" or "me," but there is no unchanging, substantial,
isolated self to be found there of the sort our minds keep working
to establish.

The mere thought of self, of "I," is sufficient to organize our experience and personality so we can function successfully at home or

work. "I am Dr. Jones and I am here to examine your X-rays." That is helpful to know. The problem is that our minds superimpose a further belief in a self that stands apart from thought. We commonly say, "I am thinking…," implying that there is someone separate from the thinking who does the thinking. But upon investigation, the Buddha taught, no such thinker, separate from thought, can be found. The "thinker" is the product of the thinking, not the other way around.

We have difficulty facing the simple truth that our sense of self is made up each moment by changing thoughts, because our minds are so accustomed to the mistaken belief in the self as unchanging thinker and grasp so tightly to that belief. Yet upon investigation, the truth becomes obvious. If you encounter someone you hate, you suddenly seem to become a hateful "self" in that instant, don't you? If you encounter someone you adore, you seem to become an adoring "self" in that moment. The sense of self changes so radically and so quickly because it is created by thought within each momentary context. The continuity of thought and memory gives us the impression that the "thinker" hasn't changed; when actually, the stream of thought that makes the "thinker," the sense of self, has been changing continually.

Try snapping your fingers rapidly. Thoughts of self are like the finger snaps, which occur rapidly and in continuity. But just as there is no unchanging snap behind all the momentary snaps, likewise there is no unchanging self, no thinker, behind all the thoughts of self. Yet, over the course of our lives, thoughts flow from our fundamental, innate awareness in whatever patterns of self-centered concern our minds have grown accustomed to. And our minds grasp tightly to this ego-centered orientation, seeking safety there. But instead of providing authentic safety, that orientation only leads to recurrent fear and suffering.

Life Becomes the Struggle to Support the False Sense of Self

Through such patterns of self-grasping, life becomes an ongoing struggle, because each situation feels like it must be interpreted to establish an unchanging, concrete self that doesn't actually exist! Within the subsequent flow of self-absorbed thought, other beings are reduced to narrow objects of self-interest, as if there were nothing more to them. Each encounter and each other being is interpreted to make this merely fabricated sense of self feel more real, more substantial. When others seem to prop up this fragile sense of self, we like them. When others seem to undercut it, thus making it feel less real, we dislike or hate them, since the act of hating makes the self feel real. And those who seem irrelevant to our sense of self, such as strangers on the street, appear to have no value at all. So we don't care about them.

Beings are not merely the narrow, distorted identities that our ego-centered minds label onto each, as if this one were really just a "stranger," nothing more; as if that one were really just "annoying," nothing more. Simply put, through the lens of self-grasping, we constantly mistake our own reductive thoughts of everyone for the actual people. We mistake our restricted and partial thoughts of self and other for the fullness of self and other. Identifying with those reductive thoughts, we cling tightly to the world that they create, unaware that it is a mental creation.

This mistake is hard for us to notice, because it is not only an individual but also a social construction in which we are all complicit. "Sally said that! Isn't she stupid?" "Isn't Jim a jerk?" "Bob's a real team player. Don't you agree?" Our conversations make it seem, in the moment, as if each person is merely the reductive label that he or she has been called. Nothing more. And that helps us to construct narrow group identities that prevent us from feeling empathy and compassion for those outside our own group.

By continually mistaking our limited thoughts of beings for their full reality, we hide from ourselves the tremendous capacity of goodness that dwells in the very nature of their minds. We are like an astronaut in space who has the opportunity to gaze upon the vast mystery of the universe but instead keeps looking at himself in the mirror, obsessing about the shape of his nose! The world and its inhabitants are a vast, deep mystery. But instead of sensing the beauty, mystery, and holiness of each being, our minds reduce all of them in thought to narrow objects of suffocating self-concern. As others react similarly to us, we socially reinforce the habit of mistaking our distorted thoughts of each other for the fullness and mystery of each other. This is part of the classical meaning of the Buddhist term *karma* (action), the ingrained habit of re-acting to our own narrow thoughts of everyone so as to make our thought-made sense of self feel real.

As we cling to those who reinforce our sense of self, hate those who undercut it, and simply don't care about the others, we contribute unconsciously in little and big ways to all our social problems. Without conscious awareness, our reactions to others feed discord and violence in our families and communities and a general spirit of mutual distrust. Our behaviors fuel manifold addictions, grasping on to whatever substance or distraction seems to pacify troubling thoughts of self and other for a little while. As a social dynamic, many individuals, each seeking to establish and reify their own sense of self, come together in large groups and nations to consume far more resources than they need and to seek economic and political dominance over other groups. Thus, individual patterns of self-centeredness, hatred, fear, and apathy translate socially into economic oppression, massive environmental damage, and recurrent war. This is the suffering of samsara in its modern form. Individual and social life caught in the delusion of self-grasping becomes endless struggle, mutual distrust, fear, and conflict.[7]

The Purpose of Spiritual Practice

So it is self-centered confusion that hides the great, innate capacities of goodness that abide in the nature of our minds, in our buddha nature. In this light, the purpose of spiritual practice becomes clear. We practice to become receptive to the tremendous capacity of wisdom and love that is hidden in our being, to let the practice bring these qualities out with such force that they start to release us from the ego-centered causes of suffering in our minds, freeing us finally to become what we had most deeply intended—a real benefactor for this world. The goal of the path is to rediscover our original nature of pure awareness prior to the momentary confusions of self-clinging and to bring out its abiding qualities: the wise equanimity that senses others as undivided from self, love and compassion for all in that light, deep inner peace, joy, and the creative, liberating power to benefit many others.

A wonderful scene in the movie *Harry Potter and the Chamber of Secrets* illustrates our situation. In a duel with another young wizard, a snake is hurled at Harry Potter. The snake, baring its fangs, hisses menacingly at the children. Suddenly Harry makes strange hissing sounds that the snake seems to understand, causing him to retreat. Harry thinks he spoke English, telling the snake not to harm anyone. But Harry's friends later inform him, to his surprise, that he was actually speaking in snake language, "parsel tongue," a language normally incomprehensible to humans. Harry is stunned! *"How can I speak a language I didn't know I could speak?"* he asks.

Similarly, the "language" of love and wisdom, deep down, is a language that we already know. We each have a hidden capacity to speak an intuitive language that communicates with others' hearts and minds below the "radar" of self-concerned thinking. Under the right conditions, we find access to it, as Alison Luterman did in her corner store. The spiritual practices in this book can trigger our ability to speak a language of the heart that we didn't know we knew. Like the clerk in the corner store, they can help us awaken to a goodness we didn't know we had, to recognize it in others, and to evoke it from them.

But just understanding this intellectually is not enough. Someone can hear Buddhist teachings such as these, be inspired by them, believe them, and think that by identifying with this new set of beliefs he has become a spiritual person. That would be a mistake. When I was a teenager, I loved to listen to Bob Dylan. One of my favorite songs had this verse:

> I don't want to fake you out,
> take or shake or forsake you out.
> I ain't lookin for you to feel like me,
> see like me, or be like me.
> All I really wanna do
> is baby be friends with you.

The song expresses an unconditional acceptance of persons without trying to get them to conform to your own needs. This was appealing to me as a teenager, in a world of peer pressure and social judgment. Because I identified strongly with the song's words as I sang it, I believed that I was actually practicing their meaning. But to identify yourself with a *belief* in unconditional acceptance for all persons is quite different from embodying such an attitude in your responses to all of them. Ironically, I see in retrospect, I looked down on all sorts of people and groups simply because they did not show sufficient appreciation for Bob Dylan and his songs!

These days, we tend to think that merely to *believe* strongly in the good constitutes *being* good, especially with regard to religious and ethical matters. That mistake gives us an unrealistic sense of our own group as the good ones, the ones who share our belief in the good (and therefore, like us, *are* good) as opposed to the others. In this way we unconsciously disrespect and endanger others (and ultimately ourselves) in the name of the good.

For authentic spiritual progress, something has to interfere with all such patterns of self-centered deception, undercut them so decisively that our innate capacity for self-transcending, all-inclusive love can actually manifest—an actual *power* of goodness, not just a *belief* in goodness. That requires effective methods of practice that are not just forms of individual and social identification with self-protective beliefs.

Nonconceptual and Conceptual Practices

In sum, great powers of goodness are hidden in us, but our habits of thought obstruct and hide them from us. What are we to do? Stop thinking? That won't work. Even if we could become that quiescent and stop thoughts for quite some time, there would still remain in our minds the subtle tendencies to fixate on experience and grasp on to dualism. Such tendencies are not overcome just by stopping thoughts for a time.

We have to learn to let our innate pure awareness come to self-recognition, to thoroughly sense its own empty, cognizant, and limitless nature and to stabilize in that recognition. Then the energies of our self-centered thoughts and emotions can be freed to take expression as enlightened attitudes and activities of compassion. That is the path to enlightenment. But how is it to unfold?

Two kinds of practice empower this process—nonconceptual and conceptual. *Nonconceptual* meditation is an intuitive knowing that is not delimited by conceptual patterns of thought—innate pure awareness itself is what does the knowing. *Conceptual* practices employ special forms of thought, image, and attitude to harmonize us with the mind's infinite nature by evoking its innate enlightened qualities— qualities such as boundless love, compassion, tranquillity, joy, and equanimity. As the nature of mind is realized, those qualities are embodied in ways that communicate enlightenment to others.

Nonconceptual Practice

> There is no thought that is something other than voidness; if you recognize the void nature of thoughts at the very moment they arise, they will dissolve. Attachment and hatred will never be able to disturb the mind. Deluded emotions will collapse by themselves. No negative actions will be accumulated, so no suffering will follow.
>
> Dilgo Khyentse Rinpoche[8]

> Innate wakefulness, nonconceptual wisdom, nondual primordial awareness—Buddha mind—is suddenly unsheathed the moment dualistic mind dissolves.
>
> Nyoshul Khen Rinpoche[9]

In nonconceptual meditation, we just rest in the nonconceptual nature of mind—the vast expanse of cognizance and openness that is beyond all conceptual and ego-centered frames of reference. Initially, we need to learn how to "get out of the way"—how to let our ordinary, dualistic patterns of thinking and grasping on to "self" and "other" relax so much that they begin to fall apart by themselves. All experiences of subject and object are traced back to the nondual clarity of their fundamental nature. Like ocean waves settling back into their own watery essence, all thoughts and patterns of experience are permitted to settle into their own cognizant, empty nature, where they are recognized as spontaneous expressions of primordially pure awareness (Tibetan: *rig pa*).

In Dzogchen tradition, such nonconceptual meditation is also called *cutting through* (Tibetan: *trekcho*). This does not mean that we

try to cut off thoughts. Rather, we learn to relax all tendencies to fixate on or grasp at subjects and objects of thought. To "cut through"
in this sense is to let everything be just as it is. We can learn to let be
so profoundly that grasping on to dualism simply collapses by itself.
In that moment, chains of self-clinging thought and emotion are cut
and innate pure awareness is "unsheathed"—freed from conceptual
fixation. That nonconceptual awareness recognizes all thoughts, feelings, and perceptions nakedly as its own radiant expressions, like the
sun recognizing its rays. Instead of forming ego-centered thought
chains, thoughts self-release naturally within that recognition, as patterns of luminous emptiness, like patterns drawn on water.

Nonconceptual meditation is also called *ultimate* practice, because
it reveals the ultimate nature of mind as an infinite expanse of cognizance and all-penetrating openness. The nonconceptual awareness that manifests through such practice is also called transcendental
wisdom (Sanskrit: *prajnaparamita*), because it transcends all conceptual, dualistic, and ego-centered frames of reference. It liberates the
mind from all such fixations and grasping tendencies. When the
word *wisdom* is used throughout this book, it refers to such nonconceptual awareness or to ways of knowing that evoke and express it.

Conceptual Practices

> ...mind-training, loving-kindness, prayers, exchanging one-
> self and others, and so forth—these practices may seem con-
> ceptual and relative, but they actually include the absolute
> truth that is the very nature of Dzogchen: vast openness, big
> mind, purity, freedom, and non-grasping.
>
> Nyoshul Khen Rinpoche[10]

It is easy to talk about "relaxing all tendencies of grasping" so as
to awaken to infinite, nonconceptual awareness and its boundless

excellent qualities. But our habit is to hold on to ourselves continually within a process of self-centered thought. How can we learn to surrender ourselves so profoundly? How can we learn to trust the mysterious reality that lies beyond the narrow confines of ego enough to release ourselves into it?

Tibetan traditions are well aware of this problem. Somehow the conceptual mind of thought and imagination, our minds as we now experience them, have to be enlisted in the process of awakening. Conceptual thought must be used as a bridge to nonconceptual wisdom, as a support for it rather than as an obstacle. For centuries, Tibetan masters such as Nyoshul Khenpo have taught conceptual practices (mind training) that use thought and image to help people relax their grip on themselves, relinquish their fear of the mystery, and harmonize themselves with the infinite nature of their minds.

Receptive Devotion and the Boundless Extending of Love

Two kinds of conceptual practice are especially effective to help carry the mind past its limitations. The first is cultivation of a strong devotion and receptivity to the qualities of enlightenment. The second is the extending of love and compassion to innumerable beings.

Reverent devotion to the qualities of enlightenment strengthens our receptivity to them and empowers our will to be offered up to them and to their ultimate ground—the infinite, undivided nature of mind. To extend love boundlessly to beings helps us sense all beings as undivided from ourselves in the infinite, undivided nature of mind.

Such conceptual practices are also called *relative* practices, because while they are not in themselves the infinite nature of mind, they help our finite, thinking minds open to that nature. Importantly, reverent devotion and impartial love don't just prepare the ego-centered mind to realize its infinite nature. When that nature is realized, loving compassion and reverence become natural ways to express and embody it for others, so that they may recognize their own enlightened potential. Such enlightened communication occurs in countless ways, even very subtle ones.

For example, my teacher Nyoshul Khenpo was revered both as an enlightened master and a learned scholar of Dzogchen tradition. For years he suffered from an illness that prevented him from speaking. And when he did recover his ability to speak, his voice remained very hoarse and barely audible. But the power of his realization was so great that he became renowned for his ability to communicate the power of enlightenment to others, mysteriously, without speaking. Twelve years ago Lama Surya Das invited Khenpo to give a teaching in Cambridge, Massachusetts, at Harvard University. Hundreds of people, including scholars, students, and well-known Buddhist teachers from throughout New England flooded the room and spilled out into halls nearby, anxious to hear the words of such a renowned master. But after Khenpo was formally introduced and the audience was waiting with baited breath for his words, he didn't speak! He folded his hands in a reverent gesture of homage to all the enlightened ones. Then he just sat there silently before them, relaxed and unmoving. Yet over the next ten minutes of silence the natural ease, tranquillity, and reverence that his body expressed, and the gentle power of his compassionate presence, quietly uplifted the minds of the audience. Then he gave a short talk, barely above a whisper, that was translated by Lama Surya Das.

Khenpo passed away years ago. Yet even today, just to recall his body sitting with such ease pulls me out of my ordinary frame of mind into peace and gratitude. The qualities of natural great peace, love, compassion, receptivity, and reverence that Khenpo had practiced throughout his life had become so natural to him, so spontaneous, that his very being communicated them to others. He exemplified the liberating power of such practices first to harmonize the mind with its boundless nature, then to embody its vast qualities in the most direct and simple ways.

Relative practices that extend love and compassion all-inclusively are developed throughout the rest of this book. I will say something further here about the devotional practice of reverent receptivity, with reference to Tibetan tradition.

Tibetan Buddhists generally begin their meditations by recalling spiritual benefactors who embody for them the enlightened qualities of the infinite, nonconceptual nature of mind. Their reverence and receptivity to the qualities of these benefactors becomes so strong that they learn to trust the mysterious, infinite ground of those qualities: the vast expanse of openness and cognizance beyond self-clinging. Through the power of such receptivity and trust, they are enabled to release their egos into the infinite nature of mind itself.

Tibetans do this by envisioning their spiritual benefactors—their lamas and buddhas and bodhisattvas—as a radiant field of refuge before them. Then they receive the luminous blessings and energies of their benefactors' enduring love, compassion, liberating wisdom, and spiritual power into their whole being. The warm, radiant energy of those qualities helps them to relax their ego-centeredness, to melt away their self-protectiveness, and to sense the radiant ground of those qualities as absolute goodness. Pulled beyond themselves in this gentle way, they merge joyfully into oneness with their benefactors within that ground, which is the infinite, nonconceptual nature of mind beyond separation (buddha mind, *dharmakaya*). In this way, a conceptual practice of devotion to the goodness of spiritual benefactors, and to the infinite ground of that goodness, provides the most effective entry into nonconceptual meditation.[11]

We have already begun to practice in a similar way. We are learning to receive the radiant love of our benefactors (including spiritual benefactors) so fully that it helps melt away our frozen egos, release us from our self-protective stance, and let us merge with our benefactors in the luminous ground of their unconditional love—innate pure awareness. To receive the blessing and energy of their love into every part of our being carries us gently beyond ourselves into the spirit of trust and openness that can begin to release us into the infinite, nonconceptual nature of mind. To discover our benefactors, then, is to discover our own authentic field of reverent devotion and refuge. For the love that flows from them gives us access to the ground of their love—buddha nature, pure awareness endowed with enlightened qualities, the ultimate source of protection for all.

Introducing the Meditation of Natural Awareness

Surrendering Control to the Wisdom of Natural Awareness

The main practice of this chapter is nonconceptual meditation. Instead of attempting to assert control over our experience so as to come to know it better, we do just the opposite—we give up the attempt to control anything and let our innate pure awareness do the knowing. This is done by relying upon the natural power of body, breath, and mind to enable all aspects of experience to calm, settle, and clarify by themselves. The senses are left wide open, the awareness unrestricted. Then the thinking mechanism that fixates narrowly on "self" and "other" can no longer sustain itself, permitting the nature of mind, infinite innate pure awareness, to reveal itself. As this innate awareness recognizes the empty, radiant nature of all experiences, all thoughts and emotions naturally self-release like ripples on water, and the natural great peace of enlightenment dawns. Nonconceptual meditation is a practice of deep receptivity and profound allowing—letting all be just as it is.

Reverent Devotion Helps the Mind Surrender to Its Pure Nature

But for most of us it is *not* easy to let be so fully into nonconceptual reality! It is the receiving of love, a conceptual practice of reverence, receptivity, and devotion, which evokes enough trust in the basic goodness of reality that we can take refuge in that reality and relax into its mystery. So we start the following meditation by receiving love deeply from our benefactors and by merging into oneness with them in the luminous, insubstantial ground of that love beyond separation. Then we can relax more subtle tendencies of holding on to ourselves by surrendering to the natural powers of our body, breath, and mind. As we thus learn, little by little, to let the mind relax into its own basic condition prior to conceptualization, it can begin to reveal its inmost nature.

Karmic Merit and the Importance of Dedication

The spiritual power of all such practices of reverent devotion, love, and wisdom pulls us beyond ourselves, so that the qualities of our buddha nature can increasingly manifest. Buddhists call that spiritual power karmic *merit* (Sanskrit: *punya*), meaning a force for well-being and goodness generated by powerfully good intentions and actions—a force that can lift us toward full enlightenment: the complete actualization of our buddha nature. To attain full enlightenment is to become a tremendous power of goodness for the world, inspiring many others to realize their similar potential. The karmic merit from virtuous practices also strengthens our inner capacity for happiness and joy. But we don't want to waste such spiritual power by frittering it away in trivial, self-centered ways. So we conclude every practice of love, devotion, and wisdom by dedicating its merit, its spiritual power, to our complete realization of enlightenment for the sake of all beings.

The meditation below thus has three parts: (1) receiving the wish of love and merging with our field of refuge, (2) letting the natural power of body, breath, and mind further release us into natural awareness, and (3) dedicating the karmic merit—the spiritual power of the meditation—to full enlightenment for the sake of all. All three parts can be completed in thirty to forty minutes. Be sure to allow a short pause at each demarcation, to give you time to explore and relax into each phase of the instruction.

Meditation: Letting Be in Natural Awareness

Part 1: Refuge—Receiving the Blessing of Unconditional Love

Sit in a relaxed way with back straight, on cushion or chair, eyes open, softly gazing slightly downward. Recall your benefactors—ones remembered from your personal life and revered spiritual beings who extend their love to all. Envision their smiling faces before you. Recall them as sending you the wish of love and remember its simple meaning: the unconditional wish for you to have deepest well-being, happiness, and joy.

Imagine their wish as a gentle radiance, like a soft shower of healing rays. Bathe your whole body and mind in that tender energy, all the way down to your toes and fingertips. Bask in it.

Trusting this wish of love more than limiting thoughts of yourself, receive it into your whole being. Absorb the healing radiance and energy of love into every cell of your body, every corner of your mind. Bathe in this; heal in this; rest in this.

After a little while, join your benefactors in their wish for you. While receiving the radiance of their love, mentally repeat their wish with reference to yourself: "May this one have deepest well-being, happiness, and joy." Affirm the wish repeatedly for yourself while accepting your benefactors' love even more deeply into body and mind, communing with them through its radiance.

Finally, drop the visualization and just relax into oneness with that loving luminosity, releasing all frames of reference. Deeply let be into that gentle, luminous wholeness beyond separation of self and others. Enjoy just being—at ease, at rest, complete.

Part 2: Letting Be in Natural Awareness

Notice where you still feel any grasping within the body— in the back, neck, hips, or anus, perhaps. Wherever you feel such grasping, let that gently release itself. Relaxed and calmly alert, allow all bodily sensations to come and go as they will, permitting everything to settle naturally in its own way. Let go of any sense of control. Just surrender to the natural power of the body, letting it embody you. Feel the gentle shift from controlling to allowing, from holding on to the body, to just being embodied. Enjoy bodily awareness in that way for a little while.

❧

Now notice any grasping on to the breathing process any- where—in the abdomen, chest, or throat. Let that relax, allowing the breath to come under its own natural power, breathing you. Sense the gentle shift from controlling the breath to allowing it, from holding on to the breath to just being breathed. Feel the breath all the way in, all the way out, as it breathes you.

After a little while, notice any grasping within the mind to the thinking mechanism, identification with chains of thought about self and other, grasping on to them as frames of reference. Let that feeling of holding on release itself, so as to unwind deep inside. Without identifying with thoughts of the past or the future, without conceptualizing the present, just let all thoughts and sensations arise and dissolve under their own power, in their own way. Cut the "kite string" on thoughts and let them fly freely even as they arise.

In this way, let the mind unfurl naturally, of itself, and fall totally open—at ease, unrestricted, free of any focus or directedness, three hundred sixty degrees all-pervasive, wide open. Raise the gaze of your eyes to look gently ahead, taking in all at once, totally expansive. Let all be just as it is, in complete openness and acceptance.

Sense the openness of awareness, infinite and without center, in which all phenomena self-arise and self-dissolve, beyond clinging, beyond thinking, beyond reference point—boundless openness and cognizance, all-pervasive like the sky. Let this vast expanse of fundamental awareness sense all that appears as its own radiant expression, like the sky sensing its own rainbows. Rest as that sky-like nature of mind—all phenomena permitted to self-arise and self-release within the infinite expanse of openness aware.

Part 3: Dedicating the Spiritual Power for All

Feel the power of this practice to pull you, even momentarily, beyond self-grasping patterns of thought and reaction, to open you toward the tranquillity, freedom, and goodness of your inmost being. Prayerfully dedicate all such spiritual power to the deepest well-being and liberation of all beings, each like you in needing and wanting such joy and freedom.

Good work! Have a rest.

Calm Abiding and Liberating Insight

As a practitioner does this meditation over the course of many days and months and becomes more adept at letting all be in complete openness, the mind can increasingly settle, calm, and self-clarify into a spacious state of profound, natural tranquillity. When this stage is reached, the meditation is called *calm abiding* (Sanskrit: *shamatha*). There is stillness, peace, and quiet power in this state of mind, with a wonderful feeling of wholeness. Self-centered emotions, worries, and anxieties settle out, and one feels spacious, joyful, and blessed. Thinking may stop entirely for a while. And one may experience a basic lightness of being, a sense of vast openness and blissful energy.

But this is not yet recognition of the mind's nonconceptual nature. For while calmly abiding in this way, the mind continues subconsciously to conceptualize a subject and an object, someone (subject) who is paying attention to her state of mind (object). And as long as that conceptual dualism is maintained, a subtle fixation and grasping accompanies it, a form of holding on, which obscures the infinite nature of mind. Because of that, when not formally meditating, all the provocations of one's life continue to trigger deluded, self-centered thoughts and reactions. The very root of one's delusions—the conceptual tendency to grasp on to self and on to dualism—has not yet been cut by the actual recognition of the ungraspable, empty nature of mind.

As the practice continues to deepen, one's ego orientation can further relax and release itself, which allows more subtle, subconscious forms of conceptualization and clinging to relax themselves and self-dissolve. Experiences of subject and object are traced back to the nondual clarity of their essential nature. Like waves settling into their own watery essence, all patterns of experience, as they arise, settle naturally into their own cognizant nature, where they are recognized as spontaneous expressions of radiant emptiness. The primordial, infinite expanse of openness and awareness, beyond all conceptualization, begins to disclose itself. At this point calm abiding is deepening into an actual recognition of the mind's infinite nature. That recognition is called *liberating insight* (Sanskrit: *vipashyana*). It is the dawning of nonconceptual awareness, transcendental wisdom.

At this stage, energies of mind that had fueled deluded emotions start to be freed to manifest as qualities of innate, pure awareness: boundlessly inclusive love, compassion, and joy, deep tranquillity, and other liberating powers. Ego-centered reactions that had inhibited such qualities begin to release their grip. Instead of forming thought chains, arising thoughts self-liberate naturally as patterns of luminous emptiness like ripples on water. At this point in practice, one learns to recognize the fundamental nature of mind, and to abide within it, more often and more fully. One becomes increasingly accustomed to that way of being. This permits the innate enlightened qualities of fundamental awareness increasingly to manifest.

Sharp Inquiries that Help Bring Out Liberating Insight

The above description of progress might give the impression that the transition from calm abiding *(shamatha)* to liberating insight *(vipashyana)* occurs by itself. And that is possible for someone who has accumulated tremendous karmic merit in the past. But to help this transition, most practitioners need also to rely on incisive ways of investigating experience; sharp modes of inquiry, which have been passed down to us by lineage masters. At the proper time in our meditation practice such inquiries can break down the subconscious fixations that obstruct liberating insight, helping to release the mind from calm abiding into insight. And even when liberating insight dawns, old conceptual habits tend to resurrect themselves in subtle forms of fixation and clinging, like ice forming over water. Then the same modes of inquiry are used to revivify the insight or, as Lama Surya Das likes to say, "to break apart the ice of subtle conceptualization and let the waters of awareness flow freely."

Inquiry is a form of questioning, which is a conceptual form of practice. But it uses concepts in a special way, to break down conceptual fixations and turn attention to the nature of mind beyond conceptualization.

Sometimes such an inquiry is launched in a spontaneous encounter between master and student. The lama may pose a question that suddenly turns the student's attention in to her experience, breaking apart conceptual frames that she had unconsciously assumed.

For example, before I had children, I stayed for a period of time with one of my Tibetan teachers, Gen Lobsang Namgyal. One day, I found him staring with fascination at a diagram of an atom in a book that someone had given him. The diagram showed how the atom was composed of subatomic particles, themselves formed from fields of energy. He beckoned me to come over.

"Is this what you call an 'atom'?" He asked, pointing to the illustration.

"Yes," I said.

"But then," he said, gesturing toward the fields of energy depicted in the diagram, "show me; where *is* it?"

I stared at him, dumbfounded.

"There *is* no atom," he declared. "'Atom' is just a name, a concept."

Suddenly, it felt as if my mind and its narrow grip on the world just collapsed. There is nothing that could be pointed to as an atom in the diagram—just fields of energy upon which a label "atom" could be put. Yet our minds habitually grasp to the things we experience, like "atom," as if they stand on their own, apart from such labeling. Geshe Lobsang looked knowingly at me, pointed to a couch, and said: "Rest a while."

I rested on the couch for the next few hours in a state of deep tranquillity, ease, and spaciousness. From that blissful state of awareness, conceptual frames of reference kept attempting to erect themselves, as if to provide something to grasp or hold on to. But even as they arose, they just collapsed back into a state of nonconceptuality and total openness. Geshe Lobsang's inquiry into the "atom" had provoked a glimpse of recognition.

Years after the incident with Geshe Lobsang, on a cold winter day, my five-year-old son Jonathan and I were spending time together in the yard. Jonathan picked up a thin sheet of ice that had formed on the ground and stared at it with fascination. Then he raised it above his head with great flourish and dropped it on the hard ground where, to his delight, it broke into many pieces. Suddenly, like in the moment after Geshe Lobsang's question, my entire frame of reference collapsed into nonconceptual openness. After some time, Daddy ambled back to the house to rest awhile!

As we practice over months and years, through the blessings of our spiritual benefactors and the incisive modes of inquiry that they impart, the persons and things all around us begin to manifest as messengers of wisdom. The world starts to reveal itself as our ultimate teacher and benefactor.

Over the centuries in Tibet, various methods of sharp inquiry have been passed down from masters to students in a systematic way. A few that I have found helpful are presented below. They are part of the Dzogchen foundational practice to help distinguish the difference between the narrowly ego-centered mind and the infinite nature of mind. You can approach these inquiries as your own fresh encounter with the wisdom of Tibetan masters who have transmitted them through the centuries to us.

Inquiring into the Arising and Dissolving of Phenomena

> In order to conquer the high ground of the uncreated nature of mind, we must go to the source and recognize the origin of our thoughts.
>
> Dilgo Khyentse Rinpoche[12]

> We can make...productive inquiries, such as, when a thought arises, noticing: "That's a thought. Where does it arise from?...Where did it go?"
>
> Nyoshul Khen Rinpoche[13]

After you have practiced for many days the three-part meditation presented earlier in this chapter of receiving love, letting be in natural awareness, and dedication, you can add the following further instruction to your practice.

At the end of the main part of the meditation, just before the dedication, your mind is resting in total openness. Right then, as you are meditating, let the following questions direct your attention sharply into the nature of your experience.

Many phenomena appear—thoughts, feelings, perceptions. From where do they arise? Let thoughts arise now—*from where* are they arising? Each thought presents the appearance of a subject and an object, a self (thinker) and an other (something thought about). *From where do those thoughts arise, those impressions of self and other?* Sift through experience guided by that question. Don't just think *about* the question. Rather, as if you were in a sandbox sifting through the sand with your fingers to *feel* how it is, *sift through present* experience to sense whether any source for the thoughts can be found. Let the investigation penetrate your mind.

After some time, pose this further question: Where are phenomena dissolving—all these thoughts, feelings, perceptions? Let thoughts occur—*is there any place that they go when they disappear?* Where do the thoughts, all those impressions of self and other, dissolve within experience? *Sift through* experience to sense if any destination can be found. Explore this for a short while, letting the investigation penetrate your mind.

If you should feel something happen—a kind of shift in consciousness, a sense of coming to a stop, of being struck dumb, of a crack or a gap in the heart of your world, relax deeply into that. Plumb that gap between thoughts; trace the radiance of experiences to their empty, infinite ground. Release thus into centerless openness and cognizance, releasing all frames of reference. Relax and let all be just as it is—all phenomena allowed to self-arise and self-release within the sky-like expanse of openness aware. Just rest like that for a little while.

That would complete the main part of the meditation. Then dedicate the liberating power of the practice toward your complete enlightenment for the sake of all beings.

Such a sharp inquiry into experience helps penetrate subconscious habits of grasping to "self" and "other" as if they were self-existent things standing apart from cognition and designation. Inquiring like this into the arising and dissolving of experiences can expose and momentarily interrupt our subconscious assumption that we confront a world that stands apart from our experience of it.

Actually, the only self and world we experience are the patterns of thought, perception, and feeling whose essential nature is radiant emptiness. And, more than we had noticed, all those beings that we had reacted to in fear, aversion, and clinging had been mistaken all along for our own limited thoughts of them. Patient practice of this meditation over months and years, with guidance from those who have deep experience of it, can increasingly bring out the innate capacities of our mind's nature: an all-encompassing awareness whose love and compassion are naturally all-inclusive and unrestricted by thoughts of partiality.

This inquiry into the source and destination of experiences is one important way Tibetan teachers have helped their students to undercut their subconscious fixations.[14] If that line of inquiry doesn't evoke a fresh curiosity to investigate your experience, try one of the other lines of inquiry presented below. Choose the inquiry that first captures your interest, and explore it in the meditation over many days. In time, this can help you further appreciate the other lines of inquiry, which can then be explored in daily practice for many more days, deepening your experience of the meditation of natural awareness.

Alternative Lines of Inquiry

At the end of the main part of the meditation, just before the dedication, your mind is resting in total openness and spaciousness. Right then, as you are meditating, let the following questions direct your attention sharply into the nature of your experience.

Who?

Who is experiencing? Is there someone separate from the experiences—separate from the thoughts, feelings, sensations? Or is your sense of self only a patterning of experience itself, just a momentary impression made by the flow of thoughts? *Who or what is experiencing?* Turn attention directly toward the experiencer and relax directly into it. If the sense of "self" and "other" collapses momentarily, plumb that gap. Let go completely there, relinquishing all frames of reference, and let be for a little while in utter openness.

Shape, Center, and Boundary

With eyes open, many shapes appear. But does the awareness that is experiencing them have any shape? Does your awareness have any boundary? Any divisions? Is there a "me" at the center of awareness, separated from all the rest? Or is that impression of a "me" just a pattern of thought? Does awareness per se actually have a shape, or a boundary, or a center? Explore such questions, letting the investigation penetrate you thoroughly.

Color

With eyes open, many colors appear. But does the awareness that experiences all those colors have any color? Or is awareness like a clear crystal, permitting colors to come through it while having no color itself?

Location

With eyes open, many things appear to be located here and there. But does the awareness that experiences those things itself have a location? Is your awareness outside of you? Inside of you? But aren't "outside" and "inside" concepts that appear within awareness? *Where* is this awareness in which thoughts of "inside" and "outside" appear? Does awareness even *have* a location? Explore this deeply for a while, letting the investigation penetrate you thoroughly.

For each such inquiry, don't just think *about* the question. Rather, let the question direct your attention into your present experience to sense how it is, like sifting through sand with your fingers. The point is not to ruminate over the question or to think up some correct answer. The point is to permit something fresh to happen, a spontaneous opening to occur, a momentary short-circuiting of accustomed chains of thought and grasping.

If you should feel something happen—a kind of shift in consciousness, a sense of coming to a stop, of being struck dumb, of a crack or a gap in the heart of your world, relax deeply into that. Plumb that gap between thoughts; trace the radiance of experiences to their empty ground.

Release thus into centerless openness and cognizance, relinquishing all frames of reference. Relax and let all be as it is—all phenomena allowed to self-arise, self-release within the sky-like expanse of openness aware. Just rest like that for a little while.

After you've explored one of the inquiries above and followed its *entire* instruction, you have completed the main part of the meditation. You can then dedicate the liberating power of the practice to enlightenment for all.

Daily Practice and Typical Difficulties

What to Do about Distracting Chains of Thought

Our habit of mind is to think continually about this and that. When we first enter into meditation, the energy of this habit makes our minds wander down pathways of thought and emotion, one thought triggering the next in a chain. For all our meditations, the teaching on this is clear. When you notice you are distracted in this way, gently bring your attention back to the meditation instruction at hand. For example, when receiving love, if you become distracted into chains of thought, as soon as you notice that happening, just bring your attention back to the meditation instruction of receiving love. Later, when resting in total openness, if you find yourself lost in chains of thought, thinking about this and that, return to the instruction of cutting the "kite string" on thoughts. Simply return to the meditation instruction at hand.[15]

Thoughts are the radiant expression of our mind's clear, quiescent, and infinitely spacious nature. They arise from that nature and dissolve into it. Our job is not to struggle with them or to try to stop them, but merely to allow them the freedom to self-dissolve into their own radiant, empty ground, like ocean waves dissolving back into their own wateriness.

The Receptivity of Reverent Devotion Deepens Trust in the Nature of Mind

Initially, as noted, it is difficult to relax and let be nearly as fully as instructed. We don't trust the mystery beyond self enough to fully relax into it. The more deeply we learn to receive the unconditional love that accepts us just as we are, the more we can trust and let be into just what is, to relax into an intuitive knowing beyond anxieties of self-concern. For this reason, I strongly recommend becoming proficient in the devotional practice of receiving love as presented in chapter 1 before focusing more primarily on the letting be practice of this chapter. Receive the love of benefactors for at least twenty or thirty minutes each morning, and recall it several times during your day for many days. This will prepare the mind to trust and relax into the meditation of this chapter.

Along the same lines, some meditators initially feel anxiety when introduced to the sharp inquiries above, a fear to look into experience in such a penetrating way, sensing that it may undercut something that they don't feel ready to let go of (one's narrow sense of self grasped as separate from one's world). If you feel such fear, again, deepen your experience of receiving love in daily practice. The more we allow ourselves to receive such love, strengthening our trust in its source, the more we can allow such inquiries to direct our attention toward its source: the insubstantial nature of mind.

Then when you feel prepared and receptive, you can begin the natural awareness meditation of *this* chapter. Do it daily for at least several weeks, including one or more of the inquiries, before shifting to the meditation of the next chapter. Of course, you can read on through the book! But typically we read faster than we progress in meditation. So do each chapter's meditation daily for several weeks or months, shifting to the next chapter's meditation only as you feel ready to do so.

The Need for the Karmic Power of Love and Compassion

> What we normally call the mind is the deluded mind, a turbulent vortex of thoughts whipped up by attachment, anger and ignorance. This mind, unlike enlightened awareness, is always being carried away by one delusion after another.
>
> Dilgo Khyentse Rinpoche[16]

Real progress toward calm abiding and insight can unfold through the meditation instruction and inquiries of this chapter. But progress means that the practice shows us more of our minds. Progress means that we become far more conscious of entrenched habits of self-centered thinking, grasping, and emoting. As we thus see more of ourselves, we may initially feel discouraged, thinking we are uniquely deluded! But there is no reason for discouragement. We are no different from those before us who awakened to the freedom in the nature of their minds.

Before their enlightenment, even the great Buddhist masters were deluded like the rest of us, otherwise they wouldn't understand so well what we are going through! Instead of getting discouraged as we see more of ourselves, we should rather recognize a different implication. We need something to empower the mind to further relinquish its deep-seated grasping. Often, our minds just don't have enough spiritual power to lift us so fully beyond ourselves. This is why great practitioners of the past have spent time "accumulating karmic merit" by doing a variety of intensive, repeated practices of devotion and extending love. Such practices purified the obscurations of their minds and evoked the spiritual power from the nature of their minds (karmic merit) to carry them past entrenched habits of clinging. The practices of extending boundless love and compassion that unfold in the following chapters help to meet this critical need. Buddhist traditions of Tibet and India have considered such cultivations tremendously powerful sources of karmic merit.

> As at the end of the rainy season, the sun, rising into the clear and cloudless sky, banishes all the dark spaces and glows and shines and blazes forth:…so, O monks, none of the means employed to acquire karmic merit has a sixteenth part of the value of love.
>
> Shakyamuni Buddha[17]

Also, to cultivate boundless love and compassion doesn't just harmonize the mind with its infinite nature. When the nature of mind is recognized, boundless love and compassion become the natural way to express it. Therefore, wisdom and love are integrated within each meditation of this book, so each may increasingly inform and empower the other. In this way, the spiritual path can unfold with a *wise* sense of ease and naturalness and a *loving* sense of commitment to all—the sort of qualities that Nyoshul Khenpo embodied in his simple presence.

Nonconceptual Practice Supports All Other Qualities on the Path

> When one realizes [this] natural state, the true nature of all beings, there is naturally a welling up of inconceivable spontaneous compassion, loving-kindness, consideration and empathy, because one realizes there is no self separate from others.... Everywhere that suffering and delusion arise, compassion arises to release and alleviate beings suffering from that delusion. That is the spontaneous outflow of the genuine realization of the true nature.
>
> Nyoshul Khen Rinpoche[18]

In sum, we have struggled so long—reacting to so much of our experience of self and world through self-grasping anxiety and aversion. We have identified with those thought patterns so much that they just appear to *be* what we all are. And we may never notice, until it is pointed out and made vivid in nonconceptual meditation, the extent to which we were reacting to our own fabrications of self and others all along. Through nonconceptual meditation, we start to sense the vast nature of goodness that had been hidden by our ego-clinging. And we sense that this is equally true for all the others around us. Together we have been lost from our true nature and together have suffered for it. From this recognition flows tremendous loving compassion for all beings equally.

Some Tibetan Buddhist teachers do not give specific, hands-on instruction for nonconceptual wisdom practice until their students have done a great many preliminary practices of devotion, love, and mental purification. This is so students can first develop the spiritual power (merit) that is needed to engage nonconceptual wisdom. Such an approach works well for some students, but for others it can make the path seem like an endless proliferation of conceptual practices, reducing "enlightenment" in their minds to a distant, seemingly unattainable goal. Then some of them become discouraged and give up.

Other teachers give instruction in nonconceptual wisdom practice early on, so that all other practices of love and reverence can flow more naturally from that practice, as in Khenpo's quote above. Love, compassion, and devotion unfold more easily when they are informed by nonconceptual wisdom. And when informed even a little by such wisdom, they unleash far more spiritual power for the path. For this reason, following my own root teachers, I have introduced nonconceptual practice here early on.

Further Guidance for Buddhists and Non-Buddhists

The practices of this chapter are deceptively simple yet quite profound. With good guidance and much practice, over time they can actually lead to the heart of enlightenment, the nondual realization of emptiness and compassion, buddha mind, dharmakaya.

Nonconceptual awareness can only communicate itself through those who abide in such awareness, accomplished masters such as those referred to in this book. So, if the practices of this chapter ignite your interest to plumb them to their depth, you will need to seek out a teacher who has deep knowledge of them, attained from long practice with his or her own teachers. Such Buddhist teachers transmit a diversity of practices to strengthen concentration, cut through subconscious patterns of clinging, bring out capacities of compassion and devotion, and point the student to the mind's infinite nature. Such teachers can help individual students, in their uniqueness, draw upon the vast resources of Buddhist traditions so as to progress in the most effective ways.

When you read spiritual books or meet spiritual teachers who speak deeply to your own life, find out with whom they trained and how they trained, and you can start to discern your own connections to the practice traditions that call to you.[19]

Non-Buddhist meditators among you are invited to explore the practices in this book to see how they empower your own process of spiritual learning. Let your experience of each meditation in this book point you to passages in your sacred texts to discover what they may further reveal. Let meditation experience shine new light upon the central tenets, practices, and ethics of your own tradition and upon all facets of your life.

> God is love, and he who abides in love abides in God, and God abides in him.
>
> First Letter of John 4:16.

3. Letting It Out:
Unleashing Love's Power

Your Own Fulfillment Comes Through Love for Others

As the great eighth-century Buddhist master Shantideva wrote:

> All who find happiness in this world have done so by wishing for the happiness of many others. All who find unhappiness in this world have done so by aiming just for their own happiness.[20]

At first glance, this statement may seem surprising. It contradicts the assumption, so prevalent in modern society, that if we focused our attention on the happiness of others we would sacrifice our own. Shantideva claims that to focus on others' happiness is the cause of our own! But if he's right, how could society have gotten it so wrong?

As earlier mentioned, our stream of thought has been working to create an impression of an isolated "self," set apart from all others, which appears real, substantial, and thereby seemingly safe. Although we have all believed such thoughts of "self" as something isolated from and over against others, those thoughts were always mistaken. We have never existed in that way. Therefore, we can never become happy or fulfilled by pretending to exist in that way. Rather, we always existed in much deeper relationship to all others, who in their innate nature of goodness and their self-centered habits of thought are like alternative versions of ourselves. *That* is the reality of our existence.

As our spiritual practice increasingly shows us our underlying connection to all others, we begin to realize that our practice, and indeed our life, was never meant just for ourselves. Its purpose all along has been to awaken to our fullest potential for the sake of all. And we learn, gratefully, to take up that responsibility.

Getting Real: The Buddha's Teaching of Karma

It is our inner nature, buddha nature, that recognizes the reality of our connection to all. It also possesses a vast capacity of openness, love, and compassion that mirrors this reality. When we are genuinely loving, kind, respectful, and generous to others, we express that innate nature and thereby evoke our own potential for well-being and happiness. By doing so, we also evoke others' potential for kindness and well-being. When we try to find happiness through selfish actions that are possessive, callous, or hateful of others, we fall away from our innate nature of loving openness and thereby create causes for struggle, suffering, and anguish in our minds. By doing so, we also evoke others' tendencies toward self-centeredness and hatred. This is the Buddha's teaching of karma: Our wise, loving actions of mind and body empower our inner potential to be well and happy and trigger others' potential for goodness. Our deluded, selfish actions of mind and body do the opposite.

Karma—Prior Actions Affect Present Experience

Distinguishing the Inner Causes of Our Feelings from the External Triggers

Modern societies promote the idea that to acquire nice things and pleasant companions is what brings happiness. Advertisements reinforce that impression: the right drinks, the right car, the right companions are the ticket to a happy life. Believing that, some people devote their lives almost entirely to the acquisition of such things and to the endeavor to protect and keep them. What the advertisements don't show is how unhappy, even desperate, such people tend to become over the course of their lives.

As the Buddha taught, happiness comes from actualizing our inner nature of love, compassion, and wisdom. Unhappiness comes from self-centered thought and action that alienate us from that nature. People and things can trigger feelings of happiness in us, but they are not the very source of those feelings. They can trigger feelings of unhappiness in us, but they are not the very source of those feelings. It is critically important to understand that distinction for us to further access Shantideva's meaning.

Paying Attention to the Karmic Structure of Experience

When someone says or does something that upsets us, we commonly say: "He hurt me." Implicit in such a statement is the assumption that the other person *put* the feeling of "hurt" into us, the mental pain that we feel, which is why we get angry about it. But could that assumption be wrong?

For example, Susan gets angry with her co-worker Jim and snarls at him, "The presentation you just gave is stupid." Jim feels hurt and angry in return. He tells others, "What Susan said really hurt me," as if her action had inserted his hurt, his mental pain, into him. He feels justified hating her for that and expects others to sympathize. The assumption that Susan hurt him is socially reinforced through gossip: "Susan hurt Jim. I don't blame him for hating her." But did Susan actually insert Jim's hurt into him, as the gossip implies? No. Then where did Jim's hurt come from?

Jim's interpretation of Susan's action triggered his feeling of mental pain. Something in Jim's mind understood that actions like Susan's often intend harm. That mental recognition helped elicit his feeling of pain. According to the Buddha's teaching of karmic action and result, like the rest of us, Jim has done actions intending harm. In this case, he has done actions analogous to what Susan did toward him. But in the moment of Susan's criticism, he doesn't remember his own past actions. When Susan criticizes him, then Jim's subconscious mind knows what it means to intend harm by such words, since he meant to harm others with words similarly in the past. So his mind takes the words personally and feels the hurt it is predisposed to feel. That unhappy feeling is the result of Jim's own karma, his own past harmful action, and the imprints it placed on his mind. The "hurt" comes *from within his mind*. Susan's action is just the *external* condition that helped to trigger it.

Try this thought experiment. Remember a time when someone said something negative to you and you felt hurt, becoming angry. Take a moment to recall that vividly now. Doesn't it seem as though they *put* the feeling of hurt into you by their words, so you became angry? But the other's action didn't actually put that mental feeling into you, did it? Somehow, your understanding of their action evoked *from within you* what your own mind was prepared to feel. Our own past negative actions prepare our minds to interpret others' actions in a personal way that makes us feel hurt.

The same principle applies in the opposite situation. If someone hasn't done a specific kind of negative action, they tend not to take it personally when others do it, and so they don't have feelings of hurt welling up inside. Beryl, my wife's mother, is a deeply loving person. I've noticed that if someone acts in a way that would generally be considered rude, she tends not to be upset by it. For example, if a man callously pushes ahead of her in line at a cafeteria, instead of getting angry, Beryl might wonder if the man is okay. "Perhaps he has low blood sugar and needs to get food quickly," she might say. If someone else suggests that he's simply rude, Beryl will express compassion for him, perhaps saying, "How difficult it must be to go through life in such a rush." In Buddhist terms, because she has not been rude to others, Beryl has no inner experience of what it's like to callously push others aside. So she tends not to take others' rude actions personally enough to feel the hurt and anger that many of us would feel in a similar situation (though presumably, as a human being, she would feel hurt by other types of negative action). In addition, her love and compassion for whomever she meets are strong. Since love and compassion are inner causes of joy, she tends to be joyful in general, even in situations that others find difficult.

So, in the prior example, Susan's criticism was not the *very source* of Jim's feeling of hurt. Rather, his inner tendency to feel personally hurt was *triggered* by her criticism. Like Jim, we don't notice that our pain comes from within, as the fruition of our own harmful past actions that we don't presently recall. In such situations, it appears as if the other person is the sole source of our "hurt," our mental pain, not merely the external trigger of it. So it feels natural to react self-righteously with anger in return. But this further reinforces the tendency for us to feel hurt in the future when others act with anger toward us; then we react once again with anger, on and on. Thus the karmic pattern gets etched deeper and deeper in endless mutual reaction.

Furthermore, in the moment of Susan's remark, Jim saw her as hateful, which is another reason he became angry. That's because he is familiar with the look of hate from times in the past when he hated others. Susan served as a mirror for Jim's own hateful face. By reacting to her with anger and hatred, he was reacting to part of himself.

In this way, we evoke the worst from each other even while blaming each other as the sole cause of the problem. As we rationalize our hatred in discussions with others, it attains social sanction, making the false construction of hurt and hate seem real: "Susan hurt Jim. I don't blame him for hating her."

Given this karmic analysis, is Jim then to be blamed for his angry reaction to Susan? That is not the point at all. Jim, Susan, and all of the rest of us are karmically conditioned in the ways described. Since before we can remember, we've been misreacting to others as if they were the very source of our feelings, without recognizing how our feelings are connected to our own past actions. Who stands outside of this problem, in a position to blame others for it? *All* are caught in this problem, and all have contributed to it. To know that is to have *compassion* for all, not to seek someone to blame for it. As several of my students at Boston College have pointed out, Jesus expressed this kind of dynamic beautifully:

> Do not judge, so that you may not be judged. For with the judgment you make you will be judged, and the measure you give will be the measure you get. Why do you see the speck in your neighbor's eye, but do not notice the log in your own eye?[21]

Ethnic Prejudice and Hatred

Ethnic prejudice and hatred are further elaborations of this karmic structure. People learn to experience others, all grouped together, as triggers for their own mental pain. By passing on the stories of a hateful and violent past, those who belong to one group learn to associate pain with any sight or thought of the other group. All the while, they consider the other group as the very source of their pain—as thoroughly evil—but with no awareness of the role of their own past actions in all they experience. So it feels natural, as a group, to hate a whole other group as intrinsically evil and to react to them accordingly. In doing so, they evoke the same kind of response in return, perpetuating an endless cycle of mutual hate and violence.

Positive Karma

The Buddha also taught about the opposite karmic dynamic. When others are kind and loving, their actions can trigger our happiness. For example, Bonnie listens with loving attention and concern to Rob. Later Rob thinks, "Bonnie makes me so happy," as if Bonnie were the very source of his happiness. But if Rob didn't have the inner capacity to be happy at that moment, if he were suffering from severe depression for example, nothing Bonnie said would have made him happy. Her kind action triggered the happy feeling that Rob's mind was prepared to feel.

Rob had done similar kind actions for others in the past, actions motivated by his wish for the other's well-being. Because those actions expressed his innate nature of love and compassion, they strengthened his inner capacity to be well and happy. Bonnie's kindness helped trigger that capacity in Rob's mind, so he felt happy. In addition, through her loving attention, Bonnie mirrored Rob's own goodness back at him, including his own prior experiences of being kind to others. So when Rob felt her kindness, he could recognize it and naturally respond with appreciation and love. In this way, others can also evoke the best from us.[22]

The Danger of Possessiveness

In light of the human tendency to grasp on to things, let's take this example further in our imagination. Rob is not aware of the Buddha's teaching of karma, so he thinks that Bonnie is the very *source* of his happiness, not just the *trigger* for it. This means he believes his happiness depends entirely on her presence. So he begins insisting she stay around him and pay exclusive attention to him. Rob calls that his "love" for Bonnie, but it is just possessiveness. Clinging to her in that way, of course, tends to drive her away. When Bonnie tries to avoid Rob, her actions trigger feelings of mental pain in him. Again mistaking Bonnie's actions as the *main cause* of his own feelings, Rob starts to hate Bonnie for "hurting" him and berates her. As she then avoids him even more, he feels more "hurt" by her action and verbal abuse escalates into physical abuse.

All too often, as television news reports, possessiveness mistaken for love turns into hatred, abuse, and violence. And because the newscaster merely reports the final, violent actions without their causal history, many of us react to such news with unmitigated disgust for the abuser.

In this way, we hide from ourselves the fact that we have *all* been implicated in the underlying problem. Every time we mistook others for the very sources of our happiness or unhappiness, and misreacted to them with possessiveness or anger through that delusion, we have contributed to a world in which greed, hatred, and violence are daily news.

As soon as we think that other persons are the givers of our mental pain, we are already caught in anger and hatred, no matter how much we consider ourselves to be nice people. As soon as we think that others are the very givers of our mental happiness, we are already caught in possessiveness, and are on our way to violence of thought or word, if not of body.

Shantideva's Fundamental Message

In sum, as Shantideva taught, happiness and well-being flow from our innate nature of loving compassion and wisdom, through actions of kindness, generosity, patience, respect, care, and consideration for others. Until we recognize this fact, we can't find much happiness.

To seek happiness from a self-centered point of view just creates more causes for suffering, because we keep mistaking others as the main cause of our pleasant and unpleasant feelings rather than the mere triggers for them. Mistaking them in this way, we can't avoid misreacting to them in possessive or angry ways, thus eliciting their equally deluded reactions, until it feels as if we are caught in an endless struggle.[23]

To experience the world in this way is to be caught in samsara. To be freed from samsara is to be freed from the self-centered point of view, the fundamental delusion, at the heart of the problem. To be freed from delusion is to awaken to our true nature—buddha nature, the ground of deep peace. To be liberated into that ground is to unleash vast powers of love and compassion for all others who are caught in the same fundamental delusion.

Indeed, in our present condition, each instant that we fall *out* of love in connection to all, we are already ill at ease in our minds, because we've fallen from our nature of all-inclusive openness in which deep peace is found. We simply can't be well and joyful in any stable way until we awaken to what we really are, our true nature, where concern for self and other is undivided. That is Shantideva's most fundamental point.

The Human Need to Realize Our Intimate Connection to All Others

Nyoshul Khen Rinpoche explains:

> [The great Tibetan master] Milarepa sang, "When I am alone, meditating in the mountains, all the Buddhas past, present, and future are with me. [My own teacher] guru Marpa is always with me. All beings are here." We are not practicing for ourselves alone, since everybody is involved and included in the great scope of our prayers and meditations.... The natural outflow of so-called "solitary meditation or prayer" is spontaneous benefit for others; it's like the rays of the sun, rays which spontaneously reach out. This good heart, pure heart, vast and open mind, is called in Tibetan *sem karpo,*

white mind. It means pure, vast and open heart. This is innate bodhichitta. It is not something foreign to us.[24]

The path to enlightenment uncovers our hidden relationship to all others, revealing our "innate bodhichitta," our innate capacity for all-inclusive care. We are dependent upon innumerable beings for all that we are and all that we will become through spiritual practice. All others are like ourselves in their causes of suffering, their wish to be happy, and their potential for enlightenment. Ultimately, all are undivided from us in the nature of mind. As the path reveals our profound relation to all others, it also reveals our connection to spiritual teachers who preceded us in this awakening and have held the way open for us. Because such vast relatedness is given in the very ground of our being, our most basic need is to realize and embody it in love and compassion.

In other words, our deep human need is to attain the inner freedom that lets us receive love in the very depth of our being and to extend love to all others in the very depth of their being. Indeed, that is part of what learning to become "enlightened" means.

According to Buddhist traditions of Tibet and East Asia, the path to enlightenment is not a quest that issues in a solitary achievement. It is an intuitive awakening to one's implicit relation to all others. This is expressed in the doctrine and iconography of buddhahood in those cultures. Complete enlightenment manifests not just as a figure in private repose but as a luminous embodiment of all-pervasive love, compassion, joy, and liberating activity, who spontaneously communes through those radiant qualities with a vast array of bodhisattvas (beings mature in the path to enlightenment). From that array, the luminous, liberating powers of those qualities extend to beings in every direction.[25]

This image of enlightenment as a holy realm of radiant, liberating activity, blessing, and communion is not a distant metaphysical abstraction. It communicates the message that to awaken to our inmost nature and freedom is to open our hearts and minds to all others in loving compassion. Our capacity of universal love (buddha nature), the spiritual path that evokes its liberating power (bodhisattva path), and the ultimate realization of that path (buddhahood) are of one piece.

Cooperating with the Primordial Power of Good Within Us

These understandings inform our practice. Meditations of wisdom and love are not for the purpose of remaking isolated, inherently sinful persons into something different. Rather, such meditations uncover the fact that we are closely connected to all others and that our inherent nature, the very essence of our minds, is always primordially good prior to self-centered thoughts of "good" and "evil."

A tremendous force of love and wisdom has been hidden within us, obstructed by momentary (but almost continuous) chains of ego-clinging thought and emotion. Energies of love and pure awareness have been distorted by those tendencies into our self-centered, deluded emotions. Practices of wisdom and love from Buddhist traditions cut through self-centeredness and purify emotional energies into enlightened powers of insight and love that can inspire many others. We take up our responsibility to self and others first by taking real measures to awaken that enlightened potential, as in the meditation that follows.

As we enter into the meditation below, it is critical to remember that we are not struggling to become something we are not. We are learning to cooperate with what we *always were*. We enter into the meditation in that spirit—following the instructions carefully so as to cooperate with the tremendous force of good within us that has been waiting to emerge.

The meditation below will extend the wish of love first to dear ones, then very widely. It repeats the basic content of prior meditations and then builds further upon them. This serves to deepen our grounding in each part of the practice as it continues to unfold. The meditation has four parts that can be done in about thirty to forty minutes in daily practice. Be sure to pause after each demarcated section, to give yourself time to dwell on the instruction at hand.

Meditation: Extending the Love We Receive

Part 1: Refuge—Receiving the Blessing of Unconditional Love

Sit in a relaxed way with back straight, eyes gently gazing slightly downward. Recall your benefactors—those remembered from your personal life and revered spiritual beings who extend their love to all. Envision their smiling faces before you. Recall them as sending you the wish of love, the wish for your deepest well-being, happiness, and joy.

Imagine their wish as a soft, radiant shower of healing blessing. Bathe your whole body and mind in that radiance, all the way down to your fingertips and toes. Receive its gentle, healing energy. Trusting this wish of love more than limiting thoughts of yourself, receive it deeply into your being.

Absorb the healing radiance of their wish for your happiness into every cell of your body, every corner of your mind. Bathe in this; heal in this; rest in this.

After a little while, join your benefactors in their wish for you. While receiving their wish, mentally repeat it for yourself, "May this one have deepest well-being, happiness, and joy." Affirm the words repeatedly while accepting your benefactors' love even more deeply into your body and mind, communing with them through its radiance.

After a little while, drop the visualization and just relax into oneness with that loving luminosity, releasing all frames of reference. Deeply let be into that gentle, luminous wholeness beyond separation of self and others. Enjoy just being— at ease, at rest, complete.

Part 2: Letting Be in Natural Awareness

Notice where you still feel any grasping in the body. Let that gently release itself. Relaxed and calmly alert, allow all bodily sensations to settle naturally in their own way. Let go of any sense of control. Just surrender to the natural power of the body, letting it embody you. Enjoy bodily awareness in that way for a little while.

Now notice any grasping on to the breathing process. Let it relax, allowing the breath to come under its own power. Sense the gentle shift from holding on to the breath to just being breathed. Feel the breath all the way in, all the way out, breathing you.

Notice any grasping within the mind on to the thinking mechanism, identifying with chains of thought, grasping on to them as frames of reference. Let that feeling of holding on release itself, so as to unwind deep inside. Let all the thoughts and sensations simply arise and dissolve under their own power, in their own way. Cut the "kite string" on thoughts to let them fly freely, even as they arise.

In this way, let the mind unfurl naturally, of itself, and fall totally open—at ease, unrestricted, free of any focus or directedness, three-hundred-sixty degrees all-pervasive, wide open. Raise the gaze of your eyes to look gently ahead, taking all in at once, totally expansive. Let all be just as it is, in complete openness and acceptance.

Sense the openness of awareness, infinite and without center, in which all thoughts and sensations self-arise and self-dissolve—beyond thinking, beyond reference point—boundless openness and translucent awareness, pervasive like the sky. Let this vast expanse of fundamental awareness sense all that appears as its own radiant expression, like the sky sensing its own rainbows. Rest as that sky-like nature of mind—all phenomena permitted to self-arise and self-release within the infinite expanse of openness aware.

Part 3: Extending the Love We Receive

Let the soft energy of this fundamental awareness manifest by envisioning your benefactors, now behind you and just above. Open to their wish for you to have deepest well-being, happiness, and joy. Accept the healing radiance of their love into every part of your body and mind.

While continuing to receive their radiant wish, also join your benefactors in their wish for you, repeating it for yourself, "May this one have deepest well-being, happiness, and joy."

After a little while, think of someone very dear to you, for whom it feels natural to extend the wish of love, such as a close friend, relative, or pet. Envision that being in front of you. While continuing to receive your benefactors' radiant love from behind, now also let the radiance come through you to the dear one before you. As you do so, sincerely affirm the wish of love in your mind for that person: "May this one have deepest well-being, happiness, and joy." Repeatedly make that wish as the radiance comes through you, bathing him or her in its healing energy.

Envision before you a few more beings that are dear to you, letting your benefactors' radiance come through you to them. Repeatedly affirm the wish of love for them in your mind: "May they have deepest well-being, happiness, and joy."

❧

Envision more beings that are dear to you in widening circles at your own pace, letting the radiance come through you to them while repeating the wish. No matter how you have thought differently of individuals, extend the wish to them all equally. Trust this wish more than any such limiting thoughts. Repeating the wish, let its radiance illumine them all, from the depth of your heart into the full depth of their being: "May they have deepest well-being and joy, through and through."

As you continue to receive your benefactors' wish of love from behind, let its radiance come through in a much vaster way. Think that it extends to every being in all directions at once: each human, animal, insect, worm, and all other sentient beings wherever they may be. Sense your heart as like the sun, radiating the energy of this wish in all directions at once, boundlessly, infinitely. Repeating the wish, illumine every being with its healing energy: "May each being have deepest well-being, happiness, and joy, every single one."

Finally, drop the visualization and just relax into oneness with that loving, insubstantial luminosity. Release all frames of reference into boundless openness and translucent awareness, pervasive like the sky, beyond any thought of separation. Rest thus, at ease, wide open, complete.

Part 4: Dedicating the Spiritual Power for All

Feel the power of this practice to pull you beyond self-grasping patterns of suffering and to open you toward the tranquillity, freedom, and goodness of your inmost being. Prayerfully dedicate all such spiritual power to the deepest well-being and liberation of all beings, each like you in needing and wanting such joy and freedom.

Good work! Have a break.

Tips on Starting to Extend Love to Others

When you began to extend love, you were asked to think of first one, then a few beings that are dear to you, for whom it feels natural to make the wish of love. Be careful at this point to avoid inauthentic choices. Don't focus here on people you think you are *supposed* to consider dear. Bring to mind those for whom it feels natural to wish their happiness.

It is traditionally advised, when starting to extend love, *not* to focus first on people from whom you expect lots of attention, appreciation, and so forth in return. Otherwise your wish for their happiness tends to get mixed with your desire for them to fulfill your expectations. That is a form of possessiveness, not the simple wish of love that we are learning to evoke. You can include such people later in your meditation, when you have more experience with the practice; not in the beginning.

When you are identifying dear ones, if any of your benefactors come naturally to mind, you can envision them in both places—in the field of benefactors behind you and in the field of dear ones before you. That is fine.

The Thoroughness of the Love We Cultivate

Notice how *thorough* is the wish of love in this practice. When receiving love, we accept it into every part of our body and mind, all the way down to our toes and fingertips. When extending it to others, we wish them total well-being, radiating the wish into their whole being, top to bottom. Indeed, we may never have consciously received or extended love in such a thoroughgoing way.

Much of the power of the practice comes from that thoroughness. To wish for the complete well-being of others is to speak to their inmost nature—the perfection, tranquillity, and joy in the very nature of their minds that is prior to all delusions arising from ego-grasping. Their complete well-being can only be fully realized when they become freed from delusion and grasping. Thus, ultimately, the love we extend to others wishes them a depth of peace and joy that only becomes actualized as they themselves awaken to their own innate, enlightened potential. At its ultimate level of meaning, then, our wish of love is a wish for their fullest enlightenment.

At the same time, in this practice, we also wish each being every other kind of genuine relief and happiness, no matter how small: a cool breeze on a hot day, food when hungry, healing when sick, consolation when sad. In this way, our wish of love also motivates specific actions to meet concrete needs. It prompts us to serve others in manifold ways: to comfort someone in despair, to share our resources with someone in need, to be present to someone who needs us.

This thorough wish of love, which wills every layer of well-being for every person, is what very great spiritual benefactors, such as Shakyamuni Buddha, Shantideva, the Dalai Lama, and Nyoshul Khenpo have made for all beings—including each of us. Because they have done this and have practiced and taught from such an all-inclusive and powerful attitude, we find ourselves with the chance to do likewise. We can join them in the same potent wish for all and learn increasingly to embody it, "teaming up" with them in enlightened activity for this world.

The spiritual power of other very great holy figures appears to function similarly. Jesus, for example, inspires wise Christians to *participate* in his active love and service to the world, not only to worship him. Christians can practice this meditation of love as a means to empower their lives as Christians. In the meditation they can envision Christ as their fundamental benefactor and consider the spiritual power unleashed by the practice as the power of God's love, pulling them beyond themselves while incorporating them into God's loving activity and service to the world. Analogously, Jews, Muslims, Hindus, and others can explore how the meditation of love may inform and empower their spiritual lives in service to others.

The only true joy on earth is to escape from the prison of our own false self, and enter by love into union with the life who dwells and sings within the essence of every creature and in the core of our own souls.

Thomas Merton[26]

May I be a light for those in need of light. May I be a bed for those in need of rest. May I be a servant for those in need of service, for all embodied beings.

Shantideva[27]

The Vastness of the Love We Cultivate

Besides its thoroughness, notice how vast the scope of love becomes in the final step of the meditation, literally extending to all beings. Part of the power of the practice comes from that vast scope, so vast it is beyond the comprehension of self-centered thought. It opens us way up, stretching the mind past its narrow, ego-centered frames of reference. Such boundless love helps harmonize us with the infinite, sky-like scope of the mind's nature, the vast expanse of openness and cognizance. It supports our practice of wisdom, by helping us release our frames of reference and let be into what lies beyond them.[28]

The Path of Enlightenment Is the Opening of the Mind

This innate buddha-nature—the fundamental enlightened mind within each of us—is like the sky, which is unfailingly vast, pure, and unchanging. Within this profound nature, the qualities of buddhahood are like the rays of light that come from the sun.... The difference between the impure mind and the pure mind, the deluded mind and the enlightened mind, is mainly a difference of narrowness and openness. In our present deluded state, our mind is extremely narrow. For example, we live [as if] alone and rarely, if ever, consider the infinity of sentient beings.... Conversely, the enlightened Buddha is one who considers the infinity of sentient beings.... Thus the entire path—from an ordinary being to buddhahood—is the gradual opening of mind.

Nyoshul Khen Rinpoche[29]

The path of enlightenment releases the mind from its constricted self-grasping to the infinite openness of its basic nature, which is pervaded by awareness and compassion like the open sky is pervaded by the rays of the sun. The path to enlightenment involves a fundamental reorientation, from identifying ourselves with the narrow, self-centered, and shifting thoughts of the moment to the all-inclusive, abiding nature of enlightened wisdom and love. This path is the opening of the mind to the vast expanse that includes all phenomena without discrimination and to the vast love that includes all beings without discrimination.

Through the nonconceptual practice of wisdom, of letting all be in the sky-like nature of mind, we realize that we are not isolated from each other; we are not set apart from others within the undivided, cognizant ground of being. As this intuitive wisdom dawns, there is a profound sense of wholeness, of oneness with our world and its inhabitants, a natural intimacy with them all. All thought of a brittle self, holding itself apart from the others, starts to collapse into basic unity with the empty, cognizant ground of all.

Complementing that nonconceptual wisdom practice, the conceptual practice boundlessly extending love enacts our implicit connection to all other beings, expressing our solidarity with them through the will and energy that wishes them deepest well-being and happiness. Unbounded love prepares the mind for unbounded wisdom and expresses the dawning of that wisdom.

One of my most inspiring and profound teachers is Chokyi Nyima Rinpoche, a learned abbot, lama, and Buddhist leader who lives in Nepal. Rinpoche is slight of build and short in stature. Yet, mysteriously, when you meet him, there is something incredibly vast about him. He is responsible for the education and support of hundreds of monks and nuns and revered as spiritual guide to thousands of other Asians and Westerners. He has established a pioneering university center to explore new ways to train students in ancient and modern forms of Buddhist studies. He has initiated service projects in support of Asian women and children. He has introduced new ways to apply Buddhist practices to modern needs and has inspired many innovators who now lead the way in bringing methods of the East to the West. While physically small, he seems like a *huge* person in the vastness of his presence, his perspective, his energy, and his sense of responsibility for the world. When we train in the boundlessly vast scope of love and wisdom through meditation, it helps us appreciate and understand a person of such vastness. Such practice inspires us not only to admire our spiritual benefactors but to begin to emulate them.

The Very Life of Life

Nyoshul Khenpo further discusses the relationship between wisdom and love in our practice:

> If self-clinging and clinging to the reality of things remains strong, how can there be any genuine Dzogchen, which is the true natural state of freedom, openness, and primordial perfection? If you do bodhichitta practices [such as] loving-kindness…these practices may seem conceptual and relative, but they actually include the absolute truth that is the very nature of Dzogchen: vast openness, big mind, purity, freedom, and non-grasping.[30]

The more we learn to let go of ourselves into the sky-like nature of pure awareness, the more its qualities of love and compassion can naturally unfold. The more such enlightened qualities are permitted to unfold all-inclusively and unconditionally, the more we can let go of ourselves into the all-inclusive, unconditioned wisdom of the mind's nature. Thus, Nyoshul Khenpo declares, transcendental wisdom and love are mutually empowering on the path to enlightenment. Indeed, they are ultimately inseparable.

The meditation sections of this chapter proceed in that spirit and in that order. We rest in natural awareness, a nonconceptual practice. Then we let the intrinsic energy of that awareness express itself in the conceptual practices of receiving and extending love. By extending love in stages until it reaches all beings, its radiant energy helps melt away ordinary frames of reference, permitting us finally to release them and relax into nonconceptual abiding: "Rest thus, at ease, complete." Finally, we dedicate the karmic merit to fullest enlightenment for all beings.

When I was thirteen, my school required a course in religious studies. Mr. Harrison, a teacher new to the school, was assigned to teach it. And since I loathed religious study, I was prepared not to like him. But the first moment I saw him, I knew this year with him would be unusual. When he smiled at his students, he appeared to mean it—as if he were actually delighted and honored to be in our adolescent presence. He taught religious and spiritual themes in connection with world events, prominently the Vietnam war at a time when it was little questioned and the civil rights movement when it was viewed with hostility by many Americans. He also taught a "sex education" component at a time when sex was seldom discussed with children. These were the most "dangerous" areas of formal study that I had ever encountered. But somehow, Mr. Harrison took us into profound learning within every subject. Part of it was his willingness to question, with care and kindness, into almost anything. But it was his care and compassion for all the people we studied, and his obvious affection for each student, that empowered us to join him in such courageous inquiries. It felt as if he had more reverence and care for each of us than we had for ourselves, naturally evoking my reverence in response—reverence for him, for my classmates, and for myself. His class was grace filled.

At that point in my life, I thought that the people I admired for their spontaneous compassion, such as Mr. Harrison, were almost a different species. Perhaps they were born with that capacity, I thought, but I could never be like that. Later in life, as I explored the practices that my Buddhist teachers taught, it began to dawn on me that what I had admired in others had been a facet of my own nature all along, a facet that I hadn't known how to bring out. For someone like me to be given an effective way to bring out such hidden capacities seemed miraculous. It's like being shown the way into the very life of life, the very heart of your heart. To realize that this is what your spiritual benefactors and teachers are open-heartedly offering to you, despite all your suspicions and worries, is to feel tremendous gratitude.

The reader may read on through the book. But I recommend that you practice the meditation above daily for several weeks before shifting to the meditation in the next chapter as your main focus of practice.

"What About My Special Loved Ones?"

A question is often asked at this point: "Isn't there something unique about my love for my family, my intimate friends, or my pets? What is that uniqueness? Would it be lost within a practice like this, that finally extends love to all beings equally?"

To clearly define the word love helps clarify the answer to this question. *Love* here means the simple wish for someone to have well-being, happiness, and joy.

Our families, intimate friends, and pets are very special recipients for our love. Because of our uniquely close connection to them in this life, they most powerfully evoke our capacity for openness, love, and compassion. They help bring out our otherwise hidden powers of presence and care from the depth of our hearts. Importantly, our family members and close friends are *also* the ones who most vividly reveal to us how much our possessiveness is mixed with our love for them.

For example, before we have a specific practice of love and wisdom (like the meditations of these chapters), we may regularly wish members of our family happiness, but that wish is often adulterated by our desire for them to behave in ways that meet our own desires and expectations. Without a specific spiritual practice, we may have no clear means to distinguish that possessiveness, that self-centered attachment, from the authentic wish of love. When we have a daily practice of love and wisdom, over time, it helps us distinguish that difference more clearly.

By and large, we tend not to notice how often we confuse our desire to possess or control others—in the name of their well-being—for genuine love. A mother may long for her daughter to have similar interests, to take a particular career direction, or to develop the same kind of sexual identity, and so forth. But authentic love for a child is an enduring wish for her happiness no matter how that may best unfold for *her*—whether that way fulfills the parent's own perceived needs or not. As the wisdom from daily practice increasingly distinguishes that difference, it empowers our authentic love in family life while disempowering our possessiveness and the problems it causes.

Learning to extend the wish of love to all beings further informs this process. By opening the mind way past its prior parameters of self-concern, such practice shows us the possibility of extending authentic love without having to possess or control its recipients.

As we become familiar with this practice of love and wisdom over time, family life and friendships are positively transformed. The power to transform our lives is enhanced by participating in meditation retreats and workshops with others long experienced in such practices. Then, as the natural outflow of practice, family life and friendships can begin to transform into another kind of "retreat." From breakfast to bedtime, each moment of interaction can be taken into our learning to be more present, loving, unconditional, to actually be there for partners, children, or friends as they describe their workday, tell you their concerns, share a silly joke, or show you their homework. To be more present to family or friends, more deeply listening at such moments, brings them joy, which brings joy to you for learning better to be the person you had intended to be.

However, our family and close friends are certainly not different from others in their most basic condition: their mind's nature of cognizance and emptiness, their innate goodness, their self-centered tendencies of thought and reaction, their deep need for love. They became dear to us through special bonds of this life and by our consequent vision of goodness in them. But our practice also reveals our hidden bonds to all others, all of whom also hold the promise of their innate goodness.

So, indeed our family, close friends, and pets remain the special emissaries of love for us in this life—the ones who most intimately evoke and support our learning of authentic love and wisdom. And as we learn to extend love to all others in meditation, it doesn't endanger the uniqueness of our love for family and friends. It purifies and revivifies it, even as it increasingly reveals all the others as our wider "family."

4. Loving Beyond Boundaries

Love Must Be Boundless to Express What We Are

> May all beings be happy. May they live in safety and joy.... As a mother watches over her child, willing to risk her own life to protect her only child, so with a boundless heart...cherish all living beings, suffusing the whole world with unobstructed loving kindness.... During all your waking hours, may you remain mindful of this heart and this way of living that is the best in the world.
>
> Shakyamuni Buddha[31]

In our previous meditation, we began to extend love in a vast way, literally to all beings. This is inevitable, because ultimately the extension of boundless love is a natural expression of what we truly are. We are all interconnected. Our innate goodness can only manifest in dependence on many other beings—those that send us love, those that evoke our love, and those that provoke our ego reactions (which shows us more of ourselves so we can grow wiser). In addition, other persons are essentially other versions of ourselves. Our fundamental condition is the same: buddha nature, pure awareness, narrowed into ego-centered emotions and sufferings. As practice progressively uncovers our deep connection to all others, therefore, it feels increasingly natural to wish them all the same well-being we would wish for ourselves.

Our love must ultimately extend to all beings for another reason as well: our innate capacities of wisdom and love are actually that vast. When we let be deeply into natural awareness, the vast scope of our innate wisdom can reveal itself as the boundless expanse of openness aware. Then as our wish of love extends itself widely to others, it unleashes a correspondingly boundless capacity of love previously hidden in our minds. To realize the freedom and joy of coming home to what we truly are, we must let our vast potential of love and wisdom emerge. That is the path to enlightenment—the uncovering of our inmost being.

Sensing the Fundamental Goodness of All

When we receive the wish of love, the wish for our happiness, we are instructed to trust that wish more than any limiting thoughts of ourselves. When we extend the same wish to others, we learn to trust it more than our limiting thoughts of them. As in the Buddha's quote above, the quality of this love is like that of a devoted mother for her child. No matter what the child thinks, does, or is driven to do, the mother senses the child's fundamental goodness and reflects that goodness back at him.

Similarly, we are learning to wish others well-being and happiness unconditionally and to sense their underlying goodness, no matter who they think they are or what they think they are doing. This takes us beyond our usual limitations, to extend the wish of love more inclusively and enduringly than we may have previously thought possible. To extend love ultimately to all beings gives us a glimpse into the vast capacity of love that was hidden in our being all along.

Progressing from a Glimpse of Our Potential to Actualization of It

During periods of quiet meditation, we may get the impression that such a glimpse means we have reached a stable realization of boundless, unconditional love. But it is just a glimpse into our *potential,* not yet a stable realization of such love. This becomes obvious in our daily lives when we notice how often—in our thoughts, emotions, and actions—we continue to react to others in less than loving ways. It has been our habit to pay far more attention to our own self-concerned *thoughts* about other persons than to the *persons* themselves (as in the last chapter's examples of Susan and Jim, Bonnie and Rob). The previous meditation starts to evoke our potential to love beings beyond our ego-centered thoughts about them. But we need to go further. Our practice also needs to show us how our own thoughts have obstructed our potential for love, so we can cut through their obstruction and more fully release our potential.

We will use the meditation introduced in this chapter to consciously extend our wish of love to beings who have *not* been dear to us—strangers and those we dislike or hate. The ego is not used to doing that, so it typically reacts against it. In this way, our thought of others as merely "strangers," "enemies," or "my friends" becomes vividly displayed. We can actually see how our belief in those reductive labels has limited our potential for love and wisdom. Once that is seen, we can learn how to cut through those patterns of thought and belief so as to let the will and energy of our love flow far more freely and enduringly.

In the meditation that follows, we are instructed to extend the wish of love past our usual ego boundaries—first to strangers, then to those we dislike. "Strangers" here refers to beings we don't personally know, whom we neither love nor hate since we don't think we know them enough to care. Notice how many strangers there are—billions of humans of the past and present, billions of animals and insects. In comparison, the number of beings we consider our "friends" is minuscule.

"Those we dislike" are all beings toward whom we feel aversion, hatred, or fear, no matter how mild or strong this aversion may be. For the purpose of this meditation, it is important to look beyond our obvious adversaries to the vast majority of "disliked ones" toward whom we feel a subtle or subconscious aversion. For example, think of someone you may not consciously hate but whom you wish to avoid when you see him coming. That counts as someone you dislike for this practice. Or think of the aversion or fear that may arise in your mind when you encounter a person of a race or ethnic group that's had tensions with your own, coming down the street in your direction on a dark night. Or think of a political figure or group that you and your friends routinely denigrate as "obviously" immoral or stupid. These are examples of beings we dislike—even just a little or just for a moment—in our typical day.

The following meditation can be done in about forty minutes as daily practice. Pause for a little while after each demarcated section to dwell on the meditation instruction.

Meditation: Self-Transcending Love

Part 1: Refuge—Receiving the Blessing of Unconditional Love

Sit in a relaxed way. Recall your benefactors and envision their smiling faces before you. Recall them as sending you the wish of love, the wish for you to have deepest well-being, happiness, and joy.

Bathe in the healing energy of that wish, accepting it into every part of your body and mind. To trust this wish of love, the goodness it comes from, and the goodness it meets in your heart—to trust it more than limiting thoughts of yourself—is to find real refuge. Receive its healing radiance deep into your being, from head to toe.

After a little while, join your benefactors in their wish for you. Repeat the wish for yourself while accepting their radiant love even more deeply into mind and body: "May this one have deepest well-being, happiness, and joy." Commune with them through that radiance.

After some time, drop the visualization and just relax into oneness with that loving luminosity, releasing all frames of reference. Deeply let be into that gentle, luminous wholeness beyond separation of self and others. Enjoy just being—at ease, at rest, complete.

Part 2: Letting Be in Natural Awareness

Notice any grasping in the body. Let that gently release itself. Let all bodily sensations settle naturally in their own way. Surrender to the natural power of the body, feeling it embody you.

Let the breath come under its own power. Feel the breath all the way in, all the way out, breathing you.

After a little while, notice any grasping to the thinking mechanism, any clinging to thought chains as frames of reference. Let that mental grasping release itself, and just permit thoughts and sensations to arise and dissolve under their own power. In this way let the mind unfurl and fall totally open—at ease, unrestricted, free of focus, all-pervasive, with the gaze of your eyes gentle and totally expansive. Let all be just as it is in complete openness and acceptance.

Sense the openness of awareness, infinite and without center, in which thoughts and sensations self-arise and self-dissolve— beyond thinking, beyond reference point—boundless openness and translucent awareness, pervasive like the sky. Let this vast expanse sense all that arises as its own radiant expression. Rest as that sky-like nature of mind—all phenomena permitted to self-arise and self-release within the infinite expanse of openness aware.

Part 3: Extending Love Past Accustomed Boundaries

After some time, recall your benefactors and open to their wish for you to have deepest well-being, happiness, and joy. Envision them this time behind you and just above. Accept the healing radiance of their love into every part of your body and mind. Join them in their wish for you, repeating it for yourself, "May this one have deepest well-being, happiness, and joy."

After a little while, envision before you a few beings who are especially dear to you. While receiving your benefactors' radiant wish from behind, let the radiance come through you to those dear ones before you, and make the wish of love for them: "May they have deepest well-being, happiness, and joy." Affirm that wish repeatedly while letting the radiance come through you, bathing them in its healing energy.

At your own pace, increase the number of dear ones you envision before you in widening circles, extending the radiant wish of love to them all equally. Trust that wish more than any limiting thoughts of them.

Envision now also before you a stranger, someone you have seen or heard of but don't really know. Let the radiance come through you to that person while mentally repeating the wish of love for him or her: "May this one have deepest happiness, well-being, and joy." Trust this wish more than your thought of the person as "stranger." As you repeat the wish, bathe the person with its radiance through and through.

Envision more strangers. Let the radiance come through you to them while repeating the wish. Extend the wish to them equally, trusting it more than the thought of them as "strangers." Just like you, these beings need and want deep well-being and happiness. Bathe them with the radiance of love, through and through. To trust this wish of love more than your own limiting thoughts of self and others is to find real refuge.

Envision now someone whom you have disliked a little. Let the radiance come through you to that person while repeating the wish of love for him or her. Try trusting that wish more than your thought of the person as dislikable. Just like you, this person needs and wants well-being and happiness but is often caught, like you, in self-centered reactions.

Repeating the wish, bathe the person with its radiance through and through.

Try extending the wish to others whom you have disliked, feared, or hated. No matter who they think they are or how you have thought of them, extend the wish to them, trusting it more than those limiting thoughts. Bathe them with its radiance through and through.

Continuing to receive your benefactors' radiant love from behind, now let its radiance come through you in a much vaster way. Think that it extends to every being in every direction. Sense your heart as like the sun, radiating the power of this wish in all directions at once, boundlessly. Repeating the wish, bathe every being in its energy: "May every being have deepest happiness, well-being, and joy, every single one."

Finally, drop the visualization and just relax into oneness with that loving, insubstantial luminosity. Release all frames of reference into boundless openness and translucent awareness, pervasive like the sky, beyond any thought of separation. Rest thus, at ease, wide open, complete.

Part 4: Dedicating the Spiritual Power for All

Feel the power of this practice to pull you beyond self-grasping patterns of suffering and to open you toward the tranquillity, freedom, and goodness of your inmost being. Prayerfully dedicate all such spiritual power to the deepest well-being and liberation of all beings, each like you in needing and wanting such joy and freedom.

Good work! Have a break.

Becoming Conscious of Our Map of Samsara

This meditation can become a profoundly liberating practice. But at first, most of us have difficulty setting aside our customary reactions to strangers and enemies—or even different levels of dear ones—so as to wish them all happiness equally. It feels fine to make that wish for a few beloved ones but not for all the others. That's because this meditation shows us the subconscious structure of thought that had inhibited our potential for love.

A Mistaken Impression of Self

The practice of wisdom shines light on how our structure of thought inhibits this potential. Recall the wisdom-oriented inquiries of chapter 2. As we inquire into the arising and dissolving of experiences and into the shape, location, and subject of awareness, *no* substantial entity within experience can be found. All that is found is cognizant emptiness, total openness beyond conceptualizing—like the empty sky pervaded by sunlight, beyond division.

But, as Buddhist masters have taught, our self-clinging minds are intolerant of that boundless nature. A subconscious movement of anxiety and mental grasping tries to fill the insubstantial openness of experience with a narrow, concrete sense of self. In that way, our minds try to feel protected from the vast mystery of experience as it is. Our chains of thought work hard to interpret each situation so as to make our narrow, evanescent, thought-constructed sense of self feel like a concrete, substantial, and inviolate thing. Thought appropriately patterns our experience into an organized personality through labels like "I" and "me," but there is no unchanging, sub-stantial self to be found there of the sort that our minds keep work-ing to establish. Our meditations increasingly reveal this simple truth.

Mistaken Impressions of Others

That ego mechanism is also what makes it so challenging to love others just as they are and to extend love to them all. For, as the mind creates such a narrow and mistaken sense of self, it creates cor-respondingly narrow and mistaken impressions of all the others.

Those who make our sense of self feel substantial, real, and good at any particular moment trigger feelings of happiness in us. They are grasped as dear and exclusively deserving of love: "my friends." Those who seem to undercut our ego-construct of self trigger feel-ings of mental pain in us. They are grasped as inherently dislikable, deserving not love but only anger and hatred. Billions of other beings, human and animal, which don't seem to affect our ego-construct of self at the moment, are dismissed as "strangers" that don't matter enough to love or hate or even to warrant our notice.

Deluded Emotions and the Cycle of Karmic Reaction

From such narrow misperceptions of self and others flow a host of self-centered emotions (Sanskrit: *klesha,* Tibetan: *nyon mong*): attachment to others as the very source of our happiness, hatred of others as the very source of our mental pain, jealousy of others' success, prejudice, partiality, arrogance, and greed. As our strate-gies to possess our friends and repel our enemies fail to secure us any dependable happiness or sense of safety, we also sink into despair, loneliness, and depression. From this stream of deluded emotion flow harmful actions of body, speech, and thought (harm-ful karma) that trigger others' feelings of hurt, evoking their neg-ative responses in return, thus perpetuating the suffering cycle of mutual reaction.

Because our ego-centered thoughts reduce others to such fragmented images of them, we tend to treat them in precisely the ways we don't want to be treated—with callousness, disrespect, self-righteous anger, and partiality. Ironically, even as we react to others in such negative ways, our minds tend to ascribe all such negativity to them, not to ourselves.

For example, do you remember the last time you became angry when someone showed you disrespect, having viewed you as merely dislikable? Or do you remember the last time someone painfully ignored you, having dismissed you as merely a stranger? At that moment, did you remember the many times in the past that you had similarly showed disrespect or ignored others, triggering their feelings of hurt? Probably not.

In order for us to be who we think *we* are, it feels as though the others must only be who we think *they* are. To commit to our narrow thought of ourselves commits us to our narrow thoughts of those around us, rather than to the actual persons beyond those thoughts. If a stranger cuts in line ahead of me, I view him instantly as completely contemptible. Perhaps he was thoughtless at that moment, driven (like me) by his own self-concerned worries. Or perhaps he had an emergency and was desperate to get home quickly. But my mind, in that moment, commits to his complete contemptibility in order to commit to myself as completely righteous—as if I had never cut in front of others. Actually, over my lifetime I've cut in front of others many times or wanted to. That's why it annoys me so much when others do it to me.

We react against the self-centeredness that we see in others because it mirrors the self-centeredness in us that our own minds have repressed and forgotten. As long as we continue to react to others as mirrors of our own hidden negativities, our reactions reflect their worst traits back at them in turn. And their negative response again evokes the worst from us.

The Map of Samsara Is Both Individually and Socially Fabricated

Others don't experience themselves as our ego-centered thoughts perceive them, but we react to them as if they did, as if they really were only the sum total of what we think they are at the moment. As if, in a moment of anger, your spouse or child were really just someone who deserves rage and blame, not the sacred object of your care. Or as if the unknown person passing you on the street were really just a "stranger," nothing more—not a parent, sibling, or child beloved by others, not a fully dimensioned being with all the hopes, fears, and struggles of living and dying in this world. Our momentary thought says, He's just a stranger, and in that moment we believe that's *all* he is, don't we?

If I put down this piece of writing, walk outside, and encounter people on the street, some are categorized the moment I see them, prereflectively, as "my friends" (who deserve love), some as "dislikable" or "enemies" (who deserve no love), and the vast majority not personally known to me as "strangers" (who have no value; who matter no more than a block of wood). See if this is not also true for you. Our ego-centered thoughts reduce people in the moment of encounter to narrow, inaccurate labels, to caricatures, before we even have time to reflect more consciously upon them. This hides from us the fuller, much more mysterious reality of each person, affecting how we react to everyone.

Indeed, in essence, that's what "harmful karma" means. It refers to our mental and physical *reactions* to the self-centered world of "strangers, enemies, and exclusive friends" that our own minds make of everyone around us.

The nature of all persons, like your own nature, is cognizance and openness, endowed with innate capacities of goodness and wisdom, but patterned (like yourself) into self-clinging chains of thought and reaction. All persons, like yourself, need and fundamentally deserve enduring reverence, love, and care as they undergo the struggles, joys, and desperations of living and dying together in this world. No one is merely what our narrow, self-centered thoughts make of him or her—merely a "stranger," merely "unlikable," merely "my friend," merely contemptible, merely impressive or unimpressive, merely stupid or smart. Everyone is *much* more than that. And when we hear this teaching from the Buddha, deep down we know it. We recognize this truth.

The Map of Dualistic Discrimination Shuts Down
Our Capacity for Love and Compassion

Bokar Rinpoche has this to say:

> The fundamental dysfunctioning of our mind takes the form of a separation between I and other. We falsely grasp at an "I" on which attachment grafts itself at the same time as we conceive of an "other" that is the basis of aversion. This duality prevents the free and spontaneous expression of love and compassion and holds them in a potential state.[32]

By discriminating among those whom we think deserve love ("my friends") and those whom we think do not ("strangers" and "enemies"), our minds shut off our capacity for impartial love and compassion. Such discriminations hide the essential sameness of self and others—their innate capacity of goodness, their need for love. It is that underlying sameness to which love and compassion naturally respond. If we don't sense it, our minds narrowly restrict the focus of our love just to ourselves and the very few who seem to support our sense of self at the moment.

Therefore, we don't think to respond to everyone on a daily basis as if each deserved enduring reverence and love. After all, our ego-centered thoughts tell us, all around me are strangers and potential enemies, who obviously deserve apathy or aversion. As people around us react similarly, unaware they are reacting to their own narrow thoughts of others, we together construct a world where callousness, distrust, and ill will seem normal. Our daily headlines scream out the results—domestic abuse, road rage, virulent prejudice, and addictions to alcohol, drugs, gambling, or whatever distraction helps people forget their troubled thoughts of self and others for a little while.

This exemplifies what the Buddha called *samsara*—the narrowing of life's richness, essential goodness, and mystery into a mentally constructed cage of individual and social suffering.

Our preconscious discrimination of a few beings that deserve love from the vast majority that do not is the *map* of this suffering, samsaric world. All of us are caught up in our own similarly deluded maps without recognition of the fact. *It is extremely hard to see our samsaric maps for what they are,* fabrications of deluded, self-centered thought and emotion, since they are not just individual but also social constructs, viewed as real by social consensus. When everyone around me believes that only a few people deserve love while most deserve just to be ignored, disliked, or feared, I become accustomed to reacting similarly. And as I treat others callously in that way, I receive the feedback that reinforces my impression of them, react accordingly, and thereby condition others around me to the same deluded view. This is why most of us find it hard to believe we could ever realize unconditional, all-inclusive love as a real human possibility. This is why our initial attempt to extend love beyond our familiar boundaries, to seeming strangers and enemies, is not so easy.

What to do? We are constantly in a struggle with ourselves and others mediated by our own false, limited thoughts of each other. And we are so accustomed to this falsity that we don't even recognize it most of the time. How could we ever find our way out of such a problem?

The Human Capacity to Transcend the Samsaric Map

But human beings are not just robots. We do have the potential to connect at a more fundamental level and to ignore our patterned, reductive judgments of each other. Here are two true stories, initially published as letters written to a literary journal, which illustrate this possibility. In the first, a boy exposes the arbitrary nature of society's labels for people by not acknowledging those labels:

> My twelve-year-old son Alex was born with Down syndrome, an unfortunate name for his condition, for if there's one thing my son is not, it's down. He begins each day by rushing into our bedroom and joyfully hollering, "Good morning!" He greets his teachers with the same excitement and never fails to give them a hug. In fact, he hugs just about everyone he meets, seeming to sense which people are most in need of one....
>
> I am an outcast in the Down-syndrome community because I do not aggressively discourage Alex's hugging. He will fall prey to a child molester, I am told. He must learn to behave like regular children, they say.
>
> But he's *not* a regular child. And child molesters don't seem to have any trouble preying on regular children. Why should I deny him one of the greatest pleasures in his life? The best thing he has to give the world is his boundless, unprejudiced affection.
>
> One afternoon, my two boys and I were walking downtown. A young man was coming toward us on the sidewalk. He was covered in tattoos and projected a fierce attitude to match. I went to pull my children out of his path, but Alex got ahead of me. I watched in horror as my son bellowed, "Hi!" and wrapped his arms around the young man's legs. I waited for the man to push him away, or perhaps even strike him.

But the man, not much more than a boy himself, instead gave Alex a gentle pat on the head. His attitude softened, and he quietly replied, "Hi." With a sweet, sad smile, he moved to the edge of the sidewalk so we could pass.[33]

Alex's mother acknowledges her son's gift—his ability to affirm the fundamental goodness of people by loving them impartially. To love so inclusively is to suggest that the labels that govern society's reactions to people, labels like "stranger," are merely conventional and therefore can be dispensed with.

Alex's mom and the "fierce" young man, like the rest of us, began to react through fragmented concepts of each other. But suddenly Alex enacted what it's like to respond to others as essentially good, beyond all reductive labels. With a hug, he momentarily liberated everyone from their usual reactions, their suspicions and fears of each other.

Alex's spontaneous affection for the young man as another human being, fundamentally good, naturally evoked the young man's kind response. Suddenly the truth seemed so obvious—what we all want is respect and love. And when someone extends those to us without judgment, he evokes our respect and love. Alex's "disability" apparently gave him the super-ability to transcend the limitations of established social prejudice—to love and evoke love beyond customary boundaries.

In the second story, a veteran nurse named Lucy becomes conscious of her limiting assumptions, and the human reality beyond them, in a moving way:

I thought I was having a pretty good day at work. I knew what to do for my patients, and they seemed appreciative. My hair was behaving. I wasn't eating too much chocolate, and I was treating everyone with kindness—everyone except the new nurse. She just rubbed me the wrong way, with her sad, insecure smile. She was a little too eager, too needy.

That evening I overheard the new nurse talking about her struggle to become pregnant. She'd finally had a child at the age of thirty-nine, she told the listener, but the little girl had needed heart surgery, and they'd lost her to an infection. By that time, premature menopause had ended the nurse's hope for another child.

Sheepishly, I asked the new nurse what her baby's name was.

Her face lit up with a mother's love. "Rebecca. She would be five next month!" She pulled out a photograph of a beautiful, bright-eyed little girl. My heart ached with shame, sadness, and awe. "Thank you," I said. What I meant was: thank you for teaching me how much I have to learn.[34]

Lucy, the veteran nurse, nicely summarizes how "self" and "other" are mutually fabricated in thought. Her thinking fabricated a narrow self with control over its world, a world of friends (appreciative patients) and a potential enemy (the new nurse). When Lucy overhears her nemesis tell her story, she suddenly awakens to the fuller human reality of the person. Instantly, Lucy's self-protective world comes crashing down, and she feels only heart-wrenching empathy for the new nurse. Then she feels ashamed for having so thoroughly mistaken her narrow thoughts of the person for the person. And she feels awe, for now she sees what the new nurse is—a sacred being who transcends all such narrow labels. Lucy's final response is gratitude to her for having revealed the ever-present holiness of persons that lies beyond all the prejudice and partiality of the world's labels.

Awe and gratitude are responses to the revelation of the *real*. They are signs that someone is starting to awaken to their highest potential. That is what happened to Lucy.

But such transformative encounters are rare, unpredictable. And the fuller implication of such a revelation, the potential for us to wake up completely, is not accomplished by just a random encounter. The purpose of a meditation *practice* is to enter into an awakening process with intention, regularity, and commitment. Our meditation practice can be revisited every day to help awaken us more fully over time. As the new nurse did for Lucy, the meditation shows us our samsaric map—our reduction of others to ego-centered labels for them. And like Lucy's encounter with the new nurse, the meditation liberates our potential for awe—our potential to recognize the essential dignity, the holiness, of self and others beyond such labels.

Learning to Transcend Our Samsaric Map Through Wisdom and Love

> Recognize others as being living Buddhas, gods or goddesses—all splendid and divine in their own right.... Honor their enlightened Buddha-nature, their innate divinity. See them in a new light, beyond personal distinctions, preferences and discriminations.
>
> Lama Surya Das[35]

When we first enter into the meditation above, at some point we find ourselves holding back from extending love—to a stranger or to an enemy, perhaps. This hesitancy or resistance is what makes us conscious of the boundaries of our samsaric map. As our understanding deepens, we learn to recognize that map, how it functions and how much harm our adherence to it has done. All of us, together, have habitually mistaken our own self-centered thoughts of beings for the fullness of them. And so we have all responded with callousness and disregard, contributing to the world's problems, often in ways of which we are not even conscious.

When we practice this meditation many times, we learn to recognize our narrow concepts of others for what they are: partial and inaccurate labels. We can learn to ignore such labels and to respond more wisely to the persons beyond them. That liberates our potential for impartial love.

Within the second part of the meditation, as we rest in the wisdom of natural awareness, our minds relax their grip on the self-centered thinking that weaves the samsaric map of "strangers," "enemies," and exclusive "friends." Then, as we extend the wish for others' happiness in widening circles, the radiant power of impartial love can methodically burn through that deluded map, liberating our potential.

All beings are the same as ourselves in three basic ways: (1) They all want to be well, happy, and free of suffering. (2) They are all lost in self-centered reactions to their own narrow thoughts of self and others. (3) They all possess an innate capacity of goodness that has been obscured by the self-centered reactions.[36]

When we sense the underlying sameness of self and others in those three ways, our natural response is love. When we don't sense the sameness through prejudices and discriminations, we are lost from love. Even thugs have moments of honesty or affection, if only to smile at their child or pet a dog. In the three ways noted, they are the same as the rest of us, but because they don't recognize their sameness with all others, they don't usually act upon it.

As the radiant power of all-inclusive love burns through our samsaric map, it touches in on the sameness of beings in their innate goodness, self-clinging ways of thinking, and need for love. Because such an attitude transcends the world's partialities while expressing a deeper knowing of beings, it is far more powerful and transformative for all involved than self-concerned forms of affection.

Learning to Recognize My Own Personal Map

One of my most profound spiritual teachers, Lama Surya Das, is remarkably skillful at helping others catch on to the mysterious reality that lies beyond their samsaric maps. He has practiced under the tutelage of some of the most revered Tibetan teachers of the twentieth century and is the American lineage heir of Nyoshul Khenpo, with whom he trained in multiple three-year meditation retreats.

I first met Lama Surya after I had already practiced under the guidance of many Tibetan lamas and had become an established academic scholar of Buddhism. Though not conscious of it, I tended to look down on others who were not as learned in the Buddha's teaching, the Dharma, or who didn't practice it in precisely the way I did. I maintained a vivid mental map of who should be counted as a worthy person and who should not, based on how similar they were to me. Such discriminations were all the more firm because they were rationalized by my seeming knowledge of the Dharma. I was not conscious of how much I mistook my own self-centered thoughts of others for the persons, even in the name of the Buddha's teaching!

I admired many Tibetan teachers but was cynical about Westerners who were identified as Dharma teachers. But then I met Lama Surya Das at a short retreat in which his own transmission and teaching of Dzogchen were so potent for me that I couldn't deny their power. After I met Nyoshul Khenpo, it became clear to me why this was so. Lama Surya was one of Khenpo's closest heart disciples in the transmission of his profound Dzogchen lineage.

Over the next several years, I joined Lama Surya in many meditation retreats, and my practice progressed, although I still retained discriminatory attitudes toward others. One day, to my surprise, Lama Surya Das stopped talking to me! When he saw me coming, he wouldn't acknowledge or even look at me but would effusively attend to anyone else in the room. He refused to participate in my impure vision of others, my viewing of them "from above" as a Buddhist scholar-practitioner. Even though I was deeply insulted and humiliated by his action, some part of me knew I should continue to show up, not just run away to other Dharma and academic settings where my ego would be stroked in its accustomed ways.

Although angry with Lama Surya, I returned to meditation retreats with him. My conscious mind was enraged that he wouldn't speak to me, but below the turbulence, my mind felt empowered and blessed by his mode of abiding in pure presence and impartial care for persons. I spent months wrestling with this conundrum, Why won't he pay attention to me the way all my other lamas and Dharma colleagues have done?

One day on retreat, just after a profound meditation session with Lama Surya, something dawned on me. During the question and answer session, I raised my hand: "Please tell me if this is true. A teacher of Dzogchen is not mainly communicating with the student's *mind* (ego). Rather, he is communicating with the *nature* of the student's mind, his buddha nature." Before I'd said the last word, Lama Surya had already struck the gong, signaling affirmation. It felt as though I were suddenly released from a great weight that had been created by my own mind! Lama Surya would not cooperate with my ego's map of self and others. He would only affirm my deeper capacity to know and care for them beyond such self-centeredness. Buddha nature had become his boss, and to work with him, it would have to become mine as well.

Those who embody an all-inclusive, wise love that doesn't believe in all the world's samsaric maps are profoundly liberating figures for this world. Their very presence signals to the rest of us that our narrow labels are not the final definition of anyone, including ourselves—that all have a tremendous innate potential and worthiness. Such benefactors are the ones who change this world instead of merely promulgating its prejudices. This is the mysterious power of figures such as Martin Luther King, Gandhi, Dietrich Bonhoeffer, the Dalai Lama, and Lama Surya Das.

Please take a break now for a little while. When you feel refreshed enough to do the meditation above again, please redo it with the following further instructions.

Meditation Tips to Unleash Self-Transcending Love
Recognizing Your Own Samsaric Map

Follow the meditation instructions again, and this time, as you begin to extend the wish of love to others, notice when you find yourself holding back or resisting.

Perhaps you hold back from someone dear, who appears a bit *less* dear than others. Or perhaps you hold back from a stranger; or someone you have disliked. The moment you feel unable to wish any person deepest happiness, pay attention. Notice that what you are pulling back from is not the actual person but just your narrow thought of him, as if the thought of him *were* his full reality. Recall the story of the new nurse. Consider how the fuller reality of the person—the fullness of his life, his death, his inmost potential—transcends your narrow label for him.

As you extend love just to the edge where you find yourself starting to withhold it from someone, seize that moment to look vividly at your own samsaric map of others. See if you can discover how it swings into action and holds you in bondage. For example, the thought may come, "But she's just a jerk (for something she did), I can't wish her happiness." But is that really all she is? When pressed to look, doesn't it seem absurd to believe that another human being, in all her depth, is only a "jerk," as if she were nothing more than a piece of trash? And is that really all you are—someone who mentally reduces others to trash and completely believes such thoughts?

As your moments of withholding love show this to you, recognize the mistaken view as the mistake that it is. Recognize how we have all been mistaking the fullness of persons for the reductive labels that our own minds have put on them!

Leaning in Past the Labels and Communing Heart to Heart

With this recognition in mind, those moments when you find yourself holding back from someone can become the doorway to transformative insights and awakenings. Instead of believing your narrow thought of the person, *lean in past that thought* to the mysterious fullness and depth of the person beyond it. As you lean in past the thought, let the radiant wish for that person's well-being come through you. In this way, explore the possibility of communing with each such person heart to heart, inmost goodness to inmost goodness, below the "radar" of customary, ego-centered thinking. Learn to trust the wish of love more than your reductive thoughts of others. Learn to trust it more than others' thoughts of themselves. Learn to trust it more than limiting thoughts of yourself—as someone who doesn't have so much love to give. In this way, let yourself commune with others through that radiance.

This is a profound and precious practice, passed down to us by generations of Buddhist masters. Only such unconditional and enduring love can make us safe from the unbelievable thicket of deluded thought, reaction, and suffering in which we have all been participating.

Progressing in Daily Practice

The meditation of this chapter has the power to bring out our inmost powers of love and to remake our experience of the whole world in its light. But for that to happen we have to proceed methodically, at our own pace, in daily practice over time.

Explore the meditation at your own rate of progress. Each day, do just as much extending of love as you feel the inner power to do. First let the radiant wish of love extend to a few beloved ones. You can focus on them for several days of practice. Then as the will and energy of love strengthens, let it extend to a wider circle of dear ones and then to wider circles gradually over more days. When the will and energy of love feels powerful enough, let it extend to a stranger, then to more strangers; to a disliked one, then to more, and so on over further days of practice. In this way, over weeks and months, move stage by stage from friends, to strangers, to disliked and hated ones at your own pace.

At each such stage, whenever you find yourself unable to extend love wholeheartedly to someone or some group, recognize that you are reacting to your own limiting thought of self and other (not to the fullness of them). Then lean in past the thought and commune heart to heart, using the power of the wish of unconditional love.

If it feels too difficult to lean in past your thought that way, return to the prior stage of the meditation. *Continue the practice at the prior stage until the wish of love is so strong that it carries you more naturally into the next stage.* For example, if you find it difficult to extend love to strangers, return to the prior stage—extending love just to dear ones. When the will and energy of love grows strong enough to carry you past your focus on dear ones, let it start naturally to extend itself to strangers.

Whatever stage of extending love you reach, *always bring that part of the meditation to its conclusion by thinking that the radiant wish of love extends literally to all beings.* Then after some time, dissolve into oneness with that insubstantial radiance. Complete the practice by dedicating its spiritual power to fullest enlightenment for all.

Throughout the practice, if you feel your mind become tired while extending love, you can stop for a little while, rest the mind, and restart at the point where you left off.

Application in Daily Life

The power of love and wisdom grows stronger in us over many months of such meditation. As this happens, don't make a big show out of being loving! You are learning to bring out a more stable and enduring attitude of love than you've had before. To begin to embody this quality in life, let it express itself first in little ways, very naturally.

Start by being present within this loving attitude to your partner, children, close friends, and others you meet regularly in your daily life. Let the ongoing wish of love help you be more fully attentive, to listen more deeply. Let it help you treat those near you with more reverence, kindness, and patience, more generosity, in small ways. Let it do the same in your relationships with neighbors, co-workers, and strangers throughout your day.

Allow the power of love and wisdom to boost your energy and broaden your perspective in work and life, but avoid becoming over-excited by the spiritual power that arises from meditation and making a big show of your "love" in grandiose gestures. This just indicates a need for personal attention rather than authentic concern for the happiness and well-being of others.

As we explore the integration of this practice in our daily life, we see why daily meditation is critical to the process. When we do the meditation of love and wisdom each morning, we can draw upon it during the rest of the day by simply recalling it: Oh yes, the wish for their happiness. That's the way to be with others. What a relief it is to remember that.

How Wisdom and Love Empower Each Other

As we progress with our practice, we learn how every part of the meditation informs the whole. The wisdom of letting be allows thoughts, feelings, and sensations to self-release within the expanse of open awareness, thus interrupting the chains of ego-centered thought that weave our samsaric map. As we learn to rest in fundamental awareness, appearances of "strangers," "enemies," and "friends" can be recognized as ephemeral displays of thought. Wisdom thus undercuts the samsaric map that has inhibited our ability to receive or offer love.

Receiving love helps ease us into the wisdom of letting be. In addition, the unconditional love we receive from benefactors senses and responds to our inner worth beyond anyone's samsaric map. And that triggers our ability to offer a love to others that senses their inner worth and reverences it in them, no matter what.

In sum, wisdom interrupts our map of "friends," "strangers," "enemies," cutting through its fabrication. Love senses the most fundamental goodness in beings that was always prior to such fabrication. Wisdom strips away the self-centered conceptualization that prevents us from loving impartially. Love resonates with the underlying goodness of all beings, below the "radar" of self-centered concepts of them.

Practice the meditation repeatedly in this spirit over weeks and months. Let the receiving of love ease you into the wisdom of natural awareness. Surrender there to sky-like openness aware, beyond all reference points of self-centered thinking. Then let the energy of that awareness manifest in the vision of your benefactors' radiant love—receiving it and extending it to others. Let your benefactors' intrinsic goodness commune with your own. Let your intrinsic goodness commune with that in others, finally extending to all. When you feel yourself pull back from anyone by mistaking your thought for the person, lean in past the thought to resonate heart to heart, below the radar of your thinking mind.

As we meditate in this way repeatedly over many months, we learn to let wisdom release us into more love and love into more wisdom. Ultimately, we discover that unconditional, boundless love is the very radiance of our deepest wisdom—*rigpa,* the unconditioned, boundless nature of mind. This is the path of the bodhisattvas, holy beings who have become spiritual benefactors to the world, radiating and embodying love to all unconditionally, even to those who have done them harm. This is what the Buddha taught. This is what our world desperately needs. And this is what we can become.

The Will to Be Free and the Power of Authentic Refuge

The Buddha identified two powers of mind necessary to realize the inner freedom and joy of enlightenment. They are a strong *will to be free* (also called *renunciation*) and strong *refuge*. The *will to be free* is the profound wish to be freed from the causes of suffering in our minds. In this context, it is the wish to be free from bondage to the map that discriminates the few who deserve love ("my friends") from the many who do not (all those "strangers" and "enemies"). It is the willingness to *renounce* such discriminations.

Through meditation, as we become conscious of our own map and of how much all beings suffer from belief in such maps, a new sense of awareness and conviction emerges. We begin to shift from believing in the map to wanting to be free of its power. Even as limiting thoughts of others still arise in our minds, we are willing now to disbelieve and renounce them. When the meditation tells us not to trust such limiting thoughts but to lean in past them, it is *the will to be free* in us that says, *Yes!*

The power of *refuge* is the power of relying on the very nature of mind and its qualities, rather than on the ego-centered reactions of the mind. It is the power of relying on love, compassion, and wisdom, on the practices that bring out those enlightened qualities, and on the community of practitioners who are mature in those qualities. The *buddhas* are those who have fully awakened to the nature of mind (buddha nature) and to its enlightened qualities. So they have profound knowledge of ways that others can awaken similarly. The *Dharma* includes the nature of mind with its qualities and all the practices that bring out those qualities. Authentic *sangha* are people mature in such qualities from practice. From their own long experience of the spiritual path, they are able to inspire, encourage, and mentor others who enter into it. Those with extremely profound realization of wisdom and love serve as spiritual benefactors of the highest caliber, such as the teachers referred to throughout this book.

As our meditation practice brings out the power of this all-inclusive loving wish, we increasingly sense the truth and rightness of what is happening, no matter how outlandish it may have seemed at first. The meditation thus naturally takes us into refuge, with the instruction "to trust this wish of love more than your own limiting thoughts of self and others." To trust and rely fully upon qualities of enlightenment—impartial love, compassion, and wisdom—to take refuge in those qualities rather than self-centered thoughts in the very moment such thoughts arise, *that* is authentic spiritual refuge. To do that at any moment of the meditation is to step onto the path of enlightenment in that moment.

Thus *refuge* and *the will to be free* emerge together and empower each other. As we practice this meditation over time, we learn increasingly to distrust and renounce the partialities of our self-clinging thoughts by strengthening our reliance on the impartial love and wisdom that emerge from the mind's nature. Each time we rely more on the unconditional wish of love for beings than on limiting thoughts of them we are finding refuge in our inmost nature—buddha nature—and manifesting it. Each such moment of practice takes us farther on the path by actualizing what enlightenment really is—enduring love and wisdom beyond self-clinging.

The Will to Be Free Supports Empathy and Compassion

As we distrust and release our own deluded map of others through practice, we also sense more acutely what drives others' apathy, ill-will, and possessiveness, how others have been trapped in reaction to their own deluded maps with no more conscious awareness than we have had. From such understanding comes empathy for them rather than rigid self-righteousness. In this way, the growing renunciation of our own suffering patterns becomes compassion for others trapped in similar patterns. And with this comes more freedom to know and love persons in their depth and fullness, rather than remaining bound to habits of thought that prevent us from knowing or loving anyone deeply.

Refuge Becomes a Zone of Protection for All

The categories of "friend," "enemy," and "stranger" are also exposed as being quite arbitrary and changeable. They can shift in a flash because our minds construct and reorder these categories in dependence upon the momentary ways that others affect our sense of self. When your child, partner, or friend says or does something that displeases or challenges you, your mind can shuttle them so quickly into the "enemy" category that you don't even realize it's happening. You find yourself reacting angrily before you know it. How many times has this happened to each of us? Is this how we intended to be present to our families and friends?

In contrast, the meditation practice provides us refuge in a much more stable and enduring reality. The unconditional wish of love is not affected by changing events, by what anyone does, not even by our own shifting thoughts of others. The practice directs us to trust that wish more than our limiting thoughts. As we learn that we can return to this wish of love anytime and rely on it fully, its protective, healing power blesses our life so deeply, it is as if our loved ones are encircled in a zone of peace and protection.

We are all caught in the same basic dynamic: acting each moment as if many others didn't deserve enduring reverence and love. Recurrent individual clashes and communal conflicts are the inevitable result. To find refuge in our potential for unwavering, impartial love is to find a stable refuge for all persons, to bless them in its light as sacred beings worthy of love. It is to *extend refuge* to the many—to encircle all in a zone of healing and protection. We can sense this emerging within the meditation and we can learn to carry its protective power into every part of our world. This will be further discussed in chapter 7.

My friend Ellen sent me this note while traveling in Japan: "While we had been to Japan before, we had never visited Hiroshima. This time we did. There is a lovely peace park and a very well-presented museum at what was ground zero, [the site where the atomic bomb landed]. As we walked through the park and museum, your teachings were vividly there with me. It was so very clear that the road of 'friends, enemies, and strangers' leads directly to Hiroshima (and Baghdad, Darfur, the World Trade Center...). In spirit, you were with me at that lovely and tragic place. With love and gratitude, Ellen."

As love and wisdom empower each other in this practice, we are drawn naturally toward the place of absolute safety that is our inmost, unconditioned nature. The deepest refuge of all is found in the nature of our minds, the unchanging essence of cognizance and emptiness, *dharmakaya*. This is the unconditioned clear light of primordial, pure awareness that is beyond change and beyond dying. Love empowers the mind to release its grip on dualism and narrow self-concern, to relax into the unchanging wisdom of the deathless nature of mind, buddha nature, nirvana.[37]

Many spiritual benefactors, women and men on this path, have radiated their unconditional love and compassion to us. Through practices they passed down to us, we, too, can become aware of the liberating power of love, to receive it deeply and to extend it whole-heartedly. But how long did it take *us* to catch on to this? How lost have we been from the potential for love that we didn't know we had? Like ourselves, don't all others deserve the same patience and respect that our benefactors have shown us? Don't all the others deserve from us the same willingness to extend love to them, no matter how long it may take for them to notice or receive it? Impartial, unconditional love is its own reward, because it fulfills our profound human need to unveil our deepest goodness for the sake of all.

How Can I Extend Love to Someone Who Has Hurt Me?

One student asked me: "When extending love, I recall a person who said malicious things to me and to my family. He really hurt me. I can't make a sincere wish for his happiness."

Recall the previous chapter's discussion of karma. We commonly say, "He hurt me by what he said." But his words didn't insert the feeling of hurt into us. If our minds didn't seize his words as hurtful, we wouldn't feel such mental pain from mere words nor would we hold grudges for so long.

The problem is that we are all in the habit of misidentifying others' actions as the very source of our feelings of hurt or joy, so we respond with hatred or possessiveness. But feelings of hurt and joy occur *within* our minds, as the outflow of inner predispositions conditioned by our own past actions. Selfish actions that a person has done in the past prepare his mind to feel hurt, ill at ease, alienated from its innate nature of openness and well-being. Meditations and actions of love, compassion, and wisdom that a person has done in the past attune his mind to its innate nature, preparing him to feel at ease, joyful, and well.

When others say pleasant or unpleasant things to us, our minds then feel what they were prepared to feel by our own past actions. Others' words are just the *triggers* for our current feelings. Even if someone harshly criticizes us, if we didn't have the self-concern, the inner predisposition to feel personally hurt by the words, then we wouldn't feel hurt. Remember the example in the last chapter of my wife's mother, who showed sincere compassion for others despite their rude behavior to her.

The purpose of such karmic analysis is *not* to pinpoint blame. It has nothing to do with blame. It's to understand better where everyone is coming from—why people do so many hurtful things to each other.

Often, those we find difficult to love are the ones who have done hurtful things to us. But anyone who is hurtful has also *felt* hurt many times. He attributes his own feelings of hurt to other people, including us, so he angrily seeks to hurt us in return. Then we mistake his angry words as the very source of our mental hurt and hate him in return, continuing the cycle. This is the web of delusion and karmic reaction that everyone is caught in.

To be shown and to understand the causes for so much harm is to be given a precious opportunity—the chance, through practice, to be freed from bondage to this suffering cycle of reaction, to learn how to respond instead from the inner freedom of wisdom and impartial love. With the opportunity to realize such inner freedom comes the responsibility to do so, for the sake of all.

One day a young Brahmin priest came to see the Buddha. He was extremely upset because his older brother had become a member of the Buddha's ascetic community, thereby abandoning his family's social caste. Feeling threatened and angry, the young Brahmin disparaged the Buddha at length in blistering terms. The Buddha listened quietly and then responded with a question, "If a person brings a man a gift and the man refuses to accept it, to whom does the gift belong?" The angry man replied, "The gift would belong to the one who had brought it." "In the same way," the

Buddha explained, "I refuse to accept your angry words. They belong to the one who brought them."[38]

The Buddha's response was not a put-down. It was an act of compassion. The whole world is caught in the same delusory cycle: all beings mistake others as the very source of their mental hurts, seek angrily to hurt them in return, evoke similar responses from the others, and suffer endlessly for it. The Buddha's wise reply is an invitation to break free of the delusion and to join him in extending compassion to all who remain caught in it.

Nevertheless, our capacity to extend love and compassion unfolds at its own pace. We can't rush that natural unfolding and mustn't seek to do so. In meditation, whenever it feels too difficult to extend love to someone who has triggered hurt in us, recall the instruction to return to the previous stage of the meditation, until the will and energy of love become strong enough to carry you beyond the prior obstacle. If we proceed at our own pace, combining the practices of wisdom and love as instructed, impartial love will increasingly blossom.

When someone becomes more highly trained, it is taught, the power of her wisdom and love becomes so strong that it overwhelms inner obstacles even as they arise. If such a bodhisattva, out of habit, gives rise to a reductive, negative thought of someone, the arising of the thought correspondingly triggers her compassion for all who continue to believe such thoughts and suffer for it. And if she is confronted by an adversary who is overcome by hatred for her, it triggers her compassion, as if someone dear to her were overcome by mental illness. That is where these practices lead.

What About Very Evil People?

I am also asked, "What about very evil people, such as Hitler, Stalin, Pol Pot, Bin Laden, who have intentionally destroyed the lives of so many human beings? If we extend unconditional love to them, are we not then exonerating them from responsibility for their actions? Shouldn't we confront great evil?"

First, we need to investigate, *What* is the evil? And how does it become *great* evil? Evil ones are those most committed to reducing others to their own self-centered thoughts of them. Instead of learning to rely upon their innate capacities for love and wisdom, evil ones put complete trust in their own reductive thoughts and the deluded emotions that flow from such thoughts. This leads to extreme expressions of absolutistic self-righteousness, megalomania, virulent hatred and prejudice, the ideological reduction of whole peoples to worthlessness, and massive violence.

Those who point to Hitler as reason not to cultivate all-inclusive love, insisting that people who are that evil should never be included in such a wish, do Hitler honor by imitation. To believe that some people do not deserve a wish of love, that they are *only* to be hated, *is* the belief that Hitler embraced and took to its extreme. We do not confront someone by joining him. Too often one person's mindless hatred evokes our hatred in response, our own inner evil. And rather than acknowledge the fact that we are succumbing to the very evil we oppose, we indulge the self-deception by insisting that the evil in us is the way to confront evil.

The Seed of Evil in This World and the Seed of Good

Hatred is never dispelled by hatred in this world. It is only dispelled by love. That is the eternal law.

Shakyamuni Buddha

A raging fire can start with a small spark, something we may easily overlook. Similarly, great evil starts with a tiny spark in the mind, easily overlooked. The very instant that *anyone, anywhere,* decides that others do not deserve love, in that instant, the seed of evil has been born in this world. When that seed is well nurtured by people and societies, it evolves into the greatest acts of extreme hatred and violence. As with Hitler, all this is done in the name of the good, since the perpetrators place absolute trust in their own demonizing thoughts of others, justifying their self-created samsaric maps.

In the case of genocide, for example, tyrants equate the good with their ideological reduction of millions of people to complete worthlessness, as "enemies" and "strangers" to the extreme. This expresses the will to identify others completely with that reductive map, with *no* willingness to know the fullness of the persons beyond the labels, no willingness to acknowledge that they are fundamentally the same as oneself.

To decide that there are some who do not deserve love is the very seed of such evil. If nothing confronts that seed of evil, if nothing radically challenges it, it can grow to colossal proportions of destructiveness while always claiming to represent the good.

In contrast, the very instant *anyone, anywhere,* makes a genuine wish of love for *all* beings—no matter who those beings think they are or what they think they are doing—in that instant the very seed of good is born in this world and the very source of evil has been decisively confronted. The choice is ours.

Confronting Evil with Radical Goodness

The practices of this book are intended to confront evil. The emphasis on meditation thus far does not imply that the power for good it unleashes should not be applied to the concrete needs of the world. But we do have to practice such meditations *repeatedly* and consistently over time to permit their effective power to manifest. Specific applications will be discussed further in the following chapters, when we focus on ways to bring the power of love and wisdom into family life, community, work, service, and social action.

To speak to the question at hand, people who do evil are certainly to be confronted in concrete ways, and it is the strength of unconditional love and wisdom that can empower us to act decisively beyond the limitations of brittle self-clinging. Notice the precision of the wish of love that we are cultivating, its depth, and rigor. It is the wish for each person to have deepest well-being, *through and through,* thoroughly beyond all self-centered delusions and bondage to hatred. To wish *that* for a terrorist is to totally undermine his reactions to his own deluded map of the world—to will the destruction of the very roots of his destructiveness. There is nothing that haters detest more than someone who targets their whole rationale for hating.

Whoever has committed himself to the most evil patterns of action must be prevented from further harming. That requires forceful confrontation; one that holds the person *responsible* for his actions. But that means we are holding him responsible to his innate capacity to do *other* than evil—his capacity to do good. If those who do grave harm were viewed as *entirely* evil by nature, possessing *no* capacity of goodness to justify a wish for their inmost well-being, then we could not hold them responsible for their actions. After all, if they are *only* evil, evil is *all* that they can possibly do.

Time and again, the greatest human evils have arisen from deeply confused thought and emotion, from the unwillingness to acknowledge the underlying sameness of self and others and the capacity of good in them. Hitler, Stalin, Pol Pot, Bin Laden—that has been their path. If we want to confront them at the root of their evil, we will have to follow a decisively different path, a path that evokes a tremendous power of goodness to confront the root of evil in all our minds.

5. Pure Perception and Profound Equanimity

If you are pure within, all will be pure without,
So have pure vision regarding all things, my heart-friends!
Nyoshul Khen Rinpoche[39]

Seeing Past Our Delusions

The movie *A Beautiful Mind* chronicles the true story of John Nash, the mathematical genius who succumbed to paranoid schizophrenia and descended into a delusory world of perceiving and reacting to nonexistent people.

After many years spent recovering from his illness, Professor Nash is visited at Princeton by a representative from the Nobel Prize committee, who informs him that he has been nominated for the prize for his early work on game theory.

In a poignant scene, Nash realizes the investigator has been purposely sent to ascertain if he is sane enough to receive the Nobel Prize in public. "Would I embarrass you? The answer is possibly. You see, I *am* crazy," Nash says to the investigator, who takes in this admission. "I still see things that are not here. I just choose not to acknowledge them." At that moment, the investigator realizes that Nash has found a remarkable ground of sanity after his long struggle with his delusions.

Nash's response is instructive for us. He knows he is mentally ill, that nonexistent people continue to appear to him. But he has learned to ignore such false appearances, no matter how vividly they appear, by relying instead upon what is more real and more trust-worthy: the love of his family and friends.

We are in an analogous situation. Most of us are not schizo-phrenic, of course. But like Nash, we are haunted by a deluded vision of others without realizing that it is just the distorted creation of our own minds. For example, we tend to view most beings around us as nothing more than "strangers," unaware that "stranger" is merely the product of our own thought. But like John Nash, we can learn, indeed *are* learning, to shift our attention away from that deluded vision so as to connect with the fuller reality of the people all around us through the power of love.

In the last chapter, we were given the secret of deep sanity, a secret like John Nash's. *We don't have to believe our own narrow, reductive thoughts of people.* Even when our own thoughts tell us: "This is just a stranger," or "This person is just a jerk," we *can* ignore the thought, lean in past it, and connect with the fuller reality of the person, heart to heart. We can drop out of the fickle, changeable field of discriminatory judgments, individual and social, which deny the fullness and holiness of each being.

Isn't it exhausting to spend so much time judging everyone? Why not take a much-needed vacation from that syndrome? Why not connect with others in a more dependable way—by relying upon the enduring and impartial wisdom of love?

This is not an attempt to put on "rose-colored" glasses that hide the truth of others. It is just the opposite. We are learning to take off the Coke bottle–like glasses that have obscured the sacred truth that each person is seen accurately *only* through eyes of wisdom and love, the eyes of the Buddha in us, the eyes of God. Such pure vision is not some ideal from on high. It is our own inmost vision.

Pure Perception[40]

> Pure perception…is to recognize the buddha-nature in all
> sentient beings and to see primordial purity and perfection in
> all phenomena. Every sentient being is endowed with the
> essence of buddhahood, just as [sesame] oil pervades every
> sesame seed. Ignorance is simply to be unaware of this
> buddha-nature, like a poor man who does not know that
> there is a pot of gold buried beneath his hovel. The journey
> to enlightenment is thus a rediscovery of this forgotten
> nature, like seeing the ever-brilliant sun again as the clouds
> that have been hiding it are blown away.
>
> Dilgo Khyentse Rinpoche[41]

As Khyentse Rinpoche says, to perceive purely is to recognize
both the primordial purity of phenomena and the buddha nature
within all sentient beings. In meditation practice, as we learn to
relinquish our ego-centered and dualistic frames of reference into
the wisdom of natural awareness, we sense the essential purity and
perfection of phenomena within the infinite, open, and unchanging
nature of mind—all thoughts, feelings, and sensations recognized as
manifestations of primordial awareness, like rays of light recognized
by the sun as its own expression. This wisdom is the ultimate aspect
of pure perception.

As the meditation further unfolds, we let the energy of that vast
awareness manifest in the pure vision of love: first by recalling our
benefactors and receiving their unconditional love and then by
extending that love to all others. Through impartial, all-inclusive
love, we sense the intrinsic goodness of beings that is prior to everyone's self-centered thoughts and reactions. Impartial love knows and
reverences the intrinsic sacredness of beings, their inner dignity, their
buddha nature. This love is the relative aspect of pure perception.

The *impure perception* of ego understands others from the head, thinking, This is the good one; that one is a jerk; that one doesn't matter. Such impure perception pretends to a kind of omniscience, as if such limited thoughts captured the whole truth of others. *Pure perception,* in contrast, is a power of knowing from beyond our egos. It senses others intuitively through the wisdom and love that values each one as holy mystery, beyond the grasp of self-centered, reductive thoughts.

For this reason, as we begin to awaken to such pure perception in meditation practice, it dawns on us that we hadn't known others nearly as well as we had previously thought, even those nearest to us! Because now, rather than knowing them just through our familiar thoughts of them, we are starting to sense them from a deeper place.

Who is doing this pure perceiving? It is our inner capacity of wisdom and love that does the perceiving; our buddha nature, not our brittle, self-concerned egos. Only our inmost goodness can sense so directly the essential purity and goodness of others. We let our buddha nature, our primordial capacity of wisdom and love know others in their buddha nature, their intrinsic worthiness and holiness. We learn to "see" beings from the depth of our heart, rather than through ego-grasping consciousness.

Pure Perception Is an Active Power and an Offering to the World

The term *pure perception* can be deceptive because we might think that it denotes a merely passive kind of observing. But it is really an active power of knowing. Through the meditation, potent energies of knowing and loving that had been hidden in our minds are unleashed. Indeed, it begins to dawn on us that, as we extend love, we are not just *wishing* for others to have well-being and joy, we are actually *communing* with the primordial well-being that already abides in the nature of their minds. Our buddha nature is *communicating* with theirs, below the radar of self-centered understanding.

There is more. Pure perception not only perceives and communicates with others' inmost goodness and well-being but also *evokes* it by calling it forth from them. We can see now how this process manifests in our meditation practice: when we receive the wise love of our benefactors, our own enlightened potential of love, reverence, and joy is evoked and brought forth. In the same way, when we extend this powerful love to others, it helps awaken their enlightened potential.

In the summer of 1981, while I was a PhD student in Buddhist Studies at the University of Wisconsin, my teacher Geshe Sopa invited H.H. the Dalai Lama to Madison to give the transmission of Kalachakra, a special Buddhist empowerment. It was the first time such a teaching was to be offered in the West. My wife Barbara and I were put in charge of finding housing for all who wanted to come, including many Tibetans and high-ranking lamas traveling from Europe and throughout North America. The University kindly provided some low-cost college dorms to help house the participants, and it turned out that we had to use every available space for accommodations.

We ended up having to assign a renowned lama named Nechung Rinpoche to a dorm room that was rather dark and dingy from generations of use. Nechung Rinpoche was the type of spiritual teacher who just naturally exuded warmth and kindness, and Barbara and I loved to be near him. After the Dalai Lama's teachings were completed, we went to see him in his small room to say goodbye. He welcomed us as if we were honored dignitaries. Barbara and I were aghast at the stained and scarred walls and apologized for the shabby accommodation, but Rinpoche just looked at us wide-eyed, as if he had no idea what we were talking about. "This place is a pure realm," he declared, his face filled with gratitude and joy. Barbara and I exchanged a quizzical look, thinking, He actually means it! That dingy place was heaven for him, and the people all around were divine beings in his eyes. In spite of our initial bewilderment, his pure view became infectious. Suddenly, we too felt totally blessed to be right there, as if it truly were a holy realm, and we, with him, were pure and holy beings.

Rinpoche's pure perception was not merely a passive knowing but an active and evocative presence of love that mirrored the purity he saw in people back at them, helping them sense their own sacredness. During the course of our lives, don't we often feel like we are inhabiting a shabby place surrounded by "strangers"? That is why it is so liberating to be in the presence of a spiritual bene-factor who simply doesn't believe in such limiting ego-constructs of the world. When someone abides in a purer vision, their pres-ence signals to us that our reductive labels are false, that all those around us are holy, precious beings, every single one. For anyone to abide in such vision is to make a tremendous offering to this world, for it holds the door open for many others to also come to recognition of their true selves.

This is why benefactors such as Mr. Harrison, Nyoshul Khenpo, Chokyi Nyima Rinpoche, Lama Surya Das, Nechung Rinpoche, and others have made such an impression on me, affecting the course of my life. This is why Alison Luterman's store clerk had such a powerful effect on her. Indeed, this is what draws us to pro-found spiritual benefactors: the liberating power of their pure vision indicates that enlightenment is real, that human beings *can* discover and learn to embody the pure, enlightened vision of nirvana, right here and now, in this dingy, samsaric world.

By understanding that the meditation of love and wisdom can lead us from impure vision toward pure vision, we learn to cooperate with it and to experience it more deeply. We can increasingly let the meditation undercut our impure perception of others as merely "stranger" or "dislikable." We can lean in past such concepts by the power of wise love, as if leaning into others' hearts to sense their inner dignity. As the meditation strips away our adherence to such reductive labels, it increasingly awakens the dormant power of unconditional love and intuitive knowing within us, our buddha nature.

In the meditation of the previous chapter, we joined our spiritual benefactors in their *wish* for beings to be well. In the meditation that follows, we begin explicitly to join them in their *pure perception* of beings as primordially good. We learn, like them, to perceive, commune with, and evoke the essential goodness of beings. We learn to cooperate with this pure perception of the heart that senses others in their deep worthiness, even as we continue to learn, like John Nash, to ignore the impure perception of the head that reduces them to caricatures.

Please pause for a little while after each demarcated section, to dwell on the meditation instruction at hand.

Meditation: Awakening Pure Perception

Part 1: Receiving the Blessing of Unconditional Love

Sit in a relaxed way. Recall your benefactors, including deeply spiritual figures such as enlightened beings, your spiritual teachers, and their teachers. Envision their smiling faces before you as they send you the wish of love, the wish for you to have deepest well-being, happiness, and joy.

Bathe in the healing energy of their wish. Receive its gentle radiance into every part of your body and mind, from head to toe.

After a little while, join your benefactors in their wish, repeating it for yourself while receiving the radiant blessing of their love even more deeply: "May this one have deepest well-being, happiness, joy."

After some time, drop the visualization and relax into oneness with that loving radiance, dropping all frames of reference. Just let be into that gentle, luminous wholeness, beyond separation of self and others.

Part 2: Letting Be in Natural Awareness

Notice any grasping in the body. Let that gently release itself. Let all bodily sensations settle naturally in their own way. Surrender to the natural power of the body, feeling it embody you.

Let the breath come under its own natural power. Feel it all the way in, all the way out, breathing you.

After a little while, notice any grasping on to the thinking mechanism in your mind. Let that release itself, permitting thoughts and sensations to arise and dissolve under their own power. Thus let the mind unfurl and fall totally open—at ease, unrestricted, free of focus, all-pervasive, with the gaze of your eyes expansive. Let all be just as it is in complete openness and acceptance.

Sense the openness of awareness, boundless and without center, in which thoughts and sensations self-arise and self-dissolve—beyond thinking, beyond reference point, infinite openness and translucent awareness, pervasive like the sky. Let this vast expanse sense all that arises as its own radiant expression. Rest as that sky-like nature of mind—all phenomena permitted to self-arise and self-release within the vast expanse of openness aware.

Part 3: Letting Pure Perception Unfold

After some time, recall your benefactors, including spiritual figures and enlightened beings. Envision them this time behind you and just above. They are sending you the wish of love, the wish for you to have deepest well-being and happiness. Accept the healing radiance of their love into every part of your body and mind.

Now envision before you several beings that are dear to you. While receiving your benefactors' radiant wish from behind, let the radiance come through you to the beloved ones before you. While doing so, make the wish of love for them repeatedly: "May they have deepest well-being, happiness, and joy," bathing their bodies and minds with its loving energy.

If you find you are holding back from any beings as *less* dear than others, notice how you are encountering your own limiting thought of them, *not* the fullness of them. Lean in past that thought to commune more fully with them through the radiant wish of love—heart to heart, inmost goodness to inmost goodness. Irradiate them all equally while repeating that wish.

Now along with the dear ones, envision several strangers before you. Letting the radiance from your benefactors come through you to them, repeat the wish of love for all in front of you, bathing them with its loving energy. If you find yourself holding back from any as mere "strangers," notice how you are encountering your own limiting thought of them as "stranger," not their fullness. Trusting the wish of love more than the thought "stranger," lean in past the thought to commune more fully with them through the radiant wish of love, heart to heart. Illumine all the beings before you equally while repeating the wish.

Together with the others in front of you, now also envision several persons for whom you have felt dislike, aversion, or hatred. Letting the radiance come through, repeat the wish of love for all in front of you, bathing them with its loving energy. If you find yourself holding back from those you've disliked, notice how you are encountering your own thought of them as dislikable, not their fullness. Trusting the wish of love more than thoughts of dislike, lean in past such thoughts to commune with them through the radiant wish of love, heart to heart. Irradiate all equally while repeating the wish.

Now *imagine that the luminous field of benefactors behind you merges completely into your heart.* Sense the loving energy radiating from your heart as one with all your benefactors and one with all enlightened beings and your spiritual teachers. Let your heart, unified with those benefactors, radiate boundlessly to sentient beings like the sun, in all directions at once. Repeating the wish of love, bathe all beings in its energy while communing heart to heart with them: "May each being have deepest happiness, well-being, and joy." Let the energy of that wish overwhelm any remaining inhibitions you may have, radiating out spontaneously and all-inclusively, as if a buddha in your heart were radiating through your mind and body to all beings at once.

After some time, drop the visualization and just let go into oneness with that loving, insubstantial radiance. Release all frames of reference into boundless openness and translucent awareness, pervasive like the sky, beyond any thought of separation. Rest thus, at ease, complete.

Part 4: Dedicating the Liberating Power for All

Feel the power of this practice to pull you beyond self-grasping patterns of suffering and to open you toward the tranquillity, freedom, and goodness of your inmost being. Prayerfully dedicate all such spiritual power to the deepest well-being and liberation of all beings, each like you in needing and wanting such joy and freedom.

The Buddha Within Does the Perceiving

Merging with the Pure Perception of Our Spiritual Benefactors

At the final stage of the meditation, the field of benefactors merges into oneness with our own heart.[42] We experience the power of love in our heart as one with theirs. We can thereby discover that the heart of love within our benefactors is ultimately one with our own, and that our heart, like theirs, is also linked to the hearts of many others. Indeed, we are discovering that our inmost heart, like theirs, is the heart of a buddha.

As such practice matures, it feels as if a buddha of impartial love and wisdom long buried in us were starting to wake up and act right *through* our mind and body. It is as if a buddha within, long inhibited, were now finally allowed to unleash its knowledge and liberating energy—to radiate its vast enlightened will for the welfare of beings and to communicate with their basic goodness. At this stage of practice, we are not just *wishing* for others' well-being, we are starting to *commune* with and evoke the very source of their well-being, their own inmost potential of love and wisdom.

Such pure perception (Tibetan *dag nang*) is not something we arrive at just by thinking about these ideas or about the meditation instructions. It emerges naturally from the ground of our being through long, regular practice of the meditation. As practice brings out the innate power of pure perception and loving energy, it begins to flow beyond sessions of meditation into our ordinary day, gently informing our life, our work, and our relationships. In this subtle process, we are not just sensing beings around us through our eyes and ears but through our heart. There is a soft, natural resonance of knowing and loving that intuits the intrinsic goodness and purity of persons below the fabrications of all our reductive minds. This is how Nechung Rinpoche was present to Barbara and me. This is how anyone who takes up this practice can learn to be present to others.

To put it another way, in the moment of unconditional love it is not the ego-centered self that is viewing but the power of love viewing through you. In that moment you are surrendering "your own" point of view to the buddha's—as if you were a window for the buddha's unconditional love to shine through you. Such love feels as if it comes from beyond ourselves while also, paradoxically, from most deeply within. This pure perception, buddha vision, comes through us as we, like John Nash, learn to ignore the delusion of "enemies" and "strangers" that had closed it out.

Recognizing a Corresponding Truth in Other Traditions

The practice we are learning gives us the experiential knowledge to recognize sacred truth when we hear it, whatever its source. For example, one of my Catholic colleagues at Boston College, Father Michael Himes, describes an analogous viewpoint for becoming a window for God's love by embodying unconditional love for others. He writes, "The whole last supper discourse in John's gospel (chapters 13–17) is a magnificent reflection on love and communion. And, astonishingly, not once does Jesus ever tell his disciples to love God, although we are repeatedly told to love one another. For God is not the object of love; in a sense, God is not even the subject of love…. God is the doing, the loving." God *is* the power of unconditional love that comes through persons, willing deepest good for all.

Related to this, Fr. Himes notes, come teachings from Jesus that have shocked many people, such as: "You have heard it said that you shall love your neighbor and hate your enemy. But I tell you that you must love your enemies and pray for those who persecute you." When some ask him why, Jesus replies, "…you must do so to be children of your Father in heaven who makes the sun shine on the wicked as well as the good…" As Fr. Himes notes, "There are no bounds to God's love, so do not put any bounds to yours." To be receptive to God *means* to become transparent to the active, all-inclusive, and unconditional love that is God.[43]

Sacred Text, Image, and Practice Illumine Each Other

Our meditation practices have been transmitted down to us from an ancient past and can thus provide a window into understanding the inner meanings of ancient scriptures and iconographies. An ancient

Buddhist text called the *Tathagatagarbha Sutra (Buddha Nature Scripture)* is renowned for revealing through images what is intuited in meditation. At the beginning of the scripture, Buddha Shakyamuni enters a meditative concentration and generates a luminous vision that is witnessed by a huge gathering of beings. In the vision, an infinite array of lotus flowers appears, rises up, and fills the whole sky, emanating colorful rays of light in all directions. Hidden within each flower is a radiant, seated buddha form, completely still. Suddenly the lotus flowers open and wilt away, revealing the luminous buddhas. Each of the infinite buddhas radiates light in all directions, transporting the assembly of witnesses with ecstasy and wonder.

Shakyamuni Buddha then explains the meaning of this startling visionary image to the astonished throng. Someone with extraordinary perception, he says, is able to perceive the presence of the splendid, unmoving buddha forms concealed within the lotus flowers, even while they remain hidden from the ordinary perception of other beings. But when the lotuses open and wither away, then all beings are able to see the luminous buddha forms and come to recognize that they had been present all along.

Similarly, Buddha Shakyamuni, with his pure perception, sees through the deluded discriminations of sentient beings into their untainted, already-abiding buddha nature. He senses directly that all beings "have a tathagatagarbha [buddha nature] that is eternally unsullied and that is replete with virtues no different from my own." From this awakened perspective, he teaches the way for beings to cut through their delusions, so that they wither away like the lotuses in the vision, and thus all may realize the innate buddhaness hidden within their minds and bodies.[44]

Because our tradition is historically connected to such scriptures, we can see how text and practice inform each other. In our meditation we are discovering the innate buddha that has been hidden within our minds and bodies all along, a great capacity of unconditional love and pure awareness that discerns and resonates with the corresponding capacity that is hidden within all others. This is the dawning of pure perception. Our meditation is not just some desperate attempt to try to see other beings as good. It actually *cuts through* the obscurations of the discriminating mind that had hidden their intrinsic worth and dignity, so we can commune with them on that level.

Chapter 3 mentioned that many examples of Asian literature and iconography image the attainment of enlightenment in terms of "pure buddha realms." In such literature, buddhahood, fullest enlightenment, is not depicted as an isolated accomplishment that stands apart from beings. Rather, fully enlightened awareness manifests in a luminous buddha form that radiates its qualities of love, compassion, and liberating power to a vast circle of bodhisattvas and through them to innumerable other beings.

Such a buddha form comes to be designated in Sanskrit texts as *sambhoga-kaya. Sam* can mean "complete" or "together with, communal." *Bhoga* means "enjoyment," and *kaya* means "body." To refer to buddhahood as *sambhoga-kaya,* then, is to imply that the *complete* realization of enlightenment is experienced *communally,* embodied in *joyous* communion with many others through the wise love that wills deepest freedom for all. To be fully enlightened is to have fully unleashed the liberating power of such enlightened qualities, so that they spontaneously bless and evoke the corresponding goodness dormant in the hearts of many other beings.[45]

This imagery informs our understanding of pure perception, for with increasing practice experience we sense that we are participating in a purer dimension of reality previously unnoticed, to resonate with the deeper truth and dignity of beings below the radar of discriminatory minds. Increasingly, through practice, this mundane, everyday world is rediscovered as a "buddha realm," a pure dimension of radiant communion, each being sensed in reverence and love as holy mystery.[46] And when we encounter others who inhabit the world in this way—our mentors, teachers, benefactors—they help evoke our own capacity to do so as well.

Mirroring the Purity of Beings, Relaxing into the Purity of Things

To Reflect Others' Goodness Is to Call It Forth from Them

Pure perception, then, doesn't just view others in their basic goodness; it reflects their goodness back at them, helping them become newly conscious of it. Pure perception doesn't just perceive others; it blesses them. It isn't just passive but quietly active, triggering openings for others. Just to abide within such an attitude of unconditional love is deeply healing and beneficial for all other beings. This is why the simple process of recalling our benefactors is so transformative for us. By doing so, we experience again how they blessed us through the unconditional way they viewed us, how they evoked our best self before we were even conscious that they were doing so. Our most important benefactors didn't believe the limited ways we thought of ourselves. They saw through us to our underlying goodness, helping it to awaken.

Back in the 1980s, Barbara and I lived for about a year in India, near a learned and saintly Tibetan scholar named Geshe Tubten Tsering who taught at the Institute of Tibetan Studies in Sarnath. Under his tutelage, I studied texts on the nature of full enlightenment, buddhahood. Geshe Tsering lived in an impoverished hut, with few belongings except his sacred texts. Each morning he made offerings of milk tea to the enlightened beings, which fat little mice happily slurped up over the course of the day. He was in so much demand by students from the Tibetan Institute that they crammed into his hovel throughout the whole day, yet somehow he made time for them all. Whoever entered his little hut felt welcomed, safe, reverenced, and blessed, as if they were entering a sacred world.

While studying and engaging in philosophical debates with him, he treated me with such gentle respect and love that, when I reluctantly left at end of the day, I felt like a different person. Something was awakened in me by his presence, a deep desire to be like him and a recognition that somehow, mysteriously, I could. It made me feel grateful to be alive. In retrospect, I realize, he taught me about buddhahood not just in the way I expected, through intellectual studies, but also through the enlightened qualities he imparted from his whole manner of being. He was a remarkable teacher, whose effectiveness flowed from his unwavering and unconditional love for all whom he served.

Unconditional Love Is the Most Effective Motivation for Service

Such love is by far the most effective motive force for service to others. Without it, our activity for others is severely limited. When the primary motivation for service is ego-oriented, we tend to quickly burn out from self-centered frustration, becoming disappointed when things don't work out as expected, or people don't express enough gratitude or thanks. When the purer perception of unconditional love emerges from our meditation into our workday, it comes from beyond our egos and is focused on others' dignity and well-being beyond our self-centeredness. Through it, we begin to sense others as different versions of ourselves and can serve them from that perspective.

Through regular practice we can learn, like Geshe Tsering, to recall the wise love from our meditations and to draw on it as we work with people throughout our day. We don't have to get control over all circumstances or receive lots of recognition for our actions. It is sufficient simply to serve many others whom we are now including in the widening scope of our love. Then, regardless of the response or the results, we realize that we don't have to become burnt out, frustrated, or angry. This way of being and acting is far more effective and helpful than a lot of self-concerned "helping" activity that lacks such boundless motivation. Integration of our practice into our lives will be further discussed in chapters 6 and 7.

Pure Perception as Love and Wisdom Evokes the Same in Others

As love and wisdom inform each other through the distinct sections of our meditation, the pure perception they bring out is not just a *love* for beings in their intrinsic worthiness. It is also a penetrating *wisdom* that senses the perfection of *every aspect of experience* in its soft, radiant, and insubstantial nature, beyond the reductive thinking of self-centered mind. This is why Dilgo Khyentse Rinpoche, in the previous quote, defined pure perception in this twofold way: "Pure perception…is to recognize the buddha-nature in all sentient beings *and to see primordial purity and perfection in all phenomena.*"

When others look upon us with eyes of love and wisdom, they help evoke our own potential for those qualities. Their unconditional *love* wishes us happiness and well-being *just as we are.* This unconditional acceptance then empowers *our* minds to accept ourselves just as we are, freeing us from the struggle of trying to create a self that would feel more acceptable. When our self-grasping thereby relaxes, our minds can begin to let go of our familiar frames of reference into a deeper wisdom that senses the essential purity of each aspect of experience as a manifestation of pure awareness.

The power of one person's pure perception to evoke the corresponding love and wisdom in others, even in the most unlikely, mundane situations, is beautifully illustrated in a song called "No Mirrors in My Nana's House," composed by Ysaye Barnwell of the African-American a cappella group, Sweet Honey in the Rock. The

song is the recollection of a young girl learning through her grandmother, who is clearly her benefactor, to perceive herself and her
world in a fresh, new light:

> There were no mirrors in my Nana's house...
> And the beauty that I saw in everything,
> The beauty in everything
> Was in her eyes.

It was the wise love in her grandmother's eyes that served as her
only mirror, where she saw reflected only her own deep goodness
and beauty:

> So I never knew that my skin was too black,
> I never knew that my nose was too flat,
> I never knew that my clothes didn't fit,
> And I never knew there were things that I'd missed.
> And the beauty in everything
> Was in her eyes.

The grandmother's house stood in a poor part of town in seemingly
oppressive surroundings. Yet through the deep comfort the girl felt
in that loving home, she found herself relaxing into the intrinsic
purity and beauty of all things, beyond worldly labels:

> I was intrigued by the cracks in the walls,
> The dust in the sun looked like snow that would fall,
> The noise in the hallway was music to me,
> The trash and the rubbish would cushion my feet,
> And the beauty in everything
> Was in her eyes.

The grandmother's pure perception as love and wisdom evoked the same capacity within her granddaughter. By accepting and participating in her grandmother's *love,* the girl could relax into the fundamental goodness of her experience, her innate *wisdom,* even under what others would consider difficult circumstances.[47] In this way, pure perception as love and wisdom tends to evoke the corresponding potential in others.

The Equanimity of Wisdom Grounds the Equanimity of Love

Previously we explored how wisdom and love are emphasized in different parts of the meditation practice and how they empower each other. But they don't just alternate with one another; they also contain each other. In the heart of the meditation, the wisdom of letting be reveals the nature of experience as an infinite expanse of openness and awareness, all-inclusive, undivided, and beyond limitation. In the next part of the meditation, then, the energy of that fundamental awareness manifests naturally as a loving will that is all-inclusive and undivided, wishing the deep happiness of beings beyond limitation. In this way, boundless love is uncovered as a natural reflex of boundless wisdom itself.

Ultimate Equanimity of Wisdom

Wisdom also reveals the empty, cognizant nature of all experience to be unconditioned and unchanging. For example, ocean waves arise, manifest, and dissolve, taking various forms depending on changing weather conditions. But the essential wateriness of all those waves is never affected by those transitory conditions. Similarly, the contents of experience fluctuate in dependence upon changing circumstances, but the essential nature of all those experiences never changes. It is always empty cognizance. All thoughts, feelings, and sensations are just ephemeral patterns of insubstantial awareness, like ripples on water.

Deepest equanimity lies in the recognition of the essential sameness of all experiences. In the meditation we are learning to simply let be in natural awareness. This helps us to recognize and then to abide in the essence of experiences, their empty cognizance, rather than reacting to the shifting contents of experiences.

Someone may praise you or denigrate you. The content of those two experiences is quite different. Praise may make you feel great; criticism may make you feel angry. But the essence of both experiences, insubstantial awareness, is just the same. To recognize this essential sameness is to experience a very deep equanimity.

A small child at the beach may at first be afraid of ocean waves, feeling happy about little ones and terrified of big ones. But with practice, the child can become intimate with the *essential nature* of all such waves, their intrinsic wateriness. She can learn to lean into waves, float on them, dive beneath them, or simply rest in their essential wateriness and thereby enjoy them all. Similarly, through the wisdom of letting be, we learn that we don't have to react to the shifting contents of our experiences but can "lean into" their unchanging essence of knowing emptiness. We can let be and find rest directly in that essence.

Such tranquillity, at ease in the unchanging essence of experiences, unaffected by changing circumstances, is the ultimate equanimity that accompanies the wisdom in our practice. Since such equanimity knows directly the tranquillity of the mind's nature, unmediated by thought, we call it *ultimate* equanimity.

Relative Kinds of Equanimity within Unconditional Love

The ultimate equanimity of wisdom grounds two other types of equanimity that operate within the wish of love. We could call them *relative* types of equanimity, since they are mediated by thought— the thought of love.

The first type is the *impartiality and inclusiveness* of boundless love that includes all beings equally in its wish, with no preference for one over others. The second type of equanimity operative in such love is *freedom from expectations,* from attachment to circumstances or outcomes. Our egos may become discouraged when we wish someone who is ill to become well but his condition only worsens over time. Or our wish for an alcoholic friend to improve his life may turn into anger when he refuses to improve himself. But the unconditional wish of love comes from beyond our egos and is not affected by such circumstances. It wills the well-being of persons no matter what occurs. The sun doesn't get discouraged when there are clouds; it just keeps radiating regardless. Similarly, unconditional love just keeps radiating to all, no matter what anyone may think, say, do, or not do.

These two aspects of relative equanimity can be seen as the radiance of ultimate equanimity. Ultimate equanimity knows that all beings are the same in their essential nature of empty cognizance. Therefore the love that radiates from such wisdom is *impartial* and *all-inclusive*—viewing all beings as the same in their essential goodness and need for love. Ultimate equanimity also knows the unchanging essential nature that underlies the transitory manifestation of experiences. So the love that radiates from such wisdom does so unwaveringly, *free of expectations,* unaffected by shifting circumstances or unexpected outcomes. Such love is *impartial, all-inclusive,* and *free of expectations,* because it is grounded in the wisdom that knows the all-inclusive and unconditioned nature of mind.[48]

When someone realizes and embodies such profound equanimity, it makes others feel deeply grounded to be in his or her presence. My teacher Geshe Sopa is renowned for his calm perseverance against seemingly insurmountable obstacles. He first came to America as a refugee who could barely speak English, although he had been famous in Tibet as a great lama scholar. Over the years he rose to become one of the most respected professors of Buddhist Studies in the United States. When he invited H.H. the Dalai Lama to come to Wisconsin to offer transmissions and teachings new to the West, many of us couldn't believe what he had taken on. An incredible number of preparations had to be made in a very short time. Geshe Sopa took the responsibility to mortgage a new home with the necessary land for the event, to quickly construct a new temple, and provide housing for thousands of people. Many obstacles and problems came up, but he remained unfazed as he quietly, constantly persevered.

Eight years ago Geshe Sopa came to teach in Boston. He stayed in our home and just his simple presence made a profound impression on my older son Jonathan, who was then six years old. To this day, whenever Barbara and I talk about any Tibetan, Jonathan asks if we are talking about Geshe Sopa. Geshe Sopa was so deeply grounded in wise, loving equanimity, that Jonathan's memory, eight years later, is still pulled toward him like mental gravity.

Pure Perception in the "Real World"

Some people ask: "Pure perception that views all as worthy of love may sound nice, but what about the *real* world, where we need to identify the people we should hate and fear because they mean us harm? What am I to tell my young daughter—that she's supposed to love everyone without discrimination? In the *real* world, that will put her in harm's way."

This question concerns reality and getting in touch with what is really real. What meditation reveals to us is intended to help us do just that. The love that emerges from meditation should not be silly or naïve but wise, that is, fully in touch with who and what people really are. To be more present to others is not just to sense their innate dignity but also their various intentions, many of which, as we've discussed, are far from pure.

By becoming more conscious through meditation of our own harmful states of mind and how they work, we can learn to abide in an attitude of care when we confront another person caught in harmful states of mind. Our responses, even to harmful people, are far more effective when they express an enduring care for persons than when they just embody the brittleness of our self-centered anxieties. Indeed, many health professionals, social service providers, therapists, and police officers have borne witness to this.

One time Barbara and I were eating in a restaurant in Madison, Wisconsin, when a huge, drunken man in the restaurant became belligerent and refused to leave. Two police officers were called to the scene. Expecting them to forcefully confront and constrain the large man, I was amazed to watch them calmly approach him with genuine concern. They spoke quietly with him for a while about what it was that he really needed, then accompanied him outside in a manner of quiet dignity. Those police officers met the drunken man not with the brittle ego of legal authority but with wise care for the person they encountered. That attitude made all the difference in their effectiveness.

The meaning of these meditations clarifies when their power flows into our lives over the course of daily practice. The first question is not what to *tell* our children *about* these practices but what quality of *presence* we *embody* for our children and others. To what extent are we a source of patient, unconditional care for those who people our daily lives? The power of wise love and equanimity that flows from our practice will inform every encounter in subtle ways, whether we are with pleasant persons or difficult ones. As we sense this, we see how much our experience of others has been mediated by our thoughts and actions all along, and that the same pattern is true for all the others around us.

Given that, which *is* a better vision of the real—the vision that discriminates some persons as worthy of love and many others as not or the pure vision that views each being as worthy of love, however lost some may be in the dark places of their minds? Which vision lets us know more of the fullness and depth of persons, more of what they *really* are? Which puts us in better touch with the reality, thus helping us respond to others in ways we don't regret later? Which thereby helps us lead a more successful life?

We could speculate about such questions endlessly, but it is more illuminating to take up a spiritual practice that actually clarifies the answers by helping us to live them. If the meditations in this book facilitate that, consider taking them up in earnest. If they do not, then consider finding a practice that does. Nothing is more important than the fundamental intent behind the original question—how best to get in touch with reality and thereby help our children and others do similarly.

6. Compassion as a Liberating Power

S HABKAR RINPOCHE, A DZOGCHEN MASTER of the nineteenth century, said this to a disciple who declared that he had realized the empty nature of phenomena:

> Now I have some heart-advice to give to you: a sky needs a sun, a mother needs a child, a bird needs two wings. Likewise emptiness alone is not enough. You need to have great compassion for all beings who have not realized this emptiness—enemies, friends, and strangers. You need to have compassion that makes no distinctions between good and bad. You must understand that compassion arises through meditation, not simply from waiting, thinking that it may come forth by itself from emptiness.[49]

Compassion is a form of love. Compassion empathizes with beings in their suffering while wishing them deep freedom from it.

To become enlightened as the Buddha did is to unify wisdom with compassion. For when the wisdom of emptiness dawns, it reveals the subtle causes of suffering in the mind—one's tendency to grasp on to self and to all aspects of experience, as if they were substantial entities rather than empty, transient patterns of cognizance. And this dawning wisdom also reveals the suffering that all other beings, subject to the same grasping tendencies, are undergoing. Sensing in that way how self and others are similar in both the causes of suffering and the potential for freedom, it becomes natural to empathize with them and wish for their freedom from misery as if it were one's own. In this way, wisdom empowers compassion for all other beings.

The reverse is also true—boundless compassion empowers wisdom. For as the boundless quality of compassion emerges—a compassion that empathetically reaches out to all other beings in this way—it empowers one's mind to release its narrow framework of ego-centeredness for the infinite wisdom beyond it, the limitless expanse of openness and cognizance. Thus, Shabkar Rinpoche declares, a practitioner who begins to realize the wisdom of emptiness learns how to integrate it with boundless compassion in order to realize the fullest potential of enlightenment.

The Significance of Compassion

Buddhists throughout Asia express the significance of compassion through stories, many of which center on Shakyamuni Buddha and his disciples. One such story concerns a remarkable woman who entered the Buddha's spiritual community after discovering tremendous compassion and wisdom through her own suffering.

Kisa Gotami was a poor village woman who longed desperately for a child of her own. When she finally gave birth to a baby boy, she was overjoyed. But while still a toddler, the child became ill and quickly died. Gotami was completely overcome with grief. Unable to accept what had happened, she placed her child's body on her hip, as if he were still alive, and wandered from house to house through her village, desperately pleading: "Please, give me medicine for my son!" At first astonished by her behavior, some villagers began mocking her, asking, "What medicine can there possibly be for the dead, Gotami?"

Finally, an old man took pity on Gotami and told her that there was a great sage with tremendous, unmatched powers called the

Buddha, who was teaching near their village. "You should go and ask him," he said. Filled with hope and excitement, still carrying her son's dead body, she rushed off to where the Buddha was teaching.

Breathless, she fell before the Buddha and beseeched him, "Please, blessed one, give me medicine for my son!" Recognizing Gotami's spiritual potential, the Buddha said, "You did well, Gotami, to come here for such medicine. But first, go back to the village and visit every house there. At each house where nobody grieves for the dead, fetch mustard seeds. Then return to me with those seeds."

Thinking the Buddha planned to use the mustard seeds to conjure a cure for her son, Gotami excitedly returned to the village. At the first house she said, "The Buddha told me to get mustard seeds from every home where no one grieves for the dead. Please give me mustard seeds for my son's medicine." But the householder replied, "Alas, Gotami, we grieve for our little daughter who died last year." Gotami went to the next house, "Please tell me no one here grieves for the dead so that I may gather mustard seeds." The man there said, "Alas, Gotami, we grieve over our dear son who died a few months ago." At the next house she was told, "Alas, Gotami, we grieve for our beloved parents."

And so her fruitless search continued until it struck her: *everyone* in the village, indeed every living being, undergoes intense grief like her own! In that moment her self-concerned sorrow transformed into empathy for the grief that all beings experience, and her wish to be free of her personal suffering transformed into the wish for all to be free. She felt intense compassion for all beings that, just like her, suffer by grasping on to things that they must inevitably lose. It dawned on her, "*This* is what the Buddha, in his compassion for all of us, has seen!" She was now ready to commend her son's body to the funeral pyre and go back to the Buddha with her new insight.

Upon her return the Buddha smiled at her and asked, "Gotami, have you brought me mustard seeds?" "Oh blessed one, I am done with mustard seeds," she replied. "Just give me refuge." The Buddha welcomed Gotami into his community of nuns, where the force of her compassion for all who grasp on to transient things empowered her to progress rapidly on the liberating path of insight into impermanence and suffering.[50]

Gotami's story illustrates the progressive development of compassion. At first, Gotami was self-absorbed in her personal grief and suffering to the brink of madness. But the practice she received from the Buddha revealed her own experience as the doorway to empathy for others. For Gotami to realize the liberating power of her own suffering, she had first to experience it in its full intensity, then to recognize in *her* suffering what so many others were similarly undergoing. "This is what the Buddha has seen!" she exclaimed, for she had begun to share in the Buddha's vision of universal compassion. Such compassion—knowing beings in their common root of suffering and their common potential for freedom from it—naturally wills freedom equally for them all.

According to tradition, Gotami was an exceptional disciple who quickly became a leader in the early Buddhist community.[51] It takes most of us a bit longer to realize such all-inclusive, wise compassion, but we all have the same potential to do so.

What Is Essential for the Development of Compassion

His Holiness the Dalai Lama says two things are essential for such profound and impartial compassion to arise: (1) strong empathy for beings by sensing each to be as dear as one's family and (2) deep insight into the nature of the suffering that all are undergoing.[52]

Strong Empathy for Beings that Senses Each as Dear

On the first point, the dearness of beings reveals itself to us through our practices of the prior chapters. Such meditations help us sense beings through the heart of love (pure perception) instead of through the egocentric judgments of the head (impure perception). We perceive others' dearness by attending to their essential goodness, their holiness beyond reduction to anyone's limited labels for them. This perception is further empowered by reflecting on the kindness of beings; how every aspect of your well-being has depended upon many others, beyond what you had noticed. All of your food, clothing, shelter, possessions, your abilities to read, write, speak, and reason were all received or learned in utter dependence upon others. Such reflection on the implicit kindness of others can become extremely extensive, finally encompassing all other beings as our ultimate field of benefactors.[53]

Insight into the Nature of Suffering

The Dalai Lama's second point concerns the need for insight into the nature of suffering in order to generate authentic compassion. The Buddha explained three levels of suffering: obvious suffering, the suffering of transience, and the suffering of ego-conditioning. As we inquire into the levels of suffering, they become progressively more subtle. *Obvious suffering* includes the intense pains and miseries of life that normally come to mind when the word "suffering" is invoked: severe illness, violent injury, the sufferings of dying, disabling grief, and so forth. Societies tend to think of compassion for others only when their suffering is of this obvious kind. We tend not to view others with compassion as they experience moments of happiness during pleasant circumstances. But clinging to such temporal happiness is an example of what the Buddha identified as the second level of suffering: the misery inherent in relying on changeable circumstances for one's happiness and well-being.

"All accumulations end in dispersion; all risings in fallings; all meetings in partings; and all life in death," said the Buddha. Within the usual stance of self-grasping, the very things that we cling to for our happiness—such as wealth, loved ones, pleasurable possessions, and personal power—all transform into conditions of suffering as we lose them throughout life and approach our death. Although such things can trigger transient feelings of happiness, they are not its source. The *suffering of transience* is the futile attempt to hold on to passing things as if they were the *very* source of our happiness and well-being, when deep down we know we will lose every one of them. The actual source of well-being is the love, compassion, and wisdom that are always available within the nature of our minds. The ephemeral pleasures of transient suffering come and go with changing circumstances. But through spiritual practice love, compassion, and wisdom can become enduring powers that can be relied upon in *all* circumstances.

The suffering of transience takes expression in the daily turmoil of painful feelings and emotions as we try to find security by holding on to things, circumstances, and people—daily anxieties over obligations, deadlines, and security, fears over how others perceive us, oscillating feelings of inadequacy, guilt, loneliness, longing, annoyance, discouragement, self-centered pride, and despair.

The third level of suffering, the *suffering of ego-conditioning,* is the basis of the other two levels and the most subtle. It is the suffering inherent in the mind's constant struggle to establish a substantial, fixed self that doesn't really exist. It arises in the moment-by-moment creation of an isolated sense of self that interprets everyone and everything around it as part of its struggle to make itself feel real and secure. This level of suffering is the continual subconscious anxiety that fuels all our self-centered reactions.

Ultimate safety and peace are found only within our primordial nature, when we are at rest in the unconditioned essence of our mind, the luminous empty nature that is intrinsically tranquil. Each moment that we don't recognize that unchanging nature—and identify instead with the shifting reactions of self-centeredness—we are oppressed by feelings of longing, anxiety, and fear. It is like being tossed about by ocean waves instead of resting unperturbed like the ocean in its bed, at ease in the unchanging wateriness of all the waves. We are painfully tossed by our conditioned reactions to experiences, instead of resting at ease in the unconditioned essence of the experiences. As we begin to recognize the mind's innate, tranquil nature in meditation, we become conscious of this third level of suffering. For then we are able to sense by contrast how even an instant of ego-grasping, by obscuring such inner peacefulness, is a form of suffering.

It is because the Buddha had insight into all three of these levels of suffering that he had equal compassion for all beings. Not just for those who are undergoing intense, obvious suffering right now but for all beings, even those who seemingly enjoy passing moments of happiness and for those who ignorantly seek happiness by hurting others. He understood how all are caught in layers of suffering and ego-conditioning beyond what they see. Therefore the eyes of the Buddha see them automatically with compassion.

When someone becomes enlightened, it is said, just to *see* a sentient being is to have spontaneous compassion arise from the depth of awareness that discerns the layers of suffering operating in each being. The meditation below helps us gain insight into those three levels of suffering so our own vision of beings may be brought closer to the Buddha's.

Becoming Conscious of Our Own Suffering
as Doorway to Compassion for Others
The Dalai Lama recommends a clear progression in the cultivation of compassion:

> One thing specific to the contemplation of suffering is that
> it tends to be more powerful and effective if we focus on our

own suffering and then extend that recognition to the suffering of others...[54]

Dzogchen Ponlop Rinpoche reiterates that progression from self to other:

Compassion must start by sensing our own suffering. If it does not, then seeing the suffering of others will be merely conceptual.[55]

To connect with what others are going through we have to become vividly and newly aware of what we ourselves are going through, in all the layers of our being. If we don't have awareness of our own layers of struggle and fear and suffering, we can't establish a clear connection to what others are experiencing. To truly empathize with others, we must be able to sense from within the layers of suffering that all share. Not just in terms of what we are currently feeling but also on more subtle levels: our personal struggles to hold on to what is dear, to maintain security, to avoid loss and death.

We saw this progression of self-awareness in Kisa Gotami's story. It was the final acknowledgment of her own grief that transformed into compassion for all others. But Gotami was not so self-aware when her quest began. Similarly, many aspects of our own suffering are hidden from our view. There are layers of anxiety, pain, and grief that are suppressed and lost from our conscious awareness because of our aversion to such feelings. We don't allow ourselves to become conscious of them unless we have a way to do so that feels profoundly safe and healing. Until we have such a way to become conscious of our suppressed, painful feelings, we can't sense the corresponding layers of pain in others so as to generate compassion for them.

Learning to Cradle Our Suffering with Compassion

We all tend to view our sufferings in a very narrow personal way, believing that our experience is unconnected from the suffering of all other beings, as if no one else has ever suffered like this before. By assigning Gotami the "mustard seed" quest, the Buddha helped her find a safe way to explore her personal suffering as her connection to that of others. Analogously, our practice of receiving love gives us a safe way to become further conscious of our own suffering as a basis for compassion. In the meditation below, we are instructed to receive loving compassion into each aspect of our suffering. To cradle each layer in such healing energy gives our minds permission to become conscious of further, more subtle layers. As we sense the similarity of self and others in such layers, it becomes natural to extend loving compassion to them as well. Through this practice, we learn to sense the underlying traces of anxiety and grief that shadow beings even during their moments of pleasure, and to hold them in the compassion that wills their deep freedom. As occurred for Gotami, eventually it can dawn on us, This is what the Buddha, in his compassion for all, has seen!

Meditation: Realizing Wise Compassion

Part 1: Receiving the Radiant Blessing of Compassion

Sit in a relaxed way. Recall your benefactors, including inspiring spiritual figures such as the Buddha. Envision them above you and just behind. They are sending you love in the form of compassion, the radiant wish for you to have deepest freedom from suffering. Bathe in the loving energy of that wish. Receive its healing warmth into every layer of your suffering, gradually step by step.

Receive the gentle radiance of compassion into physical

pains, letting all such areas of tension relax under its healing warmth.

Bring to mind daily anxieties about how you are going to survive or meet all obligations. Sense what it's like for someone to undergo such anxieties, then receive the healing energy of compassion into those feelings.

Experience your worries over finances, employment, security, or health. Sense what it's like for someone to undergo such anxieties, and receive the gentle radiance of compassion into them.

Experience your fears over what others think of you and receive compassion into those visceral feelings.

In a similar way, step by step, receive your benefactors' radiant compassion into:

feelings of self-doubt or inadequacy;
feelings of sadness or guilt;
feelings of loneliness or loss;
feelings of anger or betrayal;
feelings of despair or hopelessness;
feelings of addiction;
your longings or sense of incompleteness.

Sense what it's like for someone to undergo such feelings, then cradle each one in the soft, healing energy of compassion.

Bring to mind your fears of severe illness, injury, pain, or death, and receive compassion into those anxieties. Bring to mind fears you have for your loved ones and pets in their vulnerability and mortality, and receive compassion into those feelings.

Receive the gentle radiance of compassion into your inmost patterns of grasping to self, of trying to hold on to anything at all.

Finally, relinquish the visualization and totally surrender to loving compassion by merging into oneness with the radiance and releasing all frames of reference. Experience luminous wholeness, beyond separation of self and others, deeply letting all be.

Part 2: Letting Be in Natural Awareness

Let all bodily sensations settle naturally in their own way. Surrender to the natural power of the body and feel it embody you. Let the breath come under its own natural power, breathing you. Release all grasping on to thoughts of past, present, or future, permitting thoughts and sensations to arise and dissolve under their own power. Thus let the mind fall totally open—at ease, unrestricted, free of focus, all-pervasive, with the gaze of your eyes totally expansive. Let all be just as it is in complete openness and acceptance.

Sense the openness of awareness, boundless and without center, in which thoughts and sensations self-arise and self-dissolve—beyond thinking, beyond reference points, infinite openness and translucent awareness, pervasive like the sky. Let this vast expanse sense all that arises as its own radiant expression. Rest as that sky-like nature of mind—all phenomena allowed to self-arise and self-release within the infinite expanse of openness aware.

Part 3: Extending Radiant Compassion

After some time, recall your benefactors, including deeply spiritual figures. Envision them behind you and just above, sending you love in the form of compassion, the radiant wish for you to have deepest freedom from suffering. Bathe in the compassionate energy of that wish. Receive its healing radiance like a gentle shower into every part of your mind and body, from head to toe. Join your benefactors in their wish for you: "May this one have deepest freedom from suffering." Mentally repeat that wish for yourself as you receive the healing energy even more deeply into your body and mind.

Now envision several beings that are dear to you in front. While receiving your benefactors' radiant wish from behind, let the radiance come through you to the beloved ones before you, sensing their layers of suffering as similar to your own. Repeat the wish of compassion in your mind while radiating its healing energy to those in front of you: "May they have deepest freedom from suffering." Gradually, at your own pace, extend that radiant wish to more dear ones in front, illumining their bodies and minds with its compassionate energy.

Now, envision several strangers in front along with the dear ones, sensing them as similar to you in their layers of suffering. Let the radiance from your benefactors come through you to them while repeating the wish of compassion for them in your mind: "May they have deepest freedom from suffering." Trust this wish more than your thought of them as "strangers" while illumining them with its compassionate energy. At your own pace, extend that radiant wish similarly to more strangers in front, bathing them completely in its compassionate energy.

Now, along with the dear ones and strangers, envision several people you have disliked, hated, or wanted to avoid. Sense them as similar to you in their layers of suffering and their wish to be free of it. Let the radiance come through you to them while repeating the wish of compassion for them: "May they have deepest freedom from suffering." Trust this wish more than your thought of them as dislikable, illumining them with its compassionate energy. At your own pace, extend the wish similarly to more and more people you have disliked, hated, or wanted to avoid.

Now *imagine that the luminous field of benefactors behind you merges completely into your heart.* Sense the compassionate energy radiating from your heart as one with all your benefactors and one with all enlightened beings and your spiritual teachers. Let your heart, unified with all those benefactors, radiate boundlessly to sentient beings like the sun, in all directions at once. Repeating the wish of compassion, bathe all beings with its energy while communing heart to heart with them: "May each being have deepest freedom from suffering." Let the energy of that wish overwhelm any remaining inhibitions you may have, radiating out spontaneously and all-inclusively, as if a buddha in your heart were radiating through you to all beings at once, evoking their deepest freedom in the nature of their minds.

After some time, drop the visualization and just let go into oneness with that compassionate, insubstantial radiance. Release all frames of reference into boundless openness and translucent awareness, pervasive like the sky—beyond any thought of separation. Rest thus, at ease, complete.

Part 4: Dedicating the Liberating Power for All

Feel the power of this practice to pull you beyond self-grasping patterns of suffering and to open you toward the deep tranquillity and goodness of your inmost being. Prayerfully dedicate all such spiritual power to the deepest well-being and liberation of all beings, each like you in needing and wanting such joy and freedom.

Tips for Progressing in the Meditation of Compassion and Wisdom

Focus First on Receiving Compassion and Letting Be in Natural Awareness

To receive the compassion of spiritual benefactors, including enlightened beings, is profoundly healing for our minds. But it is also much more. It lets our basic goodness communicate with theirs, and thus to awaken. To merge with benefactors and sense their compassionate energy as our own is to discover their buddha nature as undivided from our own and to begin to unleash its spontaneous energies. Finally, to dissolve into oneness with that empty radiance, beyond reference points, is to join our spiritual benefactors in the infinite ground of compassion and wisdom they have realized, the nature of mind. In this way, by receiving our benefactors' blessing we are learning, like them, to unleash the liberating power of enlightenment from the ground of our being.

Explore this compassion and wisdom meditation at your own rate of progress. Remember that your field of benefactors includes enlightened beings, whose wish of compassion is continuous, unconditional, and all-inclusive. You are always included in their wish, no matter what. During the initial weeks of daily practice, focus on the first two parts of the meditation as follows: first take time to *receive* the light of your benefactors' compassion gradually into all layers of your suffering, then merge into oneness with that radiance, and relax into natural awareness beyond reference points, the second part of the meditation.

Some people say they are afraid to pay so much attention to their own suffering. But that's because they are focusing on the suffering alone, divorced from the compassion. For many of us, before entering into this meditation, to become conscious of our suffering implied feeling isolated from others in our personal pain; to feel terribly alone. But that is *not* how this meditation takes us into our suffering. In this meditation *we learn how to experience suffering while cradling it in the light of compassion.* This *transforms* the experience, because the compassionate energy we receive is so deeply healing.

Therefore, it is important to focus on *receiving* the healing rays of compassion into each layer of your suffering and anxiety. Don't just focus on your feelings of distress alone, as if unrelated to that receiving. The energy of compassion helps heal parts of ourselves we had not previously acknowledged, so we can become newly conscious of them.

There is no need to rush the process. We are enabled to become more conscious of feelings of pain, fear, and despair as we sense the safe, healing power of the unconditional care in which they are held. Let each such feeling come to rest in the gentle, healing warmth of loving compassion from your benefactors. By gradually sensing more layers of suffering in that way, you are sensing similar layers in others, which empowers empathy for them.

By receiving compassion into each aspect of our suffering as instructed, we become increasingly aware of all three levels of suffering that were explained above. These are the *obvious sufferings* of body and mind, the *sufferings of transience,* which include fears, longings, and resentments evoked by clinging to transient things for our happiness, and the *suffering of ego-conditioning,* which is the misery inherent in grasping on to a narrow self and its frames of reference. To become conscious of those three levels of suffering makes us aware of similar levels in others, empowering our compassion for them.

In each such session, receive the healing energy of compassion into all the layers of your suffering for ten or twenty minutes, then release into oneness with that radiance, and relax into the wisdom of natural awareness, the second part of the meditation. Then, after some time, just dedicate the liberating power of the practice.

When Ready, Extend Compassion Progressively

After a few weeks focusing in that way on the first two parts of the meditation, you can add the third part of the meditation and begin extending the wish of compassion as instructed. When you have truly familiarized yourself with your own layers of suffering, it becomes absolutely natural to empathize with others in their similar layers of difficulty and to extend compassion to them. For several weeks, radiate compassion in each session to dear ones in widening circles, then merge with your benefactors, radiate to all beings, and dedicate the liberating power. After a few more weeks, when compassion for many dear ones feels strong, you can extend it in each session also to strangers in widening circles, then merge with your benefactors, radiate to all beings, and dedicate. After several more weeks, when compassion for many strangers feels strong, extend compassion in each session also to disliked ones before merging with benefactors, radiating to all, and dedicating.

When Familiar with Compassion, Alternate It with Meditation on Love

After you have become familiar with the meditation of compassion, you can alternate it with the meditation of love from chapter 5— morning meditation on the one, evening meditation on the other. Or you can practice the love meditation daily for a month, then practice the compassion meditation for a month. By alternating in this way, each practice continues to inform and empower the other. Love, compassion, and wisdom grow increasingly deep and strong, gradually affecting your life, relationships, and work in the world.

Discovering Kisa Gotami's Story as Our Own

Over time, through such practice, we discover Kisa Gotami's story as similar to our own. How this intuitive understanding can arise is beautifully illustrated in a letter written to a literary journal by a young mother describing a day in the hospital with her child, Robert, who is gravely ill with leukemia.

"I awaken," she says, "as a nurse enters my four-year-old son's hospital room to check his tubing and vital signs.... After fourteen days in the hospital, I have somehow put aside the disbelief that this is happening to my child." The uncertain outcome of Robert's treatment rivets the mother's attention on each fresh moment with her son, as they play together with puzzles, sit together in the hospital tulip garden, joke, color pictures, listen to music. Later, as Robert naps, she wanders down to the cafeteria while praying silently: "I have learned to pray in my head while walking. I don't blame God for having let Robert get leukemia, but I do believe God can decide how much longer Robert will live, and this is the focus of my prayer. At the start of the walk, I want Robert to live to be an old man. If not that, I at least want to see him grow up, get married, and have children. I want to see what he will look like as a teenager. I've had four years with him; I want four more. I want at least one more year—one more Christmas, one more birthday. I want to bring him home one more time, away from nurses and spinal taps and IV tubes. By the time I finish praying, the hall has become very narrow. Then the thought comes to me: *At least we have had this day.* This day of laughing and playing and music and sunshine on tulips. If Robert died tomorrow, I would be able to remember every minute of this day for the rest of my life and take pleasure in it. Some children are killed by cars, and their mothers never get to say goodbye. Some infants die suddenly and their mothers never see them grow and laugh. Some mothers are too busy or burdened to spend an entire day with their child, just playing. I realize that I am one of the lucky ones."[56]

Her silent prayer began in desperation, clinging to the vision of the life with her son she had assumed she would have. But as her prayer progressed, her heartbreak transformed into gratitude and empathy—gratitude for every moment of life now perceived as sacred and empathy for all mothers who must lose their children.

The meditation of compassion and wisdom enters us upon a similar journey of awakening. Through progressive practice, we discover that our suffering is not just a personal problem. It need not isolate us from others into narrow confines of personal pain. We can rediscover the meaning of our own suffering as a profound connection to countless others and to the dignity and sacredness of all our lives.

Compassion Must Be Grounded in Wisdom to Be a Liberating Force

The Dalai Lama notes:

As we recognize that the basis of misery is mistaken perception, this mistaken grasping at a nonexistent self, we see that

suffering can be eliminated.... Knowing that people's suffering is avoidable, that it is surmountable, our sympathy for
their inability to extricate themselves leads to a more powerful compassion. Otherwise, though our compassion may
be strong, it is likely to have a quality of hopelessness, even
despair.[57]

Compassion wishes beings to be free from their suffering. If we
don't really believe that they can be free—that deep freedom, security, well-being, and joy is a real human possibility—our compassion
tends to lapse into despair. Then it is not a liberating force for anyone. Compassion becomes a liberating force when we *know* the
freedom that it wishes for beings to be *real*.

This is why practices of wisdom were introduced early in this
book. It is the wisdom of natural awareness that knows such freedom
to be real. Even as beginners, our wisdom is empowered as each part
of the meditation helps us learn to release our self-grasping and come
to rest in the natural openness of awareness beyond reference points.
There we can sense the possibility of a freedom beyond personal suffering, a dimension of deep safety, nirvanic peace, previously hidden by ego-centered thoughts.

It is as though we had been reacting to frightening projections on
a movie screen. But when we turn our attention back toward the
movie projector, we see the tranquil source of the projections: the
empty radiance that our own minds had solidified into frightening
forms.

Similarly, through the meditation, we learn to recognize the
peaceful essence of our shifting thoughts and sensations, their
unchanging nature of empty cognizance. When we sense such
peace in the radiant essence of awareness, we also sense how
ephemeral are the ego-centered patterns of thought that had driven
our personal suffering. All such patterns are empty of substance and,

when recognized as such, need not bind our minds. Amazed, we sense that a deep, inner freedom from personal suffering *is* possible. We *can* realize the kind of freedom that the Buddha spoke of and so can others around us. Then our compassion, our wish for their freedom, is imbued with real confidence and power. Such compassion doesn't just share the sorrow of beings in their suffering. It is also a resolute will and liberating energy that communes with others at the level of their deepest freedom. And it is joy at participating in their freedom now.

Three Levels of Compassion

According to Indian and Tibetan Buddhist masters, as insight into the nature of suffering deepens in practice, three levels of compassion progressively emerge on the path of enlightenment.

They are: (1) compassion that views the obvious suffering of beings, (2) compassion that senses beings in their impermanence, and (3) compassion that knows the nature of mind. The first level is compassion that empathizes with beings in their obvious sufferings, willing them to be freed from such intense misery. The second level is compassion that senses how they suffer by grasping on to transient things for an ephemeral self, willing them to be freed from such grasping. The third level is compassion that recognizes the infinite, unchanging nature of mind and understands the suffering inherent in the lack of such recognition. At this third level, when a practitioner rests in that unconditioned nature of mind beyond the turmoil of self-grasping, a spontaneous will and energy of compassion radiates to all who have not yet found such safety in the nature of their minds. This is nonconceptual compassion, a natural reflex of deep wisdom.[58]

The following quotes beautifully express this third level, in which compassion and wisdom are spontaneously united.

As Nyoshul Khenpo explained:

When you realize the true nature of things, how can you not have incredible spontaneous compassion for all those who don't realize it?... Everywhere that suffering and delusion arise, compassion arises to release and alleviate beings suffering from that delusion. That is the spontaneous outflow of the genuine realization of the true nature.[59]

And as Dilgo Khyentse Rinpoche taught:

The source of all phenomena of samsara and nirvana
Is the nature of mind—void, luminous,
All-encompassing, vast as the sky.

When in that state of skylike vastness,
Relax into its openness; stay in that very openness,
Merge with that skylike state:
Naturally, it will become more and more relaxed—
Wonderful!

If you become accomplished
In this method of integrating mind with view,
Your realization will naturally become vast.
And just as the sun shines freely throughout space,
Your compassion cannot fail to shine on all unrealized
    beings.[60]

Nyoshul Khenpo and Khyentse Rinpoche were two of the most revered Buddhist masters of the twentieth century. But the wise compassion they realized is available to us all, if we proceed with diligence at our own rate of progress.

Wise Compassion as a Liberating Power in the World

As compassion deepens through its three levels, it becomes a real liberating power for the world. This is so in several ways.

On the relative level, such compassion is the strong wish for beings to be freed from suffering; the wish that knows their potential for such freedom to be real, whatever anyone may think of themselves or others. To be present to others within that attitude is to hold them in the comforting energy of compassion, helping to ease their troubled minds. It is to listen deeply and to respond to the basic dignity of beings that worldly gossip doesn't acknowledge.

Compassion that knows beings in all levels of their suffering motivates service for them on all levels of their need. Such service is not easily discouraged at disappointing temporal outcomes, because it holds others in their deepest potential of freedom, which is always present. In the course of such service, compassion also opens one's own mind to further qualities of awakening that benefit others by inspiration and example: joy in the meaningfulness of human life, reverence for each person, patience with self and others, gratitude, enthusiastic perseverance, and stability of mind in loving compassion.

On the ultimate level, to abide in the very ground of compassion, the sky-like nature of mind, is to commune with others in their primordial freedom, beyond dualism, beyond customary thinking, subliminally evoking their potential to awaken similarly. It is to resonate with their inmost nature of freedom, blessing them to come to their own recognition of it. It is to touch them in their hearts. Indeed, this is what our spiritual benefactors, enlightened beings, have been doing for us, long before we noticed. Their awakened buddha nature has communed with our own, blessing it to awaken similarly—to actualize itself in compassionate energy and service to others.

Compassion Confirms the Dignity of Beings While Confronting Their Harmful Tendencies

Some people think of themselves as compassionate because they always try to say and do what confirms others in their self-satisfaction. But that is not compassion. It is just an attempt to get along with everyone. Others feel they should not have compassion for everyone because political opponents and perpetrators of injustice should be confronted, justifying hatred for their opponents as the necessary motivation for confronting them.

Wise compassion reverences the inner worth of every single person. But it also sees into the layers of their suffering, including the suffering they create for themselves and others through ego-centered thought and action. Wise compassion confirms the intrinsic dignity of persons even when it confronts the harmful ways that they think and act. Such compassion challenges people in their ego-centeredness while upholding their fundamental goodness.

Some of our most profound benefactors are those who are willing, out of compassion, to become objects of our anger in order to challenge us to be better people. They do so because they see in us both the positive and negative aspects that we have not yet acknowledged. And they have the courage of compassion to confront our harmful tendencies, so our positive potential can emerge.

Bankei, a seventeenth-century Japanese Zen master, was renowned for his compassion toward the masses. One day a group of beggars who suffered from leprosy came to him for refuge. Bankei admitted them into his community, washing and shaving their heads with his own hands. One of Bankei's devout disciples, upset to see his master put himself at risk by placing his hands on the lepers, ran to Bankei with a basin of water and offered to wash his hands. Bankei, fixing his disciple in a steely gaze, refused the water and said, "Your disgust for them is filthier than their sores."[61]

It would be wrong to think Bankei had compassion for the lepers but not for his disciple. Differing circumstances called forth different expressions of the same compassion. Bankei's kindness toward the lepers confirmed their worth, despite society's revulsion for them. And by confronting his disciple's revulsion for the lepers, Bankei pointed him to a better object for his revulsion—the self-clinging reactivity of his own mind. He exposed his disciple to his own samsaric map of others, so he could learn to ignore it and manifest his own potential for all-inclusive compassion.

In this way, wise compassion confirms the inner worth of beings even when it confronts their harmful patterns of self-centeredness. It confirms what should be confirmed and confronts what should be confronted, without ignoring one for the other.

Compassion and Social Service

Such compassion greatly empowers any work we may do in social service or activism. It keeps our mind on realities that transcend our own self-centeredness, so our best intentions can be realized instead of being overwhelmed by our emotional reactions to fallible people and disappointing outcomes.

People who work in social service or activism come to retreats and workshops where I teach these meditations. They ask how to avoid burnout in their work. Many feel emotionally exhausted and embittered by difficulties with clients and co-workers, disappointing results, or obstacles from vested interests. To whatever degree ego-centeredness is mixed into our motivation to help others, I tell them, we identify with the ego's reactions to all such difficulties and become exhausted and bitter. It is our own self-centered reactions that burn us out. We are not conscious of the subtleties of our self-centeredness because they are hidden and couched within our desire to be a big help to others. Within such a mixed motivation, we don't just wish for others' well-being; we also want success in *our* way of helping them, and we want gratitude from others to confirm our image as their good helper. When such expectations are not met, we become cynical or bitter and get tired of the work.

The meditations of these chapters undercut the subconscious ways we cling to identifying ourselves as "helpers," by evoking a more enduring care for persons that transcends such self-centered concern. The power of unconditional care helps carry us beyond the limitations of the ego that reacts with frustration and impatience when faced with temporary failure, setback, or lack of appreciation.

Many who have practiced these meditations with me in recent years say that the practice has empowered their service to others beyond measure, reinforcing and strengthening their basic intention to serve. Kathy directs an urban soup kitchen for homeless people, serves hundreds of people from the streets of Boston, and has trained dozens of people in service to them. Terry does chaplaincy work in a maximum security prison with inmates whose lives are defined by the violent abuse they have given and received. Jaymati, a psychotherapist, has counseled clients overcome by self-hatred and self-inflicted wounds. Chad, a social worker, has counseled inner-city kids from violent, gang-infested neighborhoods. Ana has taught in a school for emotionally disturbed children who have never experienced a supportive family life. Julie teaches college students with severe learning disabilities, many of whom feel like complete failures in their lives.

All these care providers know how hard and exhausting such work becomes if the caregiver is immersed in his or her personal reactions to problems and difficult behaviors of clients or co-workers. So each has learned increasingly to rely upon the power of wisdom, unconditional love, and compassion that flows from daily meditation. This gives them a power of enduring connection to their clients and co-workers, no matter how little appreciation they receive or what may occur in a particular day. They have learned how to hold their clients in the vision of their positive potential, confirming their essential goodness, even when confronting their clients' harmful behaviors or limiting thoughts of themselves and others.

As daily meditation brings out the power of wisdom, loving compassion, and equanimity from beyond our egos, we can learn to recall and draw upon it throughout our day, extending compassion to others no matter what they think or do, whether or not our own temporal goals are accomplished. To recall the meditation during our workday helps keep us focused on our fundamental care for persons, instead of exhausting our energy in the tiring reactions of our egos. In this way, little by little, the wisdom and energy of compassion, beyond emotional exhaustion, empowers all our work.

Compassion and Social Activism

Social activism brings up further issues. Agents of social change campaign for and against social policies, which brings them into disagreement with those who campaign for the other side. Many assume that to take a stand against political opponents requires us to hate and vilify them, which is why much public discourse quickly becomes so vicious and polarized. But detesting one's opponents only inhibits social consensus, leaving us emotionally exhausted and sick inside from our own anger. Hate, even when promulgated in the name of the public good, alienates us from our better selves and from others, often driving away the very people that we seek to attract to our cause.

It is more effective to cultivate the love and compassion that senses others as like oneself, both in their essential goodness and in their self-centered tendencies. By maintaining humility in that knowledge we can confirm the dignity of our opponents as equal to our own, even when we confront their positions on important issues.

My wife, Barbara, models this sort of attitude for me. A few years ago a bitter political issue divided our town. Many citizens believed that the town schools were in desperate need of money to rebuild dilapidated buildings. To do this, they argued, local taxes had to be raised. Many others strongly disagreed, arguing that raising taxes would harm those on limited incomes and set a bad precedent for future budgetary problems. The issue headed for a vote. Barbara joined a movement to get out the yes vote for raising taxes. Election day arrived, and Barbara stood holding a "Yes!" sign at a spot in the center of town. Nearby was an older man, well known in the town, whom she hadn't previously met. The man had written several strongly worded letters to town newspapers criticizing the proposal to raise taxes. He stood next to her holding a sign that read, "No!" They shared that corner for hours.

Barbara and the gentleman commiserated with each other over the rigors of political campaigning in chilly weather. They entertained each other with conversation throughout the day. Occasionally, someone drove by and shouted a rude comment about either the "Yes!" or "No!" people, provoking Barbara and her neighbor to discuss the importance of respect. Each enjoyed discovering and communing with the other's humanity that day, even as each remained firm in opposing the other's political stand. Such mutual respect, on one corner in the center of town, helped anchor the political process in which the whole town was participating.

But what if you are working on behalf of victims of injustice and abuse? "Surely," many have argued, "hatred for those who harm others is a good motivation for opposing them." Wait a minute. Recall how the map of "friend," "stranger," and "enemy" has held everyone in bondage. People who oppress or abuse others conceive of them merely as "strangers" who don't matter or as "enemies" to be hated as nothing but evil. So they often justify their abuse as a social good. For us, in turn, to conceive of the abusers as "enemies" who are not fully human, deserving only of hatred and abuse, reinforces the fundamental error that they are caught in. We don't want to wind up joining them in the name of opposing them.

The practices of wisdom, unconditional love, and compassion give us a way out of this vicious cycle. Our meditations help us recognize how much we share with abusers, in our thoughts if not our physical actions, and also to recognize the potential for good that is within *all* persons. Knowing what is real, the essential sameness of self and others, compassion can respond realistically by confronting the evil in persons and confirming the potential for good in them. Self-righteous hatred, because it is out of touch with reality in its deluded projections of others, is powerless to do anything but evoke further evil from them. That's because self-righteous hatred itself is part of the dynamic of evil—a self-centered reaction to one's own reductive thought of others.

Oppressed people suffer from abuse. Those who abuse them suffer from fear in their fruitless, deluded attempt to achieve secure well-being through actions that harm many others. When compassion motivates social action, it holds both the "oppressed" and the "oppressor" in its care, seeking freedom for both from actions that hold both in bondage to suffering.

The Catholic activist Thomas Merton expressed this principle well, using the theological language of his tradition:

> The saints are what they are, not because their sanctity makes them admirable to others, but because the gift of sainthood makes it possible for them to admire everybody else. It gives them a clarity of compassion that can find good in the most terrible criminals. It delivers them from the burden of judging others, condemning other men. It teaches them to bring the good out of others by compassion, mercy and pardon. A man becomes a saint not by conviction that he is better than

sinners but by the realization that he is one of them, and that all together need the mercy of God.[62]

To wake up to our enlightened potential is to relinquish the burden of mistaking others for our reductive judgments of them, since we know how much suffering has followed from that mistake. Then we recognize how all others have made the same mistake and have suffered for it. To know that is to know that all deserve compassion, and that our own self-righteousness was just a delusion. Then strong action against injustice can be taken for the sake of all.

Letting Meditation and Daily Life Inform Each Other

Responding to the World with New Eyes of Compassion

As we practice this meditation of compassion and natural wisdom each day, it affects our perception of the world. These days, as I write, thousands of people in the world are overcome by rage, swearing themselves to the painful death of their enemies. Dozens of Iraqis are maimed and killed each day by suicide bombers who think such slaughter is their path to heaven. Millions in the Sudan have been heartlessly uprooted from their villages by brutal attacks, hundreds of thousands dying from violence, hunger, and disease. Millions of laborers, including children, work such long hours on farms and in factories for so little pay that they barely survive. Families all over the world are overwhelmed by the need to support relatives with debilitating diseases. Every day in the United States families are ripped apart by addiction and abuse. Children from impoverished homes throughout the world are forced into prostitution and slave labor. Billions suffer from mental illness, including severe depression. Each day, millions of animals undergo unspeakable suffering as they are mistreated or butchered for food.

Some of us turn away from the daily news because we feel so helpless in the face of so much misery. But if we do so, it feels as if we are hiding from the realities of our world and therefore ultimately from ourselves as part of that world.

When we do daily meditation on compassion and wisdom, instead of experiencing the daily news as enemy, it can be received as the means to inform and deepen our compassion. In a session of morning meditation, we wish beings to become free of their sufferings. Then throughout the day, when we see or hear of the terrible difficulties that others are undergoing, we can take that knowledge into our practice on the spot, wishing them freedom from their suffering, from every outer circumstance and inner layer of it. We can do this when we encounter the tragedies reported in the morning paper and the evening news. And we can do it whenever we come upon anyone in our life that is suffering or grieving.

In this way, rather than hiding from the world, we learn increasingly to open our eyes and hearts to it. Then when we sit down to meditate the next morning, the sufferings we saw the previous day inform the wish of compassion that we extend.

Classical Indian and Tibetan texts instruct practitioners to elicit compassion for beings by imagining the horrors they undergo in suffering realms of rebirth as taught in Asian Buddhist cosmologies: the tortures of hell realms, the painful hunger of wandering spirits, the fearful lives of animals. We can draw in a similar way upon the viscerally brutal images of war, starvation, abuse, and oppression that we see on television, in newspapers and movies. Instead of turning away from the horrors of the contemporary world in helplessness, we accept them into our meditation to inform and empower our compassion: "May they have deep freedom from suffering."

In this way, the suffering around us informs our meditation, and the compassion from meditation helps us respond to the suffering around us. When we hear of others' suffering or see it, we don't have to feel helpless. We can make the wish for their deep freedom from it and let the energy of that wish motivate us to ameliorate whatever suffering we can. Suffering that cannot presently be assuaged need not become an excuse to turn our heads away. We can hold suffering beings in the energy of compassion, willing their deep freedom from it, keeping them in our mind, never forgetting them until they are freed.

The Joy of Wise Compassion and Love

Such practice need not make us depressed and glum—just the opposite. It gives us a way to open to the realities around us, instead of hiding from them. It helps us awaken to more of our own humanity, in solidarity with others all around us, and to be there for others in the way we had intended. There is tremendous joy in getting real in such ways.

We are learning to be a compassionate presence for others that is grounded both in the realities of their suffering and in their potential for freedom. And we are learning to act from there. As we wish beings freedom from all the levels of their suffering, we are also learning to uphold their deepest capacity for freedom in the nature of mind. And there is great joy in that as well.

In addition, as love and compassion strengthen in practice, sympathetic joy for many others also emerges. We feel joy automatically when we see others experiencing happiness in their lives, for it is the fulfillment of our wish of love and compassion for them. Through daily practice, we increasingly experience the joy of compassion that sustains others in their potential for freedom and the joy of love that shares in their happiness.

This is why it is helpful for aspiring practitioners to meet spiritual benefactors who don't just talk about wise compassion but embody it. Such people have tremendous joy in their lives, which is part of what inspires others to practice similarly. The spiritual teachers quoted in this book really are joyful to be with, not because they've hidden themselves from the terrible realities of others, but because they uphold others' potential for goodness and freedom, no matter what.

Taking Difficulties into Compassion and Wisdom

What About the Difficult Situations that Continue to Occur in Daily Life?

The practices of love, compassion, and wisdom transform every part of our lives. The wisdom of natural awareness disentangles the layers of our personal suffering, even our subtle tendencies to grasp painfully on to ourselves and on to dualism. Love and compassion increasingly manifest as such wisdom unleashes their boundless energies. When we experience such qualities in morning meditation and recall them during our day, it lessens our self-centered reactions to people and events, for in love and compassion we resonate with others heart to heart, below the radar of self-centered suspicion, possessiveness, and anger.

The path of enlightenment, however, is not just easy and smooth. The practices themselves really challenge us. They confront our sense of self and they refute the world we thought we had known. We had defined our self, in large part, through our reductive labels of others and by our emotional reactions to those labels. Practices of wisdom and love redefine others as worthy of love no matter what and one's self as someone who can love all unconditionally. Such pure perception, at first, seems like a huge leap. It is not easy to learn, like John Nash, to ignore our self-centered delusions and rely instead on the power of loving compassion and wisdom that transcends them.

Meanwhile, whenever we are not in meditation or do not experience its self-transcending power, our ego-centered reactions occur in the usual ways. From long habit, the same situations that have triggered feelings of hurt and painful emotion continue to do so.

Indeed, upsetting thoughts and emotions can seem magnified as the peacefulness of meditation, by contrast, makes us more conscious of their disturbing qualities.

If we persevere with daily practice, the power of wisdom and loving compassion strengthens. Over time, it becomes increasingly present in our life. But in the meantime, what are we to do with our accustomed, ego-centered reactions to difficulties—all the hurtful feelings and painful emotions that continue to come up during our day?

The meditation of compassion speaks directly to this problem. Instead of interpreting feelings of difficulty in ways that intensify our self-centeredness, the practice of compassion reframes them as our connection to others. Every painful feeling we have is an example of what many others feel. To experience them in empathy with others lets us take them into the path of enlightenment.

Taking Difficulties into Compassion on the Spot

> Bodhicitta [the mind of enlightenment] arises in the personality of ordinary beings who are completely attached to samsara. The reason? Such beings constantly grasp at a "self" and thus experience intense feelings of suffering. From the depth of that personal suffering, compassion is born for other sentient beings. This process is the extraordinary cause for becoming a Buddha.
>
> Zhechen Gyaltsab Rinpoche[63]

All feelings of hurt, difficulty, and frustration can be taken directly into compassion and the path of enlightenment. To do so, we need to recall the perspective of wise compassion from our meditation practice and apply that perspective to difficult feelings as we experience them during the day and over the course of our life. Taking difficulties into compassion "on the spot" allows our own problems and sufferings to become a direct link to others, awakening our enlightened potential for empathy, unconditional care, and wisdom.

At first, practice the following steps by yourself, while becoming used to the process. After you are familiar with the practice, you will be able to apply it in almost any situation or environment, "on the spot," whenever a difficulty emerges. The important thing to remember is that you must begin from a place of actually experiencing some form of difficulty. You must be in touch with a specific manifestation of discomfort, troubling emotion, or physical pain. That shouldn't be much of a problem; if we really look, there's almost always something bothering us!

Take the time now to get in touch with an area of discomfort, however small it might be. If you have to "manufacture" a difficulty, recall a recent feeling of difficulty, such as during an unsatisfactory conversation, a physical ailment, an uncomfortable emotion, or experience of anger, disappointment, frustration, loneliness, depression.

Meditation: Taking Difficulties into Compassion

Step 1: Allow yourself to feel and experience the full depth of the discomfort and suffering occurring in your mind and your body, every layer of it. Feel what it's like for someone to undergo this experience.

Step 2: While feeling this difficulty, come to the recognition: "*This* is what so many experience. *This* very feeling." As if you are sensing what others feel. As if your personal discomfort gives you the opportunity to know directly what countless others experience.

Step 3: Recalling your benefactors above and behind you, receive the healing radiance of their compassion into your feelings of suffering. Then let that radiance come through you pervasively to all others who experience similar sufferings. Commune with them through the wish and energy of compassion: "May they have deepest freedom from suffering." Envision that the whole universe of beings is bathed in the gentle, radiant blessing of compassion, evoking their deepest freedom in the nature of their minds.

Step 4: Envision that all beings, becoming deeply free of suffering, experience great joy. Take joy in their joy, as if it were your own.

Step 5: After some time, drop the visualization and relax into oneness with the all-pervasive radiance of compassion, releasing all frames of reference into boundless openness and cognizance, the infinite expanse of the nature of mind.

[Note: if you are "on the spot" at work or driving, you need to maintain your frames of reference, so simply omit this last step.]

The circumstances of suffering differ for individuals, but the underlying feelings of misery are common to us all. Through this practice, our own feelings of difficulty pull us into vivid recognition of what so many others feel.

Without such a practice, we tend to take our sufferings personally in ways that isolate us. We generate much negative karma by clinging to our miseries, blaming others for them, or wallowing in self-pity. But this on-the-spot practice, which follows naturally from the meditation of compassion, does the reverse. It reveals our suffering as undivided from others and theirs from us. It generates tremendous karmic merit for the enlightenment path by harnessing our own suffering to open our minds in compassion to others. And that helps break open our narrow grip on self, to let the infinite radiance of compassion express the wisdom of the mind's infinite nature.

Let's go through a rather common example: Suppose a co-worker criticizes you in front of other people, igniting feelings of hurt and rage in you. Without the practice of compassion, this would be the occasion for anger to reify your sense of self in hatred for the co-worker. But through the steps above, the same emotions become the path of enlightenment.

Apply the steps above. After the incident, when you have a moment to yourself, drop the focus of attention on the person who triggered your anger. Focus instead on the *feeling* of hurt and anger. Feel what it's like for someone to undergo that, experiencing the layers of physical sensation and emotions like frustration, despair, resentment, rage, whatever comes up for you. Then come to the recognition: "*This* is what so many experience. *This* very feeling." Through your own hurt and anger, sense directly what so many others undergo.

Recall your benefactors and receive their compassionate energy into your painful feelings and emotions. Let that radiance come through you to all the others who experience similar sufferings, communing with them in the wish and energy of compassion, evoking their deepest capacity for freedom. Imagine that all others who feel these feelings become released from their self-grasping patterns of anger and hurt and experience the joy of such freedom. Take joy in their joy. Finally, if you are not in the midst of other activities, release through that radiance into the wisdom beyond self-reference.

Through such steps, rather than intensifying self-centeredness, feelings of anger and despair are transmuted into energies of compassion that bless the world.

And when you practice like this throughout the day, it informs your meditation sessions. The meditation instruction to receive compassion into feelings of hurt and anger will not be abstract. You can recall the hurt and anger you felt at your workplace the previous day and take that vividly into your next morning meditation session. *Those* are the layers of mental suffering that are to be bathed in the radiance of compassion.

When you become familiar with the compassion meditation, you can take your benefactors wherever you go. There is no reason to recall them only during formal meditation sessions. You can recall your benefactors above your head and behind you everywhere you go, radiating the power of loving compassion, cradling the painful feelings that come up in your day within the energy of their compassion, and illumining all other beings in the same radiance. In this way, the experiences of your day inform your meditation sessions, and your meditation sessions empower the rest of your day.

Difficult Emotions and People as a Crucial Part of the Path

We can do the on-the-spot practice when any difficult emotions occur. The instruction is the same for every disturbing emotion: loneliness, longing, rage, confusion, fear, grief, guilt, jealousy, feelings of inadequacy, self-hatred, ego-centered pride, and all the rest.

By taking painful emotions into the path in this way we are *not* seeking to avoid them in the name of spirituality. Usually when we experience disturbing emotions, we either want to suppress and forget them as soon as possible or to act them out and rationalize any harm that our actions may cause. The steps above provide a third alternative, neither suppressing nor enacting our painful emotions. Recall the instruction to take the time to feel your emotions, not to dismiss them, and not just to act them out. Through this practice, we become more intimate with our emotions, but instead of being driven by them into deluded actions, their energies are transformed into energies of compassion.

So we are not trying to get our difficult emotions to go away. Instead, we recognize their deeper meaning as our connection to others. In this way, rather than distracting us from the path of enlightenment, our emotions become a crucial part of that path.

Ironically, then, the people and circumstances that trigger our difficult feelings provide critical support for our spiritual path. Since we tend to suppress suffering feelings from coming to conscious awareness, unless other people trigger our difficult emotions, we can't see the painful tendencies that we share with all others. We wouldn't know the basis in our own experience for empathy with others. Whoever triggers such emotions reveals the mental suffering that connects us to all others. Indeed, one sign of progress on the path is gratitude not just to those who send us love but also to those who make difficulties for us. Both are equally crucial for our own spiritual awakening.

Taking Difficult Feelings into Karmic Purification and Compassion

The self's claims of importance are the motor driving samsara and the real enemy of awakening to a healthier way of being.... Whenever we experience harm or suffering, we can trace it to its source in our [own] thoughts and actions, and learn to be independent of the patterns that have bound us.

Tarthang Tulku[64]

[A] benefit of having problems is that you can use them to purify negative karma. Think: "All my problems come only from my negative karma."

Lama Zopa Rinpoche[65]

As explained in chapter 3, all our feelings of unhappiness and happiness are the outflow of our own karma. They are triggered by circumstances around us, but the source of such feelings is in our own mind. Feelings of unhappiness are the fruition of our own past harmful thoughts and actions that were motivated by narrow self-centeredness, hatred, possessiveness, and so forth. Feelings of happiness are the fruition of our own past positive thoughts and actions that were motivated by love, compassion, openness, and wisdom. Other persons and situations trigger feelings in us, but they do not inject them into us. To understand the teaching of karma is to know the difference between the inner cause of our feelings (our own past thoughts and actions) and what triggers them (external conditions and persons) without confusing the two.

If we do not understand karma, when someone's action triggers a feeling of hurt in us, we mistake him as the very source of our feeling and hate him for it. Then we may retaliate in anger, which triggers his feeling of hurt and evokes a hostile response, which reignites our feelings of hurt and resentment, and the cycle of harmful karma and suffering goes on.

Something similar occurs when we want things to go well for us but they don't. If we work on a project and it fails, our expectations are dashed, precipitating feelings of hurt. Mistaking the situation as the very source of our unhappy feeling rather than the trigger of it, we may look for someone to be the object of our blame and bitterness, or we may wallow in self-pity. Again, the cycle of suffering karma is continued.

But when we know the meaning of karma, we can engage feelings of hurt and unhappiness in a completely different way, by using them to purify our negative karma and to cut the suffering cycle of karmic reaction. When we feel hurt, no matter who or what triggered it, *we can accept the feeling itself as the fruition of our own past actions.* By taking responsibility and accepting our unpleasant feelings in this way, we don't reinforce our ego-centered tendencies for harmful reaction. Harmful karma from our past is burned up as it comes to fruition in our present feelings. And since there is no defensive reaction to those feelings, just deep acceptance of them, the cycle of karma is severed. In this way, our feelings of misery, rather than reinforcing harmful tendencies of karmic reaction, purify our minds of those tendencies.

Indeed, this gives us another reason to feel gratitude to those who activate painful feelings in us. When we know how to take such feelings into the practice, we realize that the people who give us trouble are helping us to progress on the path. They assist us in burning away the suffering results of our negative karma and in purifying our minds of its tendencies.

Such karmic purification is contextualized by our practice of compassion. Like ourselves, all other beings experience unhappiness as the outflow of their own harmful karma and have reacted to it with further harmful actions that only generate more suffering for them. Knowing this, we can accept our difficult feelings as an example of what all others are undergoing, generating compassion for them. Thus, by accepting our own painful feelings, we not only purify our mind but generate tremendous karmic merit in compassion for others.

Buddhist masters, drawing upon the teaching of rebirth, have explained that such practice purifies eons of negative karma from our past lives. Whatever cosmological beliefs you may have, you can feel the power of this practice to purify your mind of its entrenched tendencies of self-centered reaction and to generate positive energy in compassion for others. As we experience this spiritual power, the difficult circumstances that previously elicited only our anger or self-pity begin to evoke joy, for we are learning how to experience such circumstances in ways that fulfill the deeper purpose of life.[66]

Taking Suffering Directly into Wisdom

When the nonconceptual wisdom of natural awareness becomes strong enough through familiarity in meditation, to recall that wisdom becomes the most direct way to take difficult experiences into the path.

> Since nothing, ultimately, has any existence whatsoever, if you look at the actual nature of the disturbing emotions or suffering, you will see that they are non-arising even from the first.
>
> Zhechen Gyaltsab Rinpoche[67]

When something disturbs you, and you are caught in the turmoil of difficult emotions, recall how you suffer by identifying with the self-clinging content of your thoughts and emotions instead of recognizing their nature. Having remembered this, let yourself come into recognition of the very essence of the thoughts and emotions. Rest directly in the abiding nature of the experience, cognizant emptiness, which is already free of suffering. Rest directly in the infinite, luminous openness of all experience—beyond change, beyond grasping, beyond all reference points of personal suffering.

If this perspective doesn't feel possible yet, it means that the strength of nonconceptual wisdom from meditation has not yet developed enough to be called upon so directly in ordinary life. But if you are familiar with the sharp inquiries of chapter 2 that support wisdom, you can draw upon them in the moment of difficult emotion. As Khyentse Rinpoche explains:

> ...in that which is termed deluded, there is nothing impure, nothing to rid ourselves of. Neither is there something else, pure and undeluded, which we should try to adopt. For, indeed, when illusion dissolves, undeluded wisdom is simply

present, where it always has been…if we subject the deluded mind to analysis, and reach the conclusion that it is free from birth, cessation and abiding existence, we will discover, then and there, a wisdom which is undeluded.

Dilgo Khyentse Rinpoche[68]

When you experience thoughts of anger, for example, recall that you suffer by clinging to the self-centered content of your thoughts; from not recognizing their nature. Then recall one of the sharp inquiries you know from practice and bring it vividly to mind. Use the inquiry you've found most effective to short circuit the ego-centered mind, to undercut the grip on "self" and "other," to permit your points of reference to collapse into ungraspable emptiness and cognizance, the sky-like nature of mind.

For example, ask yourself: "From where do these thoughts and feelings arise?" Letting that question guide your attention, trace the radiance of thoughts and feelings to their empty, luminous ground. Or ask: "Where are these thoughts dissolving?" or "Where are they located?" or "Who is experiencing?" If you have begun to experience the power of such inquiries in formal meditation sessions, you can invoke them in the moment of suffering, so suffering itself becomes the stimulus to direct you toward the wisdom to be discovered in the very nature of your experience.[69]

In these ways, painful feelings and emotions become allies for our practice. They show us when we are lost in the hallucinations of self-centeredness instead of abiding in the nature of mind that recognizes them as hallucinations. They remind us to return to refuge in the Dharma, by taking our sufferings into compassion, into karmic purification, or into recognition of the empty, radiant nature of all experience.

Where there is hallucination, there is the truth, by recognizing it as hallucination. Where there is suffering, there is peace and bliss, by letting go and experiencing it for numberless suffering beings.

Lama Zopa Rinpoche[70]

Great Compassion

Great compassion *(mahakaruna)* is a Buddhist term for the fullest form of compassion. It wills the freedom of all beings *from all three levels* of suffering while sensing each one as dear. And it assumes responsibility to help them achieve such freedom, knowing it to be possible. Such universal compassion is a purified perception and will that communes with and evokes the deepest good of each being without exception, while taking all personal difficulties into the path of enlightenment for their sake.[71]

Shabkar Rinpoche expresses the qualities of such compassion in further advice to his student, following upon the quote at the beginning of this chapter:

The same number of years you spent meditating on emptiness, you should now spend meditating day and night on compassion—a compassion a hundred times stronger than that of a mother for a child burnt in a fire, an unbearably intense compassion that arises when thinking about the suffering of sentient beings.

Once such compassion is born, you must practice until you come to think, with fierce energy, "Until enlightenment, I shall do whatever is possible to benefit all beings, not omitting a single one—no matter what evil actions they commit, and now matter what difficulties I must endure."[72]

May this exhortation echo within us, motivating us to take our practice into the full depth of compassion and wisdom.

7. Living Life Anew and Embodying Deep Goodness

Summing Up Our Situation

The introduction argued that authentic love, grounded in deep wisdom, is the basis of our safety and well-being and the essential motivation to truly benefit others. In addition, I argued that the ability to embody such love is not given to just a few—anyone can realize the life-transforming power of love and compassion by entering fully enough into the requisite practices—such as the meditations presented in chapters 1 through 6.

As I also noted in the introduction, children thrive with unconditional love. They only feel at home in the world when they receive the love that upholds their essential goodness, no matter how crazy their young minds may be at times. But none of us outgrows that need. We *all* need to know that someone perceives the fundamental goodness of our being and holds us in that pure vision, even when we are most lost in the dark places of our minds. When held safe in the love of our benefactors, our own capacity to love can manifest and be extended similarly to others, holding them safe in its pure vision. Through the meditations of prior chapters, we've learned to experience love and compassion as boundless qualities innate to us—healing, liberating powers that can be drawn upon at any time.

As we've seen, however, our egos draw back from the boundless qualities of our fundamental awareness by conjuring a rigid, narrow, and substantial sense of self. Depending on whether people confirm or disconfirm that limited self-concept, the ego categorizes them as worthy or unworthy to be loved. Individually and socially conditioned in this way, our minds routinely hide the profound worth and dignity of self and others, preventing us from responding to each with care and reverence. Without a clear practice of impartial love and wisdom to cut through that basic error, we react to our labels for others rather than to actual persons, and we don't even notice the difference. People everywhere are caught in this dangerous error, the cause of much harm and a great deal of suffering.

As I write this, the recent news is that dozens of people abducted in Iraq were found tortured to death and beheaded. Elsewhere in the Middle East, rockets were fired into crowds, dismembering men, women, and children. A retaliatory airstrike maimed and killed many more. Each side, viewing themselves as the victims, self-righteously called for revenge in the name of justice. A husband and father in my city inflicted so much abuse on his middle-aged wife that she brought herself and her children to a shelter. An angry young loner, shunned by his peers, tried to kill many strangers at a local bar. Two young parents, momentarily enraged by their infant's endless crying, shook her into a coma. A gang youth fired his gun at a rival across the street, killing a three-year-old girl.

At the moment of their actions, these perpetrators paid attention just to their own self-centered thoughts of the ones they sought to harm, not to their full humanity. In the years prior to the fateful moment of these perpetrators' actions, others had done likewise to them: reacting to reductive thoughts of them rather than to their full humanity. After the perpetrators' horrific actions, many who heard the news paid attention only to their thought of the perpetrators as subhuman, calling for violent revenge in the name of "justice," with little attention to the specifics of their lives or to the potential for good in even such flawed human beings.

Note the extraordinary position our meditations have put us in. The meditations of love, compassion, and wisdom thoroughly undercut the individual and social mechanisms driving such harmful actions and reactions. They reveal *all* persons as worthy of love and ourselves as people who *can* love them unconditionally and impartially. These practices draw us into a purer way of perceiving that upholds the fundamental goodness and potential of *all* persons, however flawed, while empowering us to challenge their harmful tendencies.

When anyone, anywhere, learns to abide in such loving wisdom, they generate a zone of refuge and protection that encircles all those around them. They become a force to remake this world into a place of deep mutual reverence and appreciation. To learn to embody such wise love, and to act from there for the sake of all, is the greatest gift we can give to our families, communities, and world. To abide in such love also generates tremendous karmic power for progress in spiritual awakening and for experiencing our lives with increasing joy.

At the beginning of our practice the shift of consciousness from ego-centeredness to such pure perception may seem like a huge leap. But as we persevere with practice over time, wisdom and loving compassion become increasingly present in us, affecting everything. For the process to unfold fully, we must establish a regular meditation practice and learn to apply its power in every part of our lives. We also need the support of spiritual friends and teachers mature in the enlightened qualities that we seek to realize.

Establishing a Daily Practice

For love, compassion, and wisdom to become strong, you need a daily meditation that evokes those qualities. A session of meditation each morning establishes your frame of mind for the rest of the day.

When you are familiar with the meditations of chapters 5 and 6, alternate them to bring out the qualities of each. For example, you could do the meditation of love and wisdom daily for a month, compassion and wisdom daily the next month, and so on. Or you could do both meditations each day, one in the morning, the other in the evening.

If you don't meditate each day—in the morning if possible—you won't have anything to integrate into the rest of the day. But if you rest in natural wisdom and hold others in unconditional care during a morning session, you can return to that perspective throughout the day. Loving compassion and wisdom can then flow naturally into your relationships and interactions, infusing them with grace and ease.

Remember, the rigid sense of self that obstructs our potential to love is nothing more than a chain of shifting thoughts. So if you think, "I can't change, I'm not a loving person," remember that those thoughts are nothing more than a momentary fabrication, containing no real claim to truth. Such a thin veil of ego-centered thinking in the head is all that obscures our potential for communing with others from the heart. By recalling the perspective of morning meditation at other times of the day, we can resonate with others at heart level—below the reactivity of everyone's egos—and extend the healing energy of love and compassion to whomever we meet.

Recalling the Perspective of Morning Meditation throughout the Day

Recalling Natural Wisdom throughout the Day

In the last step of every meditation session, you merge with the radiance of love or compassion and relax into the abiding nature of mind, the sky-like expanse of openness and awareness beyond reference points. In this way, meditation each morning familiarizes you with the natural wisdom of resting in simplicity, beyond grasping on to self or any sense of separateness. During the day, you can recall this wisdom when with others and relax within natural awareness wherever you are, just as in morning meditation. To do so is to become more fully present to others, not lost in self-concerned worries, not clinging to yourself as separate from them. To abide like that while with others is to enjoy them in their very being and to listen deeply, which also brings them much happiness.

When you are outside in the natural world, gazing upon a wide-open vista or sitting by the sea, let that vast panorama pull your mind beyond its narrow posture of self-clinging into the vast expanse of natural awareness. Let the limitless spaciousness of the sky awaken your limitless "inner sky" of cognizance and openness. In this way, you can allow the infinite spaciousness of the outer world to help pull you gently into recognition of the infinite nature of mind.[73]

Recalling Love and Compassion throughout the Day

In morning meditation you also extend the wish and energy of love and compassion to many beings in widening circles as the expression of wisdom. At that time, be sure to specifically direct the radiant wish of love and compassion to all the people you plan to see later in the day and to all the places you will go: your home, workplace, the streets you will travel, the places you will visit, and so forth. Then as you see and meet people in those places throughout the day, let the contact pull you back, on the spot, into the perspective and energy of your meditation session. Morning meditation revealed your world as a holy realm—all others sensed as sacred. As you see them around you in the day, commune again with the intrinsic goodness of their being beyond reductive labels, making it natural to respond to each with reverence and care.

Key Points for Integrating Practice into Your Life

Throughout the day, at times when there's no need to plan or interact, just be present in the wisdom of natural awareness—attentive,
joyfully at ease in whatever you do, at rest in the abiding nature of
experience that is wide open, fresh, mysterious, and undivided. Let
each part of your day flow from that undivided openness, without
pulling back into a small, defended sense of self. When you need
actively to plan or to interact with people, let the natural openness
and responsiveness of that innate wisdom take expression in
thoughts and actions of love and compassion. In these simple ways,
wisdom and love continue to inform your life from morning to
night, gradually transforming your mind and body into the emis-
sary of those enlightened qualities.

Integrating Meditation into Each Part of Your Day

> We need not think that we work, have a job and family, and
> therefore cannot be true Dharma practitioners...the essence
> of Dharma is the precious bodhichitta [the spirit of enlight-
> enment], which can be cultivated in any circumstances and
> during any activity.... We can all practice the Dharma in
> mind, while being engaged in any form of activity with body
> and speech.
>
> Nyoshul Khen Rinpoche[74]

If you learn to integrate the spirit of wisdom and love into many
little moments, day by day, it transforms your life and blesses those
around you. Recall the spirit of morning meditation at meals, on a
walk, when watching television or reading the paper, when playing
games, when visiting with others, and so forth. When there is no
need to talk, simply rest in natural awareness. When interacting with

others, radiate the love and compassion of that awareness to all, as in the following examples.

At the Breakfast Table

If your partner or children join you at breakfast, commune with them in the radiance of love recalled from morning meditation, as you help them with their meals and chat at the table. If you read the morning newspaper, make the deep wish of compassion for those you read about who are suffering; take joy in those who benefit others. When you hug your children, partner, or pet before leaving for work, let the hug seal them with the blessing of love and compassion still vivid from morning meditation.

Commuting to Work

While commuting to work, recall your benefactors above your head or in your heart, and let the wish and radiance of love rain down upon all the commuters and passersby around you. When caught in a traffic jam, notice your feelings of frustration, look at the multitude of drivers around you undergoing similar misery, receive the radiance of compassion, and let its healing energy extend to them all.

Interpret red stoplights as a signal to rest for that brief interlude in natural awareness and love. When feelings of anxiety arise because of cars and trucks that whiz nearby or from anticipation of a difficult day ahead, proceed with compassion for the drivers and pedestrians all around you who experience similar anxieties.

Arriving at Your Workplace

Recall how your workplace was blessed by the radiance of love and compassion during your morning meditation and actually encounter that blessing as you arrive there—sensing the environment as a radiant holy realm. As you greet co-workers, students, or clients, continue the spirit of meditation. Recognize them as sacred beings and commune with the goodness of their being, no matter who they think they are or how you had thought of them before taking up this practice.

Many people, when with others, think they need to talk continually to feel connected. But by extending the spirit of meditation into our day, we intuit our connection to others just by communing with and taking joy in them, whether any conversation happens or not. Notice how those around you respond to such simple communion, even when it is wordless.

At Work

Start your workday before you go to work; take time during morning meditation to receive plenty of loving compassion from benefactors before resting in natural awareness and then radiating its wish and energy to clients, patients, students, or others you will serve throughout your workday. Then, as you actually meet those people, resume and inhabit that very practice: Hold them in the vision and energy of reverence and love. Mirror their fundamental goodness back at them, evoking their best potential.

If you are a schoolteacher, for example, during morning meditation, envision yourself receiving the radiance of loving compassion and letting it radiate through you to all your students. Then merge with that radiance and rest in natural awareness. Throughout your day, periodically return to this practice and inhabit it. The moment you step into the classroom, begin communing with your students heart-to-heart in pure perception, radiating unconditional care below the radar of self-concerned judgments—theirs or yours. Let your wish for your students' deep well-being help evoke their innate abilities for discernment, compassion, and joy. Sense them through the wisdom that recognizes the undivided nature of mind.

One of my Dharma students, Terry, applies these principles while mentoring and counseling prisoners. These men, often lost in hateful thoughts of themselves and angry thoughts about others, are not used to being viewed through the pure perception of Terry's practice, which senses their potential for good while holding them responsible for their lives. To be viewed in that way has been life transforming for many of them.

If you are a social activist, take your interactions with supporters and opponents as chances to strengthen such pure perception and impartial care. To uphold everyone's essential goodness and potential is to imply that the political habit of reducing opponents to nothing more than "strangers" and "enemies" is a serious mistake. To abide in such pure perception provides both an important social challenge and a protection for everyone around you.

If you feel tense, frustrated, or tired at work, take a break, even if it is only brief. Recall your benefactors above your head or in your heart and bathe the tensions of mind and body in the healing radiance of their loving compassion. Then merge into oneness with that luminosity and rest in natural awareness for however long you have. Let such love and wisdom refresh and make you more fully present to whatever you do next.

As you strategize and perform tasks, periodically recall your benefactors above your head or in your heart and let their radiant compassion extend to many others right through the activities of your body and mind.

When you attend a meeting, drop to heart level and commune with other participants in reverence and radiant compassion. When you speak at the meeting, speak from that place. Notice how such speech affects others. Contrast that to the effect on them when you find yourself speaking from a more self-centered perspective.

Notice, over time, how *any* selfishness in your actions toward others tends to evoke a self-centered reaction from them. Notice when you abide in wise love and compassion, even for a moment, how it tends to evoke the inner sanity of others.

It's important frequently to recall that you are not just a *giver* of love but also a *receiver* of it. So receive it often from your benefactors over the course of your day. As you merge daily with them in the luminosity of love and release into natural awareness, love's source is revealed again and again as the unconditioned nature of mind, wherein you and others have never been divided.

When You Feel Upset

When you feel downhearted at work, discouraged by difficulties and disappointments, or angry with a co-worker or client, remember how human such feelings are. First have compassion for yourself. Recall your benefactors' radiant wish of compassion. Bathe your body and mind in that healing energy. Recall that many others experience the same difficult feelings you are undergoing, and let the wish and energy of compassion extend to them in widening circles. Finally, as in meditation sessions, release the visualization, merge into oneness with the luminosity, and relax in natural awareness.

By integrating such meditation practices into so many moments of the day, you rediscover your work as a growing expression of impartial love and simple presence. Sense those qualities gradually empowering you to persevere with difficult people or situations. Now your work provides the opportunity to embody the awareness and care from your meditations, instead of identifying with a brittle ego that gets easily discouraged by adversities. Even if you flame up in anger in the moment of a painful incident, as we all do at times, notice your growing capacity to come back to the spirit of meditation sooner after the incident. Explore how your practice affects others: both those you serve and your coworkers.

> If we have a very pure heart and a clear, altruistic mind, we
> may encounter difficulties or sufferings, but eventually we
> are sure to reach bliss and happiness: it is the inevitable result

of having good intention, positive attitude, and purity of heart. If we have a very wicked, disharmonious, and negative mind, we may meet with temporary success, but ultimately we will have to taste the fruit of suffering.... It is only the quality of our minds that will result in happiness or suffering, both for ourselves and for others.

Nyoshul Khen Rinpoche[75]

Vocation

By integrating meditation practice into your life, you don't just learn how to function better within your current job and career. You also receive light on what you feel called to do with your life, your vocation. Practice helps clarify what kind of work may best express your growing spiritual understanding and concern.

The time may come when you don't just bring the power of meditation into your workplace but reevaluate the whole question of where you want to work in order to embody the spiritual principles most important to you. Some work environments or kinds of work more readily evoke your best potential and help you remember your spiritual practice. Others may feel too oppressive—at least at your current stage of practice—for you to function within them as a spiritual practitioner. You need to be realistic about where you are in your practice and not become recurrently overwhelmed by taking on more than you can handle in your job or in your spiritual life.

When You Feel that Others Are in Your Way

When you are waiting to be served in a restaurant or store and find yourself getting impatient and annoyed, notice the tendency in your mind to label the waiter, counter clerk, or people ahead of you in line as mere annoyances that are in your way. Catch your mind as it reduces them in that way. Recall how people everywhere in similar circumstances also diminish others and get angry, causing much tension and conflict. Receive the radiant compassion of benefactors, and let its healing energy extend through you to all those who get similarly annoyed, while wishing them deep freedom from such suffering. Remember to invoke your practice whenever you find yourself momentarily angry, thinking of another person as just an obstacle.

There is also a way to bring wisdom more directly into such situations. As you learn to abide increasingly in natural awareness, you also become more conscious of your ego reactions as soon as they arise. When it feels like someone is in your way, notice how negative thoughts form chains of self-centered thinking—as though the chains of thought were trying to make a narrow, defensive boundary around yourself. While abiding in natural awareness, instead of letting such thoughts spin into further chains, let them self-liberate as they arise. Let the thoughts spontaneously release themselves back into their own fundamental awareness, like water patterns absorbed into their own wateriness.

When you catch on to this way of experiencing thoughts, do it frequently throughout the day. Explore what it's like to abide wide open in natural awareness wherever you are, fully present to others, rather than identifying with self-concerned thought chains. See what difference that makes for the quality of your experience and for everyone around you.

Arriving Home

When you arrive home from a long day at work, try to take a short break before interacting much with family members or roommates. Use that time to rest a little in the tranquil nature of your mind. Also receive the vivifying energy of your benefactors' compassion into your whole body and mind, healing your tensions and frustrations, letting the luminosity extend to family and roommates, then to many others in widening circles. Refreshed, let this loving energy bless your subsequent interactions with family or friends during dinner preparation and throughout the meal.

Dinnertime

When you sit down for supper, don't just *say* grace, *be* the grace of natural awareness that spontaneously extends the radiance of compassion to all at the table. Let that radiance extend from your table outward to all the supper tables in the neighborhood and the world. When you pass the butter or salt to someone at the table, offer it reverently to them in their buddha nature. When you eat, offer the pleasant taste and energy of the food to the Buddha or the main benefactor at your heart, who radiates his blessing to all at your table and to everyone who sits down to eat everywhere in the world.

Sleeping Practice

When going to sleep, according to Tibetan instruction and experience, the mind passes through several natural stages that are similar to the stages of dying. At first, your attention focuses externally on yourself as you are lying on the bed in your room. As you begin to drift off, the mind relaxes and attention turns to inner phenomena: images, fantasies, and spontaneously unfolding streams of thought. As sleep deepens, all such inner phenomena absorb into a vast sense of openness and luminosity, the clear light of sleep that dawns just before dreams begin.

As you lie down at night to sleep, imagine you are resting your head in the lap of the Buddha (or your own main spiritual benefactor), and receive the healing radiance of his unconditional love and compassion into your body and mind from head to toe. As you drift off to sleep through the stages above, let this loving radiance merge with the vast openness and luminosity that dawns just prior to dreaming. Let be in that clear light, at rest in the mind's infinitely spacious, clear, and knowing nature. Such practice at bedtime helps prepare the mind to recognize its unconditioned nature at the time of death, to be liberated there into its nirvanic, tranquil essence.

Nourishing and Protecting Your Family with Wisdom and Love

Let all the rituals of family life be rediscovered as gestures of wise love. When your child wants to share the stories of his day, take that chance to be fully present and to listen with complete attention. When he tells you about his friends or teachers, quietly extend the radiant wish of deep well-being to include your child's circle of acquaintances. Do the same when your partner shares stories of the people in his or her life.

Bring the spirit of meditation into leisure time when playing with your children. Commune with them in the radiance of love and compassion as they deal the cards, take a turn on the game board, or toss a ball. In that spirit, when you look into their eyes, your gaze will naturally mirror their essential goodness even without talking.

A new father recently attended a meditation retreat with me where he was introduced to these meditations and found them inspiring. But he worried how he would make time at home for regular meditation, since his baby required so much care with bathing, bottle feeding, putting her to bed, and so forth. I told him to view those times as special opportunities to engage the spirit of meditation. "While bathing your baby in water," I said, "also bathe her in the radiant wish of love and compassion. While waiting for her to drift off to sleep, transmit your benefactors' loving energy to her, and let its radiance extend to all other babies in the world who need such unconditional care. When she is sucking milk from her bottle, let her also 'suck' the radiant wish of love from your heart to nourish her with its energy. Let this luminous wish extend to all babies, then to all others who were once babies but who *never* grow out of the basic human need for unconditional love."

When your partner or child says or does something that angers you, avoid acting out your anger in ways you will later regret. Instead, take a few moments to recall your practice. If you can, step away for a short time to feel the painful emotions you are experiencing, to sense what it's like for anyone to experience such feelings. Receive the healing energy of your benefactors' compassion into your mind and body. Recall how many other parents and partners feel similar difficulty, and let the radiance of compassion extend to them all. Finally, merge into oneness with that luminosity, and relax your mind in natural awareness. The care and wisdom evoked by such practice provide what is necessary to respond wisely to your family.

Your child's own deep need is to know she is held by love, no matter who she thinks she is or what she thinks she is doing. Such unconditional love is what makes your child feel truly at home. To hold your family in your pure perception of their essential goodness is to evoke their capacity to acknowledge their own goodness and to recognize the same in others, encircling all in a zone of protection. Extend the same pure vision naturally to friends of your child who come into your home, holding them in its protection as well.

To maintain a loving attitude doesn't mean that rules and disciplines are to be ignored. My wife and I set strict limits on television and computer time that have not always been easy to enforce. But parents maintain such disciplines best with an attitude of stable care rather than acting from flashes of rage they experience in moments when their children don't cooperate. Everyone in your family knows, deep down, that the most important thing in all situations is to love everyone involved and to challenge them as needed only from that perspective. When you act from momentary uncontrolled rage, it is *not* an act of love, and everyone, including your child, knows it. When your child consciously breaks the rules, to withdraw some of her privileges is an effective discipline only if she *knows* she is still being unconditionally loved. And she knows that only to the extent that you *embody* wise love in many little ways with her, not just by voicing it.

As you integrate spiritual practice into so many aspects of life, family members may manifest mysteriously as emissaries of wisdom and compassion. When my son Jonathan was three years old, he went through a phase of fascination with the concept of "teasing," wanting to know when any interaction fit the definition of teasing. That summer, I was away for several weeks on a silent Dzogchen retreat which included the intensive practice of self-inquiry: "Who is meditating? Who, what is aware?" At retreat's end, I called home. Jonathan answered the phone. Excited to hear my voice, he squeaked, "Daddy!"

"Yes," I replied.

"Who are you?" he asked, out of the blue.

Stunned, my mind stopped. After a brief silence, I heard Jonathan's giggling voice: "Just teasing, Daddy!"

On another occasion, when my younger son David was three, he came into the kitchen with his teddy bear and asked his mother for juice. She replied, *"After* you drink some milk, you may have some juice."

Little David began to whine, "But I want juice! I want juice! I want juice...."

Deciding to play the wise father, I picked up David's teddy bear and pretended that the bear was calling to David in a high-pitched voice, "No, *I* want the juice! *I* want the juice for *me!*"

At first David smiled, then frowned at the bear, saying, "No, the juice is for *me*."

Teddy replied, "But *why? I* want it, too."

David firmly replied, "Because you're just *pretend,* Teddy."

Teddy paused for a moment, studying David's face, and then started protesting, "No! I'm not pretend! I'm not pretend! *You're* pretend!"

David said firmly, "No *I'm* not pretend, Teddy, *you're* pretend."

Teddy began shaking and sobbing and David, with a concerned look, asked, "What's wrong, Teddy?"

Teddy said, "You mean, *I'm* just pretend, and you're *not?*"

David picked up Teddy and tenderly hugged him, saying, "It's okay, Teddy, we can *both* be pretend," leaving Dad somewhat speechless at his son's intuitive grasp of compassion and wisdom.

Sharing Spiritual Practices with Children

Spiritual practices can certainly be taught to children. My wife and I have practiced with our children in simple ways since they were small. When our boys were very little, they could relate best to some of the rituals of Buddhist practice. At the age of three, they loved to bow to the statues of the Buddha and spiritual benefactors arrayed on our altar. They jostled each other over who would help light incense first, who would help pour water into bowls and put flowers and food on the altar as sensory offerings to enlightenment. They also loved to chant simple prayers and mantras before sitting with us in silence for a few minutes.

Between the ages of five and eleven, our sons became progressively more receptive to abbreviated meditation instructions of love and wisdom. At that point, one stage at a time, we taught them how to identify their benefactors, how to receive love deeply and merge with their benefactors in that light, how to transmit the radiant wish of love in widening circles to the people and animals in their neighborhood, school, and the world.

One evening, when David was five, he came into the bathroom and put himself into meditation posture on the floor while Barbara helped Jonathan finish brushing his teeth. Jonathan laughed, but David, quite seriously, kept meditating there on the floor. After a few minutes, he said, "Wow! Meditating on love is amazing. There really is light coming out of my body." Later, I told David he could experiment like that whenever he wants and can talk with me or with Mommy about what he experiences, but otherwise it would probably be best to keep it to himself. He said, "Good. And Daddy, when you experiment, have you seen all that light in the heart?"

At thirteen, Jonathan started to enjoy participating in one-day meditation retreats, especially with spiritual teachers who have a good sense of humor, and at fourteen he's begun to voice interest in longer retreats. He has also enjoyed reading biographies of spiritual masters that give vivid descriptions of their meaningful encounters and experiences. It's important, Barbara and I have found, to gauge the child's developmental stages of spiritual interest and understanding and to introduce practices and readings as appropriate for those stages.

Once our teacher, Nyoshul Khenpo, was asked what he recommended for parents who want to teach their children the Dharma. First and foremost, he said, parents should learn to be good *practitioners* of the Dharma—to embody enduring love, compassion, patience, and wisdom. Children closely observe their parents and internalize what they observe in them, not just what they are told by them. If the parents are not really living the Dharma, he said, their children are likely to have little interest in it.

Paying New Attention to the Dignity of All

An enjoyable time to integrate meditation practice is when you are out doing errands, surrounded by people unknown to you. In the grocery store, notice all the people that your mind tends to label "stranger." Then rest in natural wisdom, simple presence, beyond clinging to any sense of separation between self and other. Or recall your morning meditation when you leaned in past the label "stranger" to commune heart to heart in love or compassion, and inhabit that perspective on the spot. Practice similarly when shopping for clothes, sitting in a restaurant, picking up dry cleaning, shopping in a mall, traveling on a bus or train, waiting at the airport, and so forth.

In time such practice begins to reveal the remarkable dignity and sacredness of everyone around you wherever you are. As this occurs, it feels as though blinders are being taken from your eyes. The label "strangers" drops away, letting you sense people freshly in the goodness of their being, while cognizant of the subtle layers of suffering in all our lives. Such compassionate perception is like beholding a painting by a great master, a work of art that mysteriously expresses the tremendous dignity of each of its figures. A few Dharma students have told me that they are sometimes so moved by the dignified presence of the people around them, on a street corner, in a bus or store, that they could weep with reverence for them all.

Thomas Merton writes about a similar experience. He had spent years in contemplative practice at a Catholic monastery in Kentucky, where he prayed, worshiped, and communed with all others in the love of God. One day he went to Louisville on an errand for the monastery. He wrote:

> In Louisville, at the corner of fourth and Walnut, in the center of the shopping district, I was suddenly overwhelmed with the realization that I loved all those people, that they were mine and I theirs, that we could not be alien to one another even though we were total strangers. It was like waking from a dream of separateness, of spurious self-isolation…. Then it was as if I suddenly saw the secret beauty of their hearts, the depths of their hearts where neither sin

nor desire…can reach, the core of their reality, the person that each one is in God's eyes. If only they could all see themselves as they really *are*. If only we could see each other that way all the time. There would be no more war, no more hatred, no more cruelty, no more greed…. I suppose the big problem would be that we would fall down and worship each other.[76]

As you sense the tremendous dignity of others, let your attention turn to the kinds of people you hadn't previously noticed—people routinely marginalized and banished to the realm of "strangers." Pay fresh attention to people in racial, ethnic, or social groups different from your own, those who are poorly clothed or homeless, those imprisoned in habits of addiction or abuse, those denigrated for their sexual orientation, and so forth. As the label "stranger" comes crashing down, let the dignity of each such person reveal itself to you, evoking your reverence and care. Recall such people later when you meditate on compassion. Remember how it felt at times in your life when others held you distastefully at a distance, when you were judged or dismissed as a stranger, even if your experience was far less severe. Let such memories help you empathize with what others are feeling, empowering your compassion and care for them.

Recently Barbara, Jonathan, David, and I took a walk in a nearby park, lingering to watch some immigrants from South America play a passionate, friendly game of soccer. Another time we passed children at play under the loving eye of parents and grandparents. How natural it is to recall the spirit of meditation in those moments, to radiate care and compassion to all those "strangers," to connect with their essential goodness while mindful of the impermanence and suffering hidden within all our lives.

The Need for Mature Spiritual Community

Anyone can realize greater love, compassion, and wisdom by regularly practicing meditations like the ones in this book. But individuals who try to practice on their own, without the support of other practitioners, usually have difficulty sustaining and deepening their practice over the long term. In order to progress in our practice, we need support from people mature in the practice, others who share in the pure perception to which we are awakening. There are several reasons for this.

The first reason is that meditations of impartial love and wisdom are extremely challenging on a personal level. These meditations not only undercut our egos in their ways of labeling and reacting to everyone, but they also challenge and shake up our attachment to a particular social and cultural identity. Because we are learning to see the world in ways that many around us do *not* share, our process of awakening can sometimes feel like a very lonely endeavor.

Most members of society are *not* regularly engaged in meditations to awaken impartial love and compassion. Social discourse routinely characterizes people as objects of apathy, indignation, or possessiveness, which reinforces our own habit of doing similarly. We find support for our self-centered visions of the world through the social chatter of the group we are in, which defines itself by distinguishing its members from those in other groups who are viewed as mere strangers. This is why people who identify most strongly with an ethnic identity, nationality, or political party often have difficulty viewing people outside their group as full human beings, equal to themselves in worth and dignity, whose fundamental needs and human potential are similar to their own. To integrate wise, impartial love and compassion into one's life is culturally subversive. It challenges the partialities assumed in every society.

Recently, I taught a course on Buddhist meditation theory at my university. Besides assigned reading, students were required to meditate each day and to write about specific ways that study and meditation illumined their lives, for most of them as practicing Christians and Jews. After months of such practice, a student reported that daily meditation was "blowing her mind," revealing a capacity for impartial care that she hadn't known she had. "But," she said, "this practice is *so* radical—it opens up a way of seeing and responding *so* different from what many others around me are thinking and saying. I can't imagine carrying this practice on just by myself, without the support of the others in this class." That student had begun to realize why spiritual community is indispensable in the world's traditions of spiritual practice and why *sangha* is one of the fundamental refuges of Buddhist tradition.

When others around us actually embody the impartial care, compassion, equanimity, and wisdom that arise from meditation, they inspire and uplift us in our own practice—the enlightened qualities they embody become *real* for us, not just abstract ideals. Those who are spiritually mature from long practice exemplify what is possible, demonstrating that we *can* realize the same qualities if we practice in a similarly whole-hearted way.

Also, inevitably there are times on the spiritual path when our individual egos go astray. As we practice these powerful meditations in a sustained way, various spiritual experiences and epiphanies occur, and we may get over-excited by them. At other times, when meditation doesn't seem to go well, we may feel overwhelmed by distraction, lethargy, or personal difficulties and feel like giving up the practice. We may sometimes get lost in personal fantasies of spiritual greatness or unworthiness, holding ourselves back from further progress through spiritual pride or self-deprecation. We may start to take ourselves much too seriously. To help cut through all such deceptive mental states, we need to rely on other practitioners who have meditated longer than us, who know firsthand what we are undergoing from their own experience. Such spiritual friends are essential to provide us with wise input, advice, and encouragement. They can also demonstrate how progressing spiritually can improve our sense of humor.

The Path of Awakening Is Intrinsically Communal

There is an even more fundamental reason why the path of enlightenment unfolds within spiritual community. The enlightenment of a buddha, by its very nature, is *not* an isolated attainment. The path of fullest enlightenment is intrinsically communal, always in relationship with others, because what we awaken to is the loving compassion that we share with others, which is grounded in the nature of mind beyond separation from others.

We awaken because others have awakened before us and radiated their wise love and compassion to us, triggering our own process of awakening. When our practice becomes strong, it similarly inspires others in widening circles of illumination. That is why, as noted earlier, full enlightenment is imaged as a luminous buddha that joyously radiates the liberating powers of love and wisdom to widening circles of bodhisattvas and beings. By integrating our meditations into our lives, we similarly awaken to widening circles of communion and pure perception, spiritual connection and community, to bless, inspire, and support each other on the path. The circle of support within one's own spiritual community provides the secure foundation from which to extend impartial, enduring love and compassion to numerous other beings.

Authentic spiritual masters emerge from within such mature spiritual communities to function as teachers under their auspices. For this reason, when you find a spiritual teacher whose teaching resonates deeply with your heart, you often discover that his or her spiritual community is also your own.

Transmission and Guidance from Awakened Teachers

Spiritual teachers, such as those quoted in this book, took up practices of wisdom and love with such dedication that they became conduits of inspiration and guidance for many others. But their development did not occur in isolation. Earlier in their lives they found teachers who embodied the enlightened qualities that they sought. From such figures, they received transmission and teaching over the years. They also relied on their teachers' spiritual communities for encouragement, advice, and support. That is how they learned to practice so effectively. Eventually their authorizing teachers and community requested them to pass on what they had learned. As the proverb says: "It takes a village to raise a child." It also takes an experienced spiritual community to raise an awakened teacher.

Recall that our practice is to awaken pure perception, to let the buddha in us perceive the sacredness of beings and the primordial purity of things. Authentic teachers of love, compassion, and wisdom have realized such perception through their training. By practicing similarly under their guidance, we seek to do the same. If no one had ever awakened in such a way, there would be little reason to believe that we could. Because others have so awakened and knowledgably transmit the requisite practices, we can do likewise. A mature relationship with a spiritual teacher is an apprenticeship in awakening.

Pure perception, as noted, is not passive. In Tibetan Buddhist traditions, the teacher's awakened buddha nature communes with and helps evoke the corresponding enlightened potential within the student. As students we cooperate with this process by envisioning ourselves receiving the liberating powers of love and compassion from spiritual teachers and benefactors, then merging with them in the infinite ground of those energies: primordial awareness. As our buddha potential awakens, it radiates the same liberating power of love and wisdom to many others.

Connecting with a Spiritual Teacher

For our practice to deepen, therefore, it is a profound help to reconnect with our teachers repeatedly so as to receive continuing transmission, inspiration, and instruction that accords with our developing experience. It is an incomparable boost to join with them in meditation retreats or workshops that they offer. There, we experience the inspiration of deep practice with them, along with the opportunity to ask questions that have arisen from our maturing experience.

How to find the right spiritual teacher(s) for you? One way to explore this is by reading books or essays written by teachers who have long trained in the spiritual tradition of your interest. You may also attend their talks, workshops, or short retreats. Your teachers would be the ones who speak most profoundly to you on all levels—whose ways of communicating open your heart and mind, triggering your own unique process of awakening. In the end only you can determine who that is. A great crowd may gather around a spiritual figure whose way of teaching is not effective for you. Your best friend may benefit from the instruction of a teacher with whom you have no such connection. You have to explore by reading, attending teachings, and going to practice settings guided by teachers, until you find someone who communicates so well to your fundamental concern that you know you have much to learn from him or her.

How to tell if a spiritual teacher is effective? Teachers can take many forms. Some are always gentle, warm and kind, yet may never truly challenge you to improve yourself. Some are more abrupt, yet may challenge your patterns of self-grasping in all the ways that help you progress. One good way to determine the effectiveness of a teacher is by observing his or her students over time. Are a number of them becoming the deep, wise, and compassionate sort of person that you seek to become? Then their teacher is guiding them well. Or are the students becoming ideologues, brittle in their beliefs, espousing the dogmas of a religion without embodying its deep qualities? Then their teacher has not been effective in their training.

Avoid teachers of any tradition who require their communities to become islands unto themselves, expecting their students to cut off communication with family and friends—not just for the period of a meditation retreat but permanently. Spiritual practice should increasingly inform all relationships, not become a means to hide from them in cult-like isolation.

In sum, we rely on awakened teachers to perceive the enlightened potential in us, commune with it, and evoke it. We rely on them to perceive and challenge the self-clinging we don't yet see in ourselves, so we can learn to offer ourselves more fully to the practices that bring out self-transcending wisdom and love. We rely on them for ongoing transmission, instruction, and advice.

In meditation sessions, as we merge into oneness with our spiritual teachers in the luminosity of love, compassion, and wisdom, we are effectively uniting with all previous generations of teachers with whom our teachers similarly united. Through this profound practice, we discover our underlying identity with generations of spiritual masters in the undivided nature of our minds. Such practice helps wake up our hidden potential to become like them.

Bodhichitta: The Spirit of Enlightenment

The Spirit of Enlightenment in Aspiration

Someone may first take interest in spiritual practice to improve his life. But practice doesn't just improve your life—it also newly defines the meaning of your life. The process of awakening is unique for each individual, but common stages of spiritual development can be discerned—progressive stages through which practitioners awaken to a deeper sense of life's purpose. What follows are a few highlights of spiritual development that I've observed in dedicated practitioners of Tibetan Buddhism, a Mahayana tradition centered on the bodhisattva path of enlightenment. Non-Buddhist readers may explore how the stages of development described here might shine light upon analogous stages of their own contemplative lives.

After a practitioner has learned to integrate the power of meditation into many aspects of her life, she increasingly senses the sacredness of everyone around her. It becomes clear that the pure perception of her meditation sessions is not just a fantasy. Rather, meditation helps unveil what had previously gone unnoticed: the intrinsic goodness and immeasurable worth of everyone.

At some point the practitioner realizes there is no reason for the basic perspective of wisdom and love to stop at the end of her meditation sessions. Those states of mind are the natural response to what meditation reveals: the intrinsic purity of things and the underlying nature of beings. We can always relax into the natural wisdom that recognizes the primordial purity of things; we can always commune with the primordial goodness of benefactors and beings in love and compassion. It's just a matter of remembering to do so, of learning better to abide in our own deepest response to what is.

Over months and years of such practice, supported by her work with spiritual teachers and community, a practitioner starts to notice significant changes in some of the members of her community. They are becoming less brittle and self-centered, less superficially judgmental, more reverent of everyone, loving, and wise. She recognizes, perhaps to her surprise, that such changes have been happening in herself as well. As she practices with her teachers and merges into oneness with them as benefactors in daily meditation, she senses more and more how the love and wisdom transmitted in

228 ❧ *Awakening Through Love*

their teaching and energy has been helping to trigger her own capacity for love and wisdom—how the awakened buddha potential in them has been evoking the corresponding potential in herself. She now realizes that she has long been held by her spiritual teachers and benefactors in a protective field of pure perception and compassion, no matter what negative thoughts she had about herself or others. Now recognizing this, she feels tremendous gratitude. She may sometimes weep with reverence and appreciation at the mere thought of her teachers.

As her nonconceptual wisdom also deepens, she learns to relax more fully into the nature of her mind beyond clinging, where she increasingly experiences the spontaneous liberation of deluded thoughts and reactions—deep, blissful freedom from the causes of suffering. "Freedom from suffering" is no longer an abstraction; she is actually learning to experience it firsthand. At the same time, meditation practice is bringing out her innate love for beings with increasing force and inclusiveness. Without equivocating, she transmits love not just to a few humans but to all; not just to humans but to all sensate creatures. In addition, her compassion for beings intensifies as she learns to abide in the unconditioned freedom of the nature of mind and understands better the layers of conditioned suffering that they undergo for not yet recognizing such freedom.

All these enlightened qualities—wisdom, love, compassion, and their liberating energy—manifest more and more strongly in her and others in her community. And she understands: "It is because our spiritual teachers accomplished these qualities that their teaching and energy are evoking our potential for the same." From her own experience she now knows the liberating power that enlightened beings embody for others. Recall the story about Kisa Gotami, the young woman who mourned the death of her child and then discovered her grief as a link to compassion for others. When this insight dawned, she exclaimed: "This is what the Buddha, in *his* compassion, has seen!" At that moment she realized how the Buddha's own realization enabled him to guide her to the same realization. At this stage the practitioner is having a similar recognition: her teachers' profound awakening is what enabled them to inspire and guide her own awakening.

And it dawns on her: "The purpose of these spiritual practices is not merely to improve my life. Rather, the purpose of my life is to accomplish these practices—to attain freedom from the inner causes of my own suffering and to completely realize the wisdom, love, and energy that are needed to help many others do the same. That is what my teachers accomplished, and that is what I must likewise do." A powerful aspiration wells up to follow in the footsteps of her teachers, her deepest spiritual benefactors, to practice so thoroughly that she unleashes the full liberating power of her enlightened potential for the sake of all.

In Buddhist traditions of India and Tibet, this dawning realization is called the arising of *bodhichitta*—the *spirit of enlightenment. Bodhichitta* is the buddha capacity long hidden in our minds by ego-clinging, which has the ever-present potential to wake up and manifest its liberating qualities. Through the stages of development noted above, the practitioner's capacity of bodhichitta begins to awaken in a decisive way, breaking into consciousness as a powerful aspiration to fully manifest its enlightened qualities. When this happens, it feels as if an enormous force of will has erupted from the depths of one's mind—the spirit of enlightenment is roaring.

Michael Himes explains something intriguingly analogous in Christian understanding. Father Himes says: "How do we discern the will of God for us?... God's will is not the will of some other person out there someplace with which we are supposed to bring our will into line.... The will of God is the will within and beneath my will.... To find the will of God, don't look 'out there'; drill down to the deepest depths of your own will, and there you will discover the will of God."[77]

When bodhichitta breaks into consciousness, it feels as though your truest, inmost will is finally manifesting, the profound aspiration to realize all enlightened qualities of your buddha nature: the inner knowledge, compassion, skillful means, and liberating power that can trigger the awakening of many others. This is what Indo-Tibetan tradition calls *the spirit of enlightenment in aspiration*. When this aspiration emerges in a powerful, steadfast way, one has become a bodhisattva. *Bodhi* is Sanskrit for "enlightenment," *sattva* for "person." A bodhisattva is a person who embodies the spirit of enlightenment.

At this point the practitioner is thoroughly disgusted with fruitless attempts to find lasting happiness by clinging to transient, conditioned circumstances. Instead, she feels a solemn responsibility to realize the unconditioned wisdom and love that actually provide lasting joy and to help many others do the same. She knows life is short and can end at any time. With an urgent sense of responsibility, she requests her teacher to formalize her entry into the bodhisattva path, by transmitting the vow that prior bodhisattvas have taken.

Taking the Vow of the Bodhisattvas

The bodhisattva vow is transmitted in a ceremony passed down from the great bodhisattva masters of India and Tibet. The student kneels before her teacher, palms pressed together, envisioning and reverencing the great masters of the past, from the Buddha to her present teacher. With all of those masters as witness, she takes refuge in the three jewels—Buddha, Dharma, and Sangha—and repeats a solemn vow after her teacher to fully realize the qualities of enlightenment for the sake of all beings. In Tibetan tradition, the vow is often recited in the words of the great Indian bodhisattva, Shantideva:

Just as buddhas of the past generated the spirit of enlightenment and progressively accomplished the training of the
bodhisattvas, so I give rise to the spirit of enlightenment and
will progressively accomplish those trainings for the sake of
the world.[78]

"I give rise to the spirit of enlightenment" expresses bodhichitta
in aspiration—the resolve to fully realize her enlightened potential
for the sake of all. Therefore, like prior buddhas and bodhisattvas—
including the spiritual teachers who guided her in this life—she
firmly vows to make her whole life into a practice of awakening.
The next phrase expresses that commitment: "[I] will progressively
accomplish those [bodhisattva] trainings for the sake of the world."
This vow impels the emerging bodhisattva to make every activity
into a means to realize her enlightened potential of wisdom and
love, thereby evoking the same potential in others.

The Spirit of Enlightenment in Action

To take this bodhisattva vow and then put it into action by training
in the practices of a bodhisattva, constitutes what Indo-Tibetan tradition calls *the spirit of enlightenment in action* (bodhichitta in action).[79]
To make such a vow is a joyful moment, for the new bodhisattva
has now stepped onto the bodhisattva path that culminates in the
enlightenment of a buddha.[80] It means she has taken up her deepest
purpose as a human being. Shantideva's next verse expresses this joy:

Now my life has borne great fruit; human life well obtained.
Today I am born into the Buddha's family. Now I am the
Buddha's child.[81]

Henceforth, each day the bodhisattva recites the vow while
visualizing the buddhas and bodhisattvas before her. Such daily

repetition imprints the bodhisattva resolve deep into the practitioner's mind, so the spirit of enlightenment may inform her life and draw her back to the bodhisattva path from lifetime to lifetime, until she is fully awakened.

Practitioners don't have to go through all the stages of spiritual progress described above before receiving this vow. Many people at an early stage of their practice request the bodhisattva vow from their teacher in order to inspire and support their development to the point of actually generating the spirit of enlightenment in aspiration and action.

After the bodhisattva has given rise to the spirit of enlightenment and taken the vow, his path unfolds by deepening his practice of wisdom and love, which comprise the ultimate and relative aspects of bodhichitta. *Ultimate bodhichitta* is the nonconceptual wisdom that recognizes the empty, infinite, and undivided nature of mind beyond all partialities. *Relative bodhichitta* is the boundless, impartial love and compassion that arise naturally from such wisdom. Wisdom and love are to be cultivated not just in meditation sessions but at all times, everywhere. Wherever you are, whatever you are doing, you are learning to be fully present to self and others within the natural state, the wisdom beyond clinging, and to commune with others and respond to them in the pure perception of love and compassion.

At this stage the spirit of enlightenment becomes the organizing principle of the practitioner's life, defining its purposes and arrangements. In order to fulfill the bodhisattva vow, one may choose to be a monk, nun, or lay practitioner. Monastics maintain hundreds of disciplinary vows that keep their lives focused exclusively on the Dharma, which helps maintain the disciplinary power and purity of the tradition for future generations. They have the opportunity to train in monasteries, traditionally the centers of intensive Buddhist learning and practice in Tibetan culture.

Tibet has also produced a great many enlightened lay adepts: powerful lamas, teachers, yogis, and yoginis, such as Padmasambhava, Yeshe Tsogyal, Machig Labdron, Marpa, and Milarepa. A lay bodhisattva trains extensively with his teachers and in centers of Buddhist learning and meditation, but then contributes much to the world by entering into all aspects of ordinary life as means of awakening. For example, in our time a lay bodhisattva may explore how family life, work life, leisure activity, and social service can support wisdom and love in self and others. Modern societies need more bodhisattva mothers and fathers, doctors and nurses, teachers, social workers, coaches, leaders, officials, and policemen. Since the contemporary world is not likely to become as heavily monasticized as Tibet, those who learn to transform lay life into a field of awakening perform an invaluable service for future generations. Many laypeople and monastics maintain intimate relationships of mutual support and learning as the Dharma continues to plant new roots in contemporary cultures.

Whether the bodhisattva is a layperson or a monastic, to accept the spirit of enlightenment as the directive force of his life redefines his approach to spiritual practice. *Before* the arising of bodhichitta, the practitioner sought to integrate spiritual practice *with* his life, as if each part of his life had its own autonomous purpose and practice was to be added on to that. For example, the practitioner thought his purpose for going to the grocery store was mainly to get groceries, and while he was there, he would also try to integrate the perspective and energy of his meditations. *After* he gives rise to bodhichitta and has become a bodhisattva, he realizes that spiritual practice *is* the main purpose of each part of life. Each situation is viewed as a means to evoke and express his enlightened potential. *Now* the main purpose for going to the grocery store is to abide in the wisdom of natural awareness, fully present, and to sense and respond to all the people around him in love and compassion. Groceries are purchased in order to support the life dedicated to such practice.

Similarly, before giving rise to bodhichitta, a practitioner may work in a job mainly to earn money for food, rent, and so forth. While there, he tries to recall his spiritual practice. After giving rise to bodhichitta, the bodhisattva goes to work each day so as to further realize and embody wisdom and compassion in action, in ways that can inspire others to realize their best potential. The money earned from work goes to support a life centered on that purpose.

One young American educator who had meditated for several years went to see his spiritual teacher, a lama. The young man, enthusiastic at how well he was integrating practice into his life, told his teacher: "The effects of these meditations are pouring into each part of my school day, transforming my work as a teacher." The lama gazed at him for a moment, then replied: "Educating others, in itself, is not your life work. Your life work is to realize your full potential for wisdom, love, and compassion. Your job as an educator is the form through which to do that." The lama was pointing to the difference between merely integrating spiritual practice with your life and recognizing the spirit of awakening as the very purpose of your life. The lama was helping the young man to realize that he could shoot higher—he could be a bodhisattva.

A bodhisattva doesn't live to eat, sleep, and have a roof over his head. He eats, sleeps, and has a roof to support a life lived in the spirit of enlightenment. He doesn't live just to undergo passing experiences. He undergoes many kinds of experiences, some pleasant, some unpleasant, as a means to draw out his wisdom, empathy, and compassion. He doesn't have a family just to fulfill his needs, expectations, or to ward off loneliness. His family serves to evoke his love, patience, wise presence, and care for them. Within family life, such attitudes are refined, tested, honed, and strengthened. Then they can be extended to many others, who also don't exist just to fulfill his own needs and expectations. The bodhisattva's family, and ultimately the whole world, are sacraments of awakening.

The Six Transcendental Virtues
of the Bodhisattva Path

To practice the bodhisattva path is to engage all situations and inter-actions as ways to evoke or express the spirit of enlightenment. This all-encompassing field of activity is encapsulated in *six transcendental virtues* (Sanskrit: *paramitas,* also translated as the "six perfections"). They are "transcendental" because they are all expressions of deep-est wisdom, the pure awareness that transcends all grasping.

Transcendental wisdom, the sixth virtue, is the stable recognition of the nature of mind: limitless openness and awareness undivided. It is also the nonconceptual wisdom of emptiness that transcends grasp-ing on to self, to other, or to action as independent from each other. From such wisdom flows tremendous love and compassion for all beings who undergo sufferings caused by grasping on to self and to dualism. A bodhisattva enacts the love and compassion of transcen-dental wisdom through the activities of the other five virtues: gen-erosity, moral discipline, patience, enthusiastic perseverance, and meditative concentration. These five areas of activity are also called the *skillful means* of transcendental wisdom, because they are ways to care for others that skillfully evoke their deepest goodness, their own potential for wisdom and love.

The division into six virtues organizes all the practices of wisdom and love previously described into six basic kinds of practice. To take one area of life as example, let's briefly explore the six tran-scendental virtues as they may take expression in the family life of a lay bodhisattva.

Generosity involves offering yourself to others by giving whatever is needed. It becomes a transcendental virtue in family life when you are fully present to your family in the natural awareness and love that transcend clinging to self and other. From that generous place of openness, acceptance, equanimity, and communion, you freely offer your time, energy, material means, protection, knowledge, and care to your family. To abide in natural awareness is to take joy in the very being of your partner, children, or other relatives, beyond anyone's map of self-concerned expectations. To be so fully present to your family and to embody that in numerous small gestures of kindness, attention, and love is a gift that blesses them to uncover and grow into their best selves.

Moral discipline means to refrain from harming others in thought or deed, cultivating the potential of goodness in oneself and others, and acting beneficially for others in numerous ways. It becomes a transcendental virtue when you recognize the empty essence of your mind's habitual reactions as they arise, so that self-centered emotions spontaneously release into their basic ground of empty awareness instead of driving harmful actions. From within that state of innate wisdom, you generate much karmic merit by communing with your family and all others in love and compassion—perceiving and evoking their innate goodness. From that perspective and attitude flow many gestures of care and respect for your partner and children: sorting the mail, washing the dishes, collecting the trash, making the bed, helping with homework—performing family tasks with full attention, presence, reverence, and joyfulness.

Patience includes patience when others present difficulties for you, patience with your own sufferings, and patience with all the challenges of spiritual practice. Patience becomes a transcendental virtue when it flows from the wisdom in the nature of mind, the unconditioned, unchanging nature of openness and cognizance that is never threatened or harmed by changing circumstances. From this wisdom flows compassionate patience with partner, children, and self, through understanding the reactivity and sufferings that trouble all who have not yet found stable recognition of their mind's nature. In addition, to practice within family life and spiritual community sometimes feels frustrating, since your own ego-clinging is regularly challenged in new ways. All such circumstances can enhance the patience of wisdom and compassion—by resting directly in the empty essence of those experiences or by recognizing each difficulty as a bridge of empathy to many others with similar difficulties.

Enthusiastic perseverance is delight in the spirit of enlightenment, in the practices that express it, and in the challenges and difficulties of spiritual life. It becomes a transcendental virtue when it flows from the boundless joy of unconditioned freedom within the natural state, beyond self-centered anxieties or inhibitions. This is a joy that recognizes the deep meaningfulness of every aspect of life. In light of the spirit of awakening, even problems and difficulties posed by others or by your own ego reactions are seen as meaningful, since they can all serve as means to purify your mind, to generate compassion, and to extend the recognition of emptiness to increasingly difficult aspects of experience. In family life, enthusiastic perseverance is delight in the meaningfulness of every activity done for your child or partner—the joy of offering yourself to them, such as by doing laundry, changing diapers, feeding children, reading them stories, and putting them to bed.

Transcendental meditative concentration, in this context, is the calm, stable power of unconditional love and compassion that expresses the innate stability found in the unconditioned nature of mind. The bodhisattva draws upon the natural power of concentration that is always available in the mind's very nature: the innate tranquillity of emptiness and pure awareness.

Transcendental wisdom, again, is the natural wisdom of infinite openness and cognizance that transcends all grasping. When operative in each of the other virtues, it turns them into *transcendental* virtues.

Besides family life, a lay bodhisattva applies the same six virtues to all other areas of life: strengthening his generosity, care, patience, perseverance, attention, and wisdom within his work life, in his service to the work of his spiritual teachers and community, in offering himself in various ways to the people of his neighborhood or town, in leisure time with family and friends, and so forth.

The bodhisattva's practice of the transcendental virtues generates the karmic merit and wisdom to take him to fullest awakening while inspiring others to realize their own corresponding potential of wisdom and love. In this way, the bodhisattva's actions help trigger the process of awakening of many others.[82]

Further Practices to Evoke and Express the Spirit of Enlightenment

With the guidance of her teacher, a practitioner of Tibetan Buddhism may enter into further practices to help purify the mental patterns that obscure her enlightenment potential, to generate vast karmic merit, and to deepen her nonconceptual wisdom. In Tibetan Buddhism, these include the foundational practices *(ngondro)* of Vajrayana: solemnly reaffirming her refuge and bodhisattva resolve, offering every part of her world to enlightenment, purifying negativities, and uniting with lineage teachers. To help further evoke the qualities of her innate buddha potential, her teacher may also assist her entry into tantric deity yogas. In addition, practitioners of the Dzogchen tradition engage in special foundational practices of body, speech, and mind, as well as other practices to elicit visionary dimensions of enlightened awareness.[83]

All such practices are ways to further realize and embody the qualities, energies, and powers of the spirit of enlightenment: the innate potential of wisdom and love that we have been cultivating throughout this book.

Epilogue

A s I sit down to write the final section of this book, I realize it is September 11, 2006, the fifth anniversary of the tragic attack on the United States by terrorists from abroad. Today, politicians across America are discussing ways to protect Americans from their enemies—mostly through strategies of self-defense. Certainly nations must take measures to protect their people. But if we want to be protected, we should focus attention not only outward toward potential sources of violence against us but also inward at our own attitudes toward the masses of people in the world, many of whom sympathize with those who oppose us.

In our economic, political, and military relations with people of other nations, do our actions express genuine concern for their lives or cynical attempts to gain control over them and their resources? It will never be enough for leaders to *posture* as if they cared about the peoples of other lands without actually acting accordingly. Unless, as a people, we genuinely wish for the well-being of people in other nations, and act courageously from that motivation over the long term, no military solution will be enough to protect us. Government and military leaders who care deeply for the peoples of other cultures, and embody that concern through concrete actions, wield *much* greater power to protect their own people. General George Marshall's reconstruction efforts in Europe after the Second World War exemplified this. Gandhi's successful work for Indian independence embodied his concern for both the Indian and British peoples.

I hope that readers from diverse walks of life, religious traditions, and cultures who enter into the meditations and teachings of this book receive inspiration and blessing for their lives. In a class on Buddhist meditation I taught last spring, students kept journals on how the meditations of natural love and wisdom informed their lives, most of them as Christians, Jews, and so forth. One student, a devout Catholic, had this entry in her journal:

> Today after meditating, I spontaneously wrote this:
> "If you steer from fear, and cling to no thing,
> you'll find freedom to give and joy to sing.
> You'll know who you are, held from above;
> you'll know the Truth that God Is.
> ...you'll know God is Love."

These meditations from Buddhism helped deepen her faith in the reality of God as unconditional, all-embracing love. From such journals, I also received inspiration and light for my own spiritual path as a Buddhist. I hope the practices in this book help people of different faiths, and no formal faith, enter similarly into a dialogue with Buddhist tradition of deep mutual learning and appreciation.

I pray that Buddhist readers among you, through the meditations of this book, find inspiration to strengthen your participation in the spirit of enlightenment and to empower your refuge in the practices, communities, and teachers that most effectively support your awakening.

I pray that these meditations inspire greater wisdom, patience, and compassion in families and communities that so desperately need more of those qualities. May these meditations help cut through the inner causes of prejudice, hatred, and violence that lie hidden in all our minds. May they empower people to realize their best potential and find joy in their work and in their service to others. May these practices support people who work for a happier and safer world: leaders in government, international service, the military, those who care for children, work for peace, assist the troubled, treat the sick, help the elderly, the homeless, and the dying, feed the hungry, protect animals and the environment. May those who practice these meditations realize the nature of their minds, spontaneously embracing all others in the soothing radiance of love and compassion. May the spirit of enlightenment bless everyone to awaken to his or her deepest potential. May the path of awakening unfold in the most effective way for each person.

To you, the reader, I make this request: please never give up on yourself. When you feel dejected, remember your benefactors and receive their radiant wish for your deepest well-being and freedom. Each one of us is held in a power of love and awareness beyond our conception. The blessings of enlightenment are always pouring forth. This troubled world is just waiting for us to receive them, to realize their source in the very ground of our being, and to extend the same blessing unconditionally to others.

Notes

1. For further discussion of the need for impartial love to respond to violence and oppression, see John Makransky, "No Real Protection without Authentic Love and Compassion," *Journal of Buddhist Ethics* 12 (2005), pp. 25–36 (online journal).

2. Nyoshul Khen Rinpoche and Lama Surya Das, *Natural Great Perfection* (Ithaca, NY: Snow Lion, 1995), p. 86.

3, Alison Luterman, "At the Corner Store," *The Sun* 324 (December 2002), p. 41.

4. Nyoshul Khenpo and Surya Das, *Natural Great Perfection*, p. 82.

5. Nyoshul Khenpo and Surya Das, *Natural Great Perfection*, p. 107.

6. Nyoshul Khenpo and Surya Das, *Natural Great Perfection*, pp. 70–71.

7. For some modern social implications of traditional Buddhist diagnoses of causes of suffering, see David Loy, *The Great Awakening: A Buddhist Social Theory* (Boston: Wisdom, 2003).

8. Dilgo Khyentse Rinpoche and Matthieu Ricard, *The Spirit of Tibet: The Life and World of Khyentse Rinpoche, Spiritual Teacher* (New York: Aperture Foundation, 2000), p. 52.

9. Nyoshul Khenpo and Surya Das, *Natural Great Perfection*, p. 79.

10. Nyoshul Khenpo and Surya Das, *Natural Great Perfection*, p. 59.

11. Tibetan Buddhist practices of refuge and union are explained in commentaries available in English. Tulku Thondup has made them accessible in *The Healing Power of Mind* (Boston: Shambhala, 1996), pp. 165–73. Also see Sogyal Rinpoche, *Tibetan Book of Living and Dying* (New York: HarperCollins, 1992), pp. 146–49, and Dilgo Khyentse

Rinpoche, *Excellent Path to Enlightenment* (Ithaca, NY: Snow Lion, 1996), pp. 29–36, 73–86. The practice in this book of receiving and uniting with our benefactors in unconditional love is intended for a wide public to find simple, direct entry into the heart of such practice and for experienced Buddhist meditators to help enhance their practice.

12. Khyentse and Ricard, *Spirit of Tibet,* p. 45.

13. Nyoshul Khenpo and Surya Das, *Natural Great Perfection,* pp. 61, 73.

14. For examples of such inquiries into the nature of mind in the Nyingma Dzogchen and Kagyu Mahamudra traditions, see, e.g., Tulku Urgyen Rinpoche, *As It Is,* vol. II (Kathmandu: Rangjung Yeshe, 2000), pp. 161–62; Nyoshul Khenpo and Surya Das, *Natural Great Perfection,* pp. 61, 73, 118; Longchen Rabjampa, *Buddha Mind,* translated by Tulku Thondup (Ithaca, NY: Snow Lion, 1989), p. 361; Dakpo Tashi Namgyal, *Clarifying the Natural State,* translated by Erik Kunzang (Boudhanath, Nepal: Rangjung Yeshe, 2001); Lama Surya Das, *Natural Radiance* (Boulder, CO: Sounds True, 2005), pp. 47–54; Ken McLeod, *Wake Up to Your Life* (New York: HarperCollins, 2001), pp. 353–410.

15. This incisive expression, "cut the kite-string on thoughts," is from Lama Surya Das.

16. Khyentse and Ricard, *Spirit of Tibet,* p. 52.

17. From the Pali *Itivuttaka* in Jack Kornfield, *Teachings of the Buddha* (Boston: Shambhala, 1993), p. 112. I retranslate Pali *punna* as "karmic merit" and *metta* as "love" to conform to the usage in this book.

18. Nyoshul Khenpo and Surya Das, *Natural Great Perfection,* p. 120.

19. For accessible modern introductions to the practice and theory of the Natural Great Perfection tradition discussed in this chapter, see Nyoshul Khenpo and Surya Das, *Natural Great Perfection;* Khyentse and Ricard, *Spirit of Tibet;* Lama Surya Das, *Natural Radiance;* Chokyi Nyima Rinpoche, *Present Fresh Wakefulness* (Kathmandu: Rangjung Yeshe, 2002); Tsoknyi Rinpoche, *Fearless Simplicity* (Kathmandu: Rangjung Yeshe, 2003); Sogyal Rinpoche, *Tibetan Book of Living and*

Dying (New York: HarperCollins, 1992); and Namkhai Norbu, *The Crystal and the Way of Light* (New York: Routledge, 1986). For classical Tibetan exposition of Dzogchen, see Longchen Rabjam, *The Practice of Dzogchen,* translated by Tulku Thondup (Ithaca, NY: Snow Lion, 2003), containing extensive translation from the collected works of the great fourteenth-century Dzogchen master Longchen Rabjam. Also see Longchen Rabjam, *The Precious Treasury of the Way of Abiding,* translated by Richard Barron (Junction City, CA: Padma, 1998) and Longchen Rabjam, *The Precious Treasury of the Basic Space of Phenomena,* translated by Richard Barron (Junction City, CA: Padma, 2001).

20. Shantideva, *Bodhicharyavatara,* 8:129, my translation.

21. *Gospel of Matthew* 7.1–3.

22. This discussion of karmic cause and effect is not exhaustive. It concerns a few key points critical to inform our practice both in meditation and everyday life. Further points will be made in following chapters. One focus here concerns the distinction made in Buddhist Abhidharma treatises between primary causes and secondary conditions for pleasant and unpleasant feelings: the primary cause of pleasant feelings being past virtue, of unpleasant feelings past nonvirtue. On this, see *Abhidharmakosha-bhashya,* 4:45–48, 56 (the manual of higher Buddhist studies by the fourth-century Indian master Vasubandhu). Also see the first Dalai Lama's commentary on chapter 4 of Vasubandhu's text: *Mdsod tik thar lam sal byed* (analyzed in John Makransky, "A Phenomenological Study of Buddhist Karma Theory," PhD research paper, 1982). A second focus here concerns *karmic results similar to the cause* (Sanskrit: *nishyandaphala,* Tibetan: *gyu tuengyi draybu*), the tendency, imprinted by one's past actions, to react similarly again and again from habit and to experience oneself also, in a broad sense, as the object of such actions. On this, see *Abhidharmakosha-bhashya,* 4.85, elaborated in Yangsi Rinpoche, *Practicing the Path,* (Boston: Wisdom, 2003) pp. 173–74, based on Tsongkhapa's *Great Treatise on the Stages of the Path.*

For further detail on karma doctrine, see Tsong kha pa, *Great Treatise on the Stages of the Path,* vol. 1, translated by the Lamrim Chenmo Translation Committee (Ithaca, NY: Snow Lion, 2000), pp. 209–46; Kangyur Rinpoche and Jigme Lingpa, *Treasury of Precious Qualities,* translated by the Padmakara Translation Group (Boston: Shambhala, 2001), pp. 43–64. For incisive contemporary Buddhist writing on karma, see *Seeking the Heart of Wisdom* by Goldstein and Kornfield (Boston: Shambhala, 1987), pp. 111–26, and *Practicing the Path,* pp. 155–94.

23. Shantideva expresses the futility of self-centered strategies for happiness in another verse: "In the desire for happiness, out of delusion, [beings] destroy their own happiness like an enemy." Santideva, *Bodhicaryavatara,* translated by Kate Crosby and Andrew Skilton (New York: Oxford University Press, 1995), 1:28.

24. Nyoshul Khenpo and Surya Das, *Natural Great Perfection,* p. 58.

25. On enlightenment taking form within a pure realm of radiant activity, blessing, and communion, see John Makransky, "Buddhahood and Buddha Bodies," in *Encyclopedia of Buddhism* edited by Robert Buswell (New York: Macmillan, 2004), vol. 1, pp. 76–79; John Makransky, *Buddhahood Embodied* (Albany, NY: State University of New York, 1997), pp. 54–59, 104–8; John Makransky, "Tathagata," in *Encyclopedia of Religion,* 2nd edition, edited by Lindsay Jones (Detroit: Macmillan, 2005), vol. 13, pp. 9015–17. For depictions in Tibetan art, see for example: Marylin Rhie and Robert Thurman, *Worlds of Transformation: Tibetan Art of Wisdom and Compassion* (New York: Tibet House, 1999), pp. 449–84.

26. Thomas Merton, *New Seeds of Contemplation* (New York: New Directions, 1961), p. 25.

27. Santideva, *Bodhicharyavatara,* 3:18, trans. by Crosby and Skilton.

28. "Of all [objects] the essential original nature is boundless; of beings likewise the essential original nature is boundless. As the essential original nature of space has no limits, just so the wisdom of the World-knowers [buddhas] is boundless. *Verses on the Perfection of Wisdom,* II.

10, translated by Edward Conze in *The Perfection of Wisdom in Eight Thousand Lines and Its Verse Summary* (Berkeley: Four Seasons Foundation, 1973), p. 14.

29. Nyoshul Khenpo and Surya Das, *Natural Great Perfection,* pp. 42–43.

30. Nyoshul Khenpo and Surya Das, *Natural Great Perfection,* p. 59.

31. From *Metta Sutta* in *Teachings of the Buddha,* edited by Jack Kornfield (Boston: Shambhala, 1993), pp. 6–8. I replace "one" with "you," implicit in the Pali, to retain more of the rhetorical power of the text.

32. Bokar Rinpoche, *Chenrezig: Lord of Love* (San Francisco: Clear Point Press, 1991), pp. 14–15.

33. Cindy Fabricius-Segal, "Blessings in Disguise," *The Sun* 333 (September 2003), p. 34.

34. Lucy Garbus, *The Sun* 342 (June 2004), p. 40.

35. Lama Surya Das, *Awakening the Buddhist Heart* (New York: Broadway, 2000), pp. 194–95.

36. On further supportive contemplations to inform love, compassion, and wisdom, see the Dalai Lama, *An Open Heart* (New York: Little, Brown and Company, 2001); Geshe Jampa Tegchok, *Transforming the Heart* (Ithaca, NY: Snow Lion, 1999); Lama Surya Das, *Awakening the Buddhist Heart.*

37. See Sogyal Rinpoche, *Tibetan Book of Living and Dying,* for an accessible introduction to the clear light nature of mind and its relation to gracious living and dying.

38. Adapted from two versions of the story that appear in the *Samyutta Nikaya* and the *Chinese Sutra of 42 Sections:* Bhikku Bodhi, editor and translator, *Connected Discourses of the Buddha: A Translation of the Samyutta Nikaya* (Boston: Wisdom, 2000), pp 255–56; Donald Lopez, editor, *Religions of China in Practice* (Princeton, NJ: Princeton University Press, 1996), pp. 365–66. I give thanks to Todd Lewis, James Benn, Franz Metcalf, Guang Xing, and Richard Hayes for finding these references for me.

39. Nyoshul Khenpo and Surya Das, *Natural Great Perfection,* p. 137.

40. A note for scholars: Pure perception (Tibetan *dag nang*) is codified in Tibetan Buddhism as one of the central practices of the Vajrayana tradition. Because Dzogchen is understood to express the very essence of Vajrayana, pure perception becomes a central theme here. Themes of pure perception are also prominent in Mahayana scriptures and commentaries that preceded and contributed to the emergence of Vajrayana traditions in India: e.g., perception by transcendental wisdom of the intrinsically pure suchness of beings and things as elaborated in *Prajna-paramita* scriptures and Maitreya texts, pure perception of the innate buddha nature of each being as elaborated in buddha nature literature, and so forth. See Makransky, *Buddhahood Embodied,* pp. 41–54, 323–35.

41. Khyentse Rinpoche and Ricard, *Spirit of Tibet,* p. 82.

42. A non-Buddhist practicing these meditations should include within the benefactors that merge into her heart whoever she believes to be most deeply spiritual figures. Buddhists identify such figures as buddhas and bodhisattvas, including their own spiritual teachers. A Christian might think instead of Christ, Mary, or the communion of saints, a Jew of most cherished prophets and rabbis, and so forth.

43. Michael Himes, *Doing the Truth in Love* (New York: Paulist, 1995), pp. 10, 11, 18. Also see John Makransky, "Buddha and Christ as Mediators of Ultimate Reality: A Mahayana Buddhist Perspective," in *Buddhism and Christianity in Dialogue,* ed. by Perry Schmidt-Leukel (Norwich, England: SCM, 2005), pp. 176–211.

44. *Tathagatagarbha Sutra* translated by William Grossnick in Donald Lopez, editor, *Buddhism in Practice* (Princeton, NJ: Princeton University Press, 1995), pp. 95–96 ff.

45. Several early Mahayana commentaries proclaim that the full enlightenment of a buddha embodies itself in three basic ways. (1) Dharmakaya (embodiment of the real) is a buddha's full realization of the infinite, empty, luminous nature of mind. Since buddhahood is one with the deep nature of reality as such *(dharma-ta),* that is its ultimate

body *(kaya)*. (2) Sambhoga-kaya (embodiment in communal joy) is the luminous energy of dharmakaya as it manifests in radiant form, to commune joyously with circles of bodhisattvas who are receptive to the joyful, liberating powers of enlightenment. (3) Nirmana-kaya (creative embodiment) is buddhahood as it creatively and spontaneously expresses liberating truth to ordinary beings through persons, phenomena of nature, ritual forms, works of art, and so forth. See Makransky, *Buddhahood Embodied,* chaps. 4, 5, and 13.

46. To participate in this purer dimension of reality broadly corresponds to what Vajrayana Buddhism describes as participation in a mandala of Buddha activity, see Chagdud Tulku's *Gates to Buddhist Practice* (Junction City, CA: Padma, 2001), chap. 16; Reginald Ray, *Secret of the Vajra World* (Boston: Shambhala, 2001), chap. 7.

47. "No Mirrors in My Nana's House," Sweet Honey in the Rock, *Still on the Journey* (Redway, CA: Earthbeat! Records, 1993).

48. We see the connection between the ultimate equanimity of wisdom and the relative equanimity operative in love and compassion in Perfection of Wisdom scriptures of early Mahayana Buddhism. For example, Conze, *Perfection of Wisdom in Eight Thousand Lines,* p. 199, shows the movement from ultimate equanimity (the wisdom that knows the undivided, ultimate nature of beings) to relative equanimity (the impartial and indomitable love that a bodhisattva extends to beings). Page 235 lists the four boundless attitudes—boundless love, compassion, joy, and equanimity, while equating the last with the perfection of wisdom itself—that which discerns the true nature of phenomena. The same occurs in the larger *Perfection of Wisdom Sutra:* Edward Conze, *The Large Sutra on Perfect Wisdom* (Delhi: Motilal Banarsidass, 1979), p. 442.

49. Matthieu Ricard, trans., *The Life of Shabkar* (Ithaca, NY: Snow Lion, 2001), p. 422. My gratitude to Bob Morrison for pointing out this passage.

50. E.A. Burtt, editor, *Teachings of the Compassionate Buddha* (New York:

Mentor, 1955), pp. 43–46; Eugene Watson Burlingame, trans., *Buddhist Legends* in the Pali text of the Dhammapada Commentary (Cambridge, MA: Harvard University Press, 1921), Harvard Oriental Series, vol. 30, pp. 165–66.

51. Ranjini Obeyesekere, *Portraits of Buddhist Women* (Albany, NY: State University of New York, 2001), p. 137.

52. Dalai Lama, *Open Heart,* pp. 91, 93.

53. See Dalai Lama, *Open Heart,* p. 92; Dalai Lama, *The Good Heart* (Boston: Wisdom, 1996), pp. 69–70.

54. Dalai Lama, *Open Heart,* pp. 93, 95.

55. Dzogchen Ponlop Rinpoche, *Trainings in Compassion* (Ithaca, NY: Snow Lion, 2004), p. 18.

56. Kathy Hall, *The Sun* 315 (March 2002), p. 35.

57. Dalai Lama, *Open Heart,* p. 102. Cf. Ringu Tulku, *Path to Buddhahood* (Boston: Shambhala, 2003), p. 61: "Compassion becomes very vivid when we see that the sufferings, although clearly omnipresent, are in fact baseless and so easy to eliminate. What separates beings from liberation is such a thin partition! And yet, by ignorance, by misunderstanding the true nature of things, they suffer intensely and needlessly."

58. Gampopa, *Jewel Ornament of Liberation* (Ithaca, NY: Snow Lion, 1998), p. 130; Zhechen Gyaltsab Rinpoche, *Path of Heroes,* vol. II (Oakland, CA: Dharma, 1995), pp. 306–7; Dzogchen Ponlop, *Trainings in Compassion,* pp. 21–22; Ringu Tulku, *Path to Buddhahood,* pp. 51, 61.

59. Nyoshul Khenpo and Surya Das, *Natural Great Perfection,* p. 120.

60. Khyentse Rinpoche, *Spirit of Tibet,* p. 86.

61. Thomas Cleary, trans., *Zen Antics* (Boston: Shambhala, 1993), p. 2.

62. Merton, *New Seeds of Contemplation,* p. 57.

63. Zhechen Gyaltsab, *Path of Heroes,* vol. II, p. 301.

64. In Zhechen Gyaltsab, *Path of Heroes,* vol. II, pp. 366–67.

65. Zopa Rinpoche, *Transforming Problems into Happiness* (Boston: Wisdom, 2001), p. 42.

66. On transmuting difficult experiences into the path of enlightenment,

also see Geshe Rabten and Geshe Ngawang Dhargyey, *Advice from a Spiritual Friend* (Boston: Wisdom, 1984), pp. 65–69; Tulku Thondup, *Enlightened Living* (Hong Kong: Rangjung Yeshe, 1997), pp. 117–29. Also see references in the prior two endnotes.

67. Zhechen Gyaltsab, *Path of Heroes,* vol. II, p. 413.

68. Dilgo Khyentse Rinpoche, *Enlightened Courage* (Ithaca, NY: Snow Lion, 1993), p. 52.

69. For examples of using such inquiries in daily life, see references in prior two notes; and Chagdud Tulku, *Gates to Buddhist Practice,* pp. 11–13, 22–23.

70. From a card that Rinpoche sent to his students in 1994.

71. Cf. Tsongkhapa's *Great Treatise,* vol. 2, pp. 44–45, which draws upon the writings of Kamalashila.

72. Ricard, *Life of Shabkar,* p. 422.

73. Cf. Surya Das, *Natural Radiance,* pp. 63–67; Tulku Urgyen Rinpoche, *Rainbow Painting* (Hong Kong: Rangjung Yeshe, 1995), pp. 59–66.

74. Nyoshul Khenpo and Surya Das, *Natural Great Perfection,* p. 46.

75. Nyoshul Khenpo and Surya Das, *Natural Great Perfection,* p. 46.

76. Thomas Merton, *Conjectures of a Guilty Bystander* (New York: Image, 1989), pp. 156–58.

77. Himes, *Doing the Truth in Love,* p. 56.

78. Shantideva and Ngul chu Thogmed, *Bodhisattva-charyavatara and Its Commentary* (Sarnath, India: Sakya Students' Union, 1982), p. 164. My translation of chapter 3, verses 22–23, from the Tibetan.

79. Many Dharma books translate the same Tibetan term, *jug pay sem,* as "engaging bodhichitta." I think "bodhichitta in action" better expresses the meaning of the term.

80. To take sincere refuge in the qualities, practices, and embodiments of enlightenment marks entry into the path of enlightenment as noted in chapter 4. But enlightenment can be viewed mainly as the attainment of one's own freedom from suffering (personal nirvana) or as the attainment of the enlightened power to trigger many others' realization of

freedom (active nirvana, buddhahood). To give rise to bodhichitta in a steadfast way is to step decisively onto the path to buddhahood, the bodhisattva path.

81. Shantideva and Thogmed, *Bodhisattva-charavatara,* p. 165, chapter 3, verse 25.

82. For more extensive contemporary presentations of the transcendental virtues (perfections), see Lama Surya Das' book: *Buddha Is as Buddha Does* (Harper SanFrancisco, 2006); Reginald Ray, *Indestructible Truth,* pp. 336–46; Yangsi Rinpoche, *Practicing the Path,* pp. 353–477. For classical presentations, see Tsong kha pa, *Great Treatise,* vol. 2, pp. 85–224; Kangyur Rinpoche and Jigme Lingpa, *Treasury of Precious Qualities,* pp. 190–268.

83. On Vajrayana foundational practices, see Jane Tromge, *Ngondro Commentary* (Junction City, CA: Padma, 1995); Patrul Rinpoche, *The Words of My Perfect Teacher* (San Francisco: HarperCollins, 1994); Dilgo Khyentse Rinpoche, *Excellent Path to Enlightenment* (Ithaca, NY: Snow Lion, 1996). On Vajrayana creation and completion stage practices in the context of Dzogchen and Mahamudra, see Reginald Ray's overview, *Secret of the Vajra World;* Dilgo Khyentse Rinpoche and Patrul Rinpoche, *Heart Treasure of the Enlightened Ones* (Boston: Shambala, 1992), pp. 55–146; Chokyi Nyima Rinpoche and Karma Chagmey Rinpoche, *The Union of Mahamudra and Dzogchen* (Hong Kong: Rangjung Yeshe, 1989); Tulku Urgyen Rinpoche, *As It Is,* vol. I (Hong Kong: Rangjung Yeshe, 1999).

Dzogchen foundational and visionary practices are just mentioned briefly in books since they are more fully taught only in meditation retreat with qualified teachers. On Dzogchen foundational practices distinguishing dualistic, ego-centered mind from the infinite nature of mind, see the section on "sharp inquiries" in chapter 2 of this book; also see Lama Surya Das, *Natural Radiance,* pp. 47-54; Tsoknyi Rinpoche, *Fearless Simplicity* (Hong Kong: Rangjung Yeshe, 2003), pp. 116-44.

Index

256 ⬿ *Awakening Through Love*

soul, 36
soup kitchens, 181
spiritual teachers
  connecting with, 225–26
  lineage and, 238
  selecting, 68
  spiritual community and, 223
  transmission and guidance from,
    224–26
Stalin, Joseph, 127, 130
stillness, 54–55
strangers
  boundless love and, 97, 101–102,
    105–108, 112–113, 118–25, 129
  compassion and, 168–69, 172,
    183–84
  delusion and, 132
  dualism and, 107–108
  embodying goodness and, 219, 220
  evil and, 129
  extending refuge and, 123–25
  pure perception and, 136, 140, 143
  samsaric maps and, 116–17
  social activism and, 209
  will to be free and, 121
subject and object, relation of, 45
Sudan, 185
suffering, xxi, 39, 41
  becoming conscious of our own,
    163–64
  boundless love and, 95, 104–105,
    108, 113
  compassion and, 157–63, 168–69,
    175–79, 186–87, 191–92, 195–99
  of ego-conditioning, 161–63, 172
  karma and, 75
  learning to cradle our, 165
  nature of, insight into, 161–63
  obvious, 161–63, 172, 176
  of transience, 161–63, 172
Surya Das, Lama, xxv, 47, 56, 112,
    114–16, 136
Suu Kyi, Aung San, xix
Sweet Honey in the Rock, 148–50
sympathetic joy, use of the term, xv

T
Tarthang Tulku, 194
*Tathagatagarbha Sutra (Buddha Nature
  Scripture)*, 144–45
teachers
  connecting with, 225–26
  lineage and, 238
  selecting, 68
  spiritual community and, 223
  transmission and guidance from,
    224–26
Teresa of Avila, 24
Teresa, Mother. *See* Mother Teresa
terrorism, 125, 127, 130, 239. *See also*
  violence; warfare
thought, distracting chains of, 62–64
Tibetan Buddhism, xv–xvi, xxii
transcendental wisdom, 235, 237–38.
  See also wisdom
transience, suffering of, 161–63, 172

U
union, practice of, xxiv, xxv
University of Wisconsin, 135

V
Vajrayana practices, 238, 248n40,
    249n46
Vietnam War, 90
violence, xvi, 76, 239–40. *See also* terrorism; warfare
  dualism and, 108
  embodying goodness and, 202
  solutions to, xx–xxii
virtues, 235–38

W
warfare, 186, 202, 239. *See also* terrorism; violence
wisdom, xx–xxii, 45
  bodhichitta and, 232
  boundless love and, 96–97,
    106–107, 112–116, 119–21
  compassion and, 157, 174–78, 184,
    187–88
  conceptual practices and, 48

About the Author

JOHN MAKRANSKY has practiced and studied Tibetan Buddhism since 1978 with Nyingma, Kagyu, and Gelug teachers of Tibet. He is a professor of Buddhism and Comparative Theology at Boston College and senior advisor to Chokyi Nyima Rinpoche's Centre for Buddhist Studies in Nepal. His research focuses on Indian and Tibetan Buddhist thought and practice, the adaptation of such teachings to contemporary contexts, and interfaith learning. John is the guiding teacher for the Foundation for Active Compassion, described below. In 2000, John was ordained a Tibetan Buddhist lama in the lineage of Nyoshul Khen Rinpoche. His books include *Buddhist Theology* (2000, co-edited with Roger Jackson). John is co-founder of the Buddhist Constructive Reflection Group in the American Academy of Religion and on the board of directors of the Society of Buddhist-Christian Studies.

Audio Recordings of Guided Meditations

Downloadable mp3 audio files of John Makransky leading the guided meditations presented in this book are available through the Foundation for Active Compassion, on its website: www.foundationforactivecompassion.org.

About the Foundation for Active Compassion

The Foundation for Active Compassion was co-founded in 2008 by a community of meditation teachers with John Makransky. Its purpose is make contemplative trainings of innate compassion and wisdom from Tibet accessible for teachers, healthcare givers, social workers, therapists, and social service agents of all backgrounds and faiths, in order to empower their lives and their work to make a better world. The Foundation for Active Compassion website (www.foundationforactivecompassion.org) is a regularly updated resource on contemplative training to empower social service and social change work, dharma practice, and interfaith learning. This website includes a schedule of workshops and retreats, a list of local meditation groups, audios, videos, and meditation texts.

About Wisdom

Wisdom Publications, Wisdom Publications is dedicated to offering works relating to and inspired by Buddhist traditions. To learn more about us or to explore our other books, please visit our website at www.wisdompubs.org. You can subscribe to our e-newsletter or request our print catalog online, or by writing to:

Wisdom Publications
199 Elm Street
Somerville, Massachusetts 02144 USA

You can also contact us at 617-776-7416, or info@wisdompubs.org.

Wisdom is a nonprofit, charitable 501(c)(3) organization affiliated with the Foundation for the Preservation of the Mahayana Tradition (FPMT).